9.00

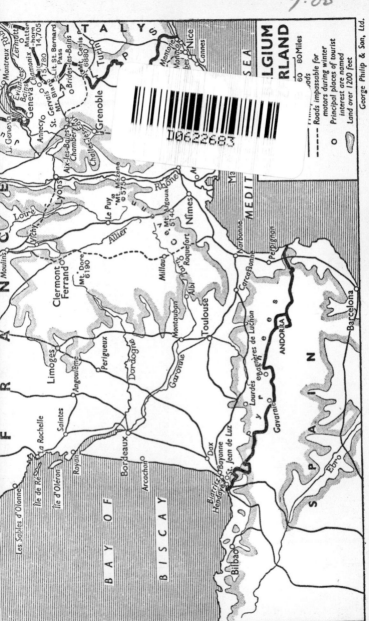

George Philip & Son, Ltd.

# TEACH YOURSELF BOOKS

# FRENCH
# PHRASE BOOK

## TEACH YOURSELF BOOKS
ST. PAUL'S HOUSE  WARWICK LANE  LONDON EC4

*First printed 1947*
*This impression 1971*

This volume is published in the U.S.A. by
David McKay Company Inc., 750 Third Avenue,
New York, N.Y. 10017

ISBN 0 340 05786 6

*Printed and bound in Great Britain for The English Universities Press, Ltd.,
by Richard Clay (The Chaucer Press), Ltd., Bungay, Suffolk*

# CONTENTS

## THE PHRASE BOOK

# INTRODUCTION

## A FEW FRIENDLY HINTS TO THE TRAVELLER

THIS French Phrase Book is intended to help the traveller to express his needs and desires so that he shall be understood. Its vocabularies cover almost every department of life, and its phrases are adapted to deal with practically all situations likely to arise when travelling abroad.

And now a few words of friendly advice as to your attitude when abroad : behave in France, Belgium or Switzerland with the same natural courtesy that you do at home, and never forget that when abroad you are, whatever your social rank may be, an ambassador of your country, which will be judged by your conduct.

You are bound to make mistakes, since every country has its own peculiar traditions, customs and social rules—e.g., in France you generally keep the lady on your left, so as to have your sword-arm free to defend her, except in a town, where you always walk close to the kerb, so as to be able to step off into the gutter if necessary ! Do not wait for a lady to smile before saluting her : take your hat off at once, as you thus show your respect. Shake hands whenever you meet an acquaintance, even if it is ten times in a day, and always say " good-bye " or some other apt greeting when you leave him ; in other words, do not *filer à l'anglaise*, " take French leave " ! In a café or restaurant ask if the seat is free before sitting down, even if it is evident, and bow with a murmured " *monsieur* " or " *madame* " or " *monsieur-dame* " to those seated at the table. Always greet with a " *bonjour, monsieur, madame* " people you meet on the stairs or elsewhere in your boarding-house, even if it happens to be the charwoman or the chambermaid : they are also human beings like yourself. Do not hesitate to start conversations in the bus, train, café or elsewhere : France is a country of social ease, so make yourself at home in it.

Do not be disturbed if the French have not the same table manners as you have; they are just as good as yours, but different. They cut up the meat, lay the knife on the plate and eat with the fork, like our friends the Americans. Why not? You will probably not find a fish knife and fork; what's wrong with an ordinary knife and fork? You may perhaps find no salt-spoon in the salt-cellar; use your knife, if necessary cleaning it on the ubiquitous piece of bread.

And do not, oh, do not, deprive yourself of the delights of French cooking by insisting on English dishes and English meals! Bacon and eggs are delicious, but so is the French *petit déjeuner* with its lovely coffee and *croissants* with fresh butter. Try dishes that look "funny" or "outlandish"; you will find most of them a revelation. Try every cheese that comes your way, especially the numerous local cheeses, many of which are a connoisseur's dream. When you find a dish that ravishes you, do not hesitate to ask your hostess, or the waiter, or the cook, for the recipe. And, if you are a housewife, try to spend a few hours in a French kitchen.

Drink wine and ask the advice of the waiter as to which wines go with which dishes. Life will put on a rosier hue if you have had a glass or two of good French wine with your lunch and dinner.

Never over-tip, but restrict yourself to 10%* of the bill or the charge, and if that 10% has already been added on as a fixed charge, then do not tip at all. Over-tipping brands you in French eyes as—to use slang—*une poire,* "a mug", and spoils the market for the native French. It is not done.

Finally you cannot go wrong in France if you are sociable, kindly, patient and tolerant; but where could one go wrong with these simple, human virtues?

*Bon voyage! Et vive la France!*

* In some restaurants, the service charge may be as high as 15%, but whatever it is, it is generally stated on the menu card. In most hotels and restaurants it is put down on the bill as "service".

## HOW TO USE THE PHRASE BOOK

In order to use the Phrase Book to the best advantage, we suggest that the traveller should proceed as follows :

1. Study carefully the Section on Pronunciation, and make yourself familiar with the phonetic symbols and the sounds they represent.

2. Then practise the pronunciation by reading out aloud from the phonetic script the vocabularies and phrases in the body of the book. It is useful, and more amusing, to do this with a friend, so that one can check up on the other. At first read slowly and very carefully, concentrating on getting each sound perfect, and then, as you become more sure of yourself and fluent, speed up the pace.

3. The Section on Grammar will be useful for reference and also, since it is brief and clear, either for brushing up your rusty school French or, if you have none at all, for introducing you to the grammar of the language.

4. Work your way through the vocabularies and phrases whenever you can spare time, so that they become familiar and fluent, and so that you know just where to find what you need when you need it.

# FRENCH PRONUNCIATION

As French spelling is, like English, in many cases not representative of the pronunciation—e.g., *vin, vain, vainc, vaincs, vains, vingt* all spell exactly the same two sounds [vɛ̃], and *sain, saint, sein, seing, ceint, cinq* all spell [sɛ̃]—it is necessary to resort to some phonetic system of representing the sounds. The system used in this Phrase Book is that of the International Phonetic Association, now recognized as the best and universally adopted.

The basis of the system is that one sound shall always be represented by one symbol and that one symbol shall always represent one and the same sound : thus [s] represents the " c " in *face*, the " ç " in *garçon*, the " s " in *si*, the " ss " in *passer*, the " sc " in *sceau*, part of the " x " in *externe*.

We give below a list of the phonetic symbols with a description of the sounds and an English equivalent, if it exists, followed by the traditional French spelling.

Before we list the symbols it will be useful to give in broad outline the main characteristics of French pronunciation. The French, when speaking, keep the muscles of the vocal organs tauter than we do in English, so that their sounds are clearer and more audible than English. They do not whisper as we do, and their lips are much more mobile, being pouted forwards and stretched or spread sideways more vigorously. The tongue is continuously in the front of the mouth in contact with the lower teeth, and in fact the tongue is always more forward in the mouth than in corresponding English sounds— e.g., t, d, l. The transition from one sound to another is more rapid than in English, and hence vowels do not tend to glide off into diphthongs, and voiced consonants, like b, d, g, v, z —which are made by vibrating the vocal chords, whereas p, t, k, f, s are unvoiced—are buzzed until the following sound is

13

pronounced. In the same way, there is no slight aspirate after p, t, k, as in many parts of England, where " pat " is pronounced " pʰat ".

## THE PHONETIC ALPHABET

### Consonantal Symbols

| Phonetic symbol. | Explanation of sound. | French spelling. |
|---|---|---|
| p | Like English " p " but no following slight aspirate. | p : *patte, pas* |
| b | Like English but more strongly vibrated. | b : *bas, bon* |
| t | Like English but no following slight aspirate, and tongue well pressed just above upper teeth. | t : *temps, tasse* th : *théâtre* |
| d | Like English but well vibrated and tongue well pressed just above upper teeth. | d : *dent, addition* |
| k | Like English but no following slight aspirate, and the tongue contacts the palate nearer the front of the mouth than in English. | c before a, o, u : *car, comme, cure* qu : *qui, que, quand* ch : *choriste* c at end of word : *chic* |
| g | Like English but the tongue farther forward and the " g " well vibrated until next sound produced. | g before a, o, u : *gant, gond, aigu* gu before i and e : *gui, gué* |
| m | Like English but well vibrated. | m : *ma, merci* |
| n | Like English but well vibrated. | n : *note, notre* |

| Phonetic symbol. | Explanation of sound. | French spelling. |
|---|---|---|
| l | Like English but tongue well forward on the teeth; never like the second "l" in "little" which is formed in the back of the mouth. | l : *laver* |
| r | Rolled as in Northern English and Scotch by vibrating the tongue; in most of France and especially in Paris it is formed like the Northumberland "burr" by vibrating the uvula. Practise this by holding your head up and doing a dry gargle. | r : *rive, terre, faire* |
| f | Like English "f". | f : *fil* <br> ph : *physique* |
| v | Like English but teeth not pressed so tightly on lower lip. | v : *verre* <br> w : *Waterloo, wagon* |
| s | Like English but tongue farther forward and hiss more energetic. | s : *sonner* <br> ss : *passer* <br> c before i, y and e *ici, cynique, cette* <br> ç : *façon* <br> sc : *sceau* |
| z | Like English but vibration throughout the sound. | s between two vowels: *rose, maison* <br> z : *azur, zigzag* |
| h | As the aspirate is used only in certain parts of France it does not figure in our phonetic transcription. | |
| ʃ | Like English "sh" in "shame". | ch : *chercher* |

| Phonetic symbol. | Explanation of sound. | French spelling. |
|---|---|---|
| ʒ | Like English " s " in " pleasure ". | j : *juger, jet*<br>g before i or e : *agir, géant* |
| ɲ | Like English "ng" in " sing " but back of tongue farther forward against the palate and tip well down behind lower teeth. | gn : *signal, montagne* |
| j | Like English " y " in " yes". | i : *copier*<br>y : *payer*<br>ll : *fille* |
| w | Like English "w" in "wing". | ou : *oui*<br>oi : *moi* |
| ɥ | This is the vowel [y] turned into a consonant by rapid utterance, just as [w] is a [u] turned into a consonant similarly. | u : *lui, nuage* |

## Vowel Sounds

*Note.*—In our transcription we have, for the sake of simplicity, not marked the length of vowels, though this causes a slight change in character. This is not a course of Phonetics but a practical, simple guide to pronunciation.

Before setting out the list of vowels as we have done for the consonants, it will be useful to show them diagrammatically—

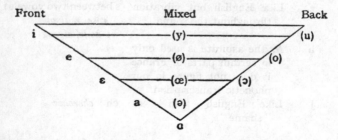

The triangle represents a section of the mouth, the lips being on the left, the back of the mouth and throat on the right. The front vowels, [i], [e], [ɛ], [a] and [ɑ] are pronounced with the lips flat, the mixed and back vowels with the lips rounded, or pouted, and this is shown by printing them in round brackets.

The position of the symbols shows the height of the tongue in the mouth—the tip or blade of the tongue in the front and mixed vowels, the back of the tongue in the back vowels—and at the same time the distance of the lips from each other. Thus as we go from [i] to [e], to [ɛ], to [a], to [ɑ], the tongue follows the lower jaw downwards as the mouth opens; and as we go from [ɑ] to [ɔ], to [o], to [u], the tongue follows the lower jaw upwards as the mouth closes step by step. The vowels [i] and [u] have the same lip opening, but in [i] the tip of the tongue is close to the palate near the upper teeth and the lips are stretched or spread at the corners; in [u] the back of the tongue is high up against the soft palate at the back of the mouth, the lips are close together and pouted or rounded to form a small circular hole. Similarly with [e] and [o], [ɛ] and [ɔ]. The mixed vowels [y], [ø], [œ] and [ə] are formed as follows : [y] is with the lips in position for [u] and the tongue in the position for [i] ; [ø], lips as for [o] and tongue as for [e] ; [œ], lips as for [ɔ], tongue as for [ɛ] ; [ə], the " mute *e* ", is a weak form of [œ] with the lips less rounded and less open.

| Symbol. | Explanation. | French spelling. |
|---|---|---|
| i | Like English " ee " in " preen " or " i " in " machine " but lips closer together and well spread at the corners. The sound does not trail off into a [j] as in English " see " = [sij]. | i : *il, fille*<br>y : *système* |
| e | Like Cockney " cat " or Scotch " cake " with a long " a ". Lips close together | é : *donné*<br>er : *donner*<br>ez : *donnez* |

| Symbol. | Explanation. | French spelling. |
|---|---|---|
| | and well spread; no trailing off. | ai : *gai* |
| ɛ | Like " ey " in English " they ", especially in the North, but no trailing off into [i] and [j], [almost the same sound as " e " in " ten "]. | è : *thème*<br>ê : *tête*<br>e before two consonants: *telle, terreur*<br>ai : *maison*<br>ay : *payer* |
| a | Like Northern English " a " in " cat ". Lips more open than in Southern English " cat " and drawn out at corners. | a : *patte*<br>à : *à, là*<br>â : *allâmes*<br>oi : *droit* |
| ɑ | Like " a " in English " father ". | a : *passer*<br>â : *mât*<br>oi : *mois* |
| ɔ | Like English " awl " but tongue not so far back in the mouth and lips wider open. | o : *loge*<br>au : *aurore* |
| o | Northern English and Scotch " o " in " no ". Small aperture, lips well pouted, no trailing off. | o : *poser*<br>ô : *bientôt*<br>au : *auguste*<br>eau : *eau, seau* |
| u | Like English " u " in " rule " but very small round aperture, lips well pouted, tongue pressed high up, no trailing off. | ou : *route*<br>où : *où* |
| y | This is formed by putting the lips as for [u] and trying at the same time to pronounce [i], or try to whistle the sound [i]. | u : *pu, brume*<br>eu : *eu, eut, eusse* |
| ø | This is formed by pouting the lips as for [o] and trying to pronounce [e]. | eu : *feu, eux, creuser*<br>œu : *œufs* |

| Symbol. | Explanation. | French spelling. |
|---|---|---|
| œ | This is formed by pouting the lips as for [ɔ] and trying to pronounce [ɛ]. | eu : *faveur* <br> œu : *sœur* |
| ə | This is a weak form of [œ]. It is like the " ir " in English " sir ", but lips slightly pouted and tongue farther forward. | e : *ce, lever* |

## The Nasal Vowels

These are formed by allowing some of the sound to escape through the nose. If you hold a small mirror under your nostrils when you pronounce the " a " in " father ", nothing will happen to the surface of the glass. If you keep your lips and tongue in the same position and sing a little through your nose you will see the surface dimmed by condensation of the moisture in the breath passing through your nose. Practise the nasals by singing them on a rising scale using : *Un bon pain blanc,* which contains the four nasal vowels.

| Symbol. | Explanation. | French spelling. |
|---|---|---|
| ã | This is simply nasalized [ɑ]. | an : *tante, antenne* <br> am : *ample* <br> en : *envoyer* <br> em : *temps, emploi* |
| 5̃ | This is nasalized [ɔ] but the lips are rather closer together and more pouted. | on : *son, fond* <br> om : *ombre* |
| ɛ̃ | This is nasalized [ɛ] but the mouth is not quite so wide open. | in : *vin, cinq* <br> im : *important* <br> ain : *vain, sain* <br> aim : *faim* <br> ein : *sein* <br> ien : *bien* <br> oin : *coin* |

| Symbol. | Explanation. | French spelling. |
|---|---|---|
| œ̃ | This is nasalized [œ] but lips only slightly pouted and mouth not quite so wide open as for [œ]. | un : *un*<br>um : *humble* |

## The Phonetic Transcription

There are one or two points which need a little explanation. French, like English and other languages, if spoken slowly and solemnly or read aloud is not the same as when spoken at a normal rate nor, especially, when spoken rapidly and carelessly. As the French in this Phrase Book is intended to be spoken by a foreigner, we have used a fairly normal but somewhat slow rate of speech. This affects the dropping of the " mute *e* " which disappears—in certain circumstances —from fairly rapid speech and from speech at a normal rate ; we have dropped it where it would sound pedantic and stiff to pronounce it. Thus *je ne sais pas* would be stiff and pedantic as [ʒə nə sɛ pɑ] ; it would be normal but careful as [ʒə nsɛ pɑ] ; it would be normal but rapid as [nsɛ pɑ] and as [sɛ pɑ] ; our version is [ʒə nsɛ pɑ], the normal and careful.

Another difficulty is the liaison, as in *les hommes* = [lezɔm]. The tendency in French, and especially in Parisian French, is to make very few liaisons—though of course one would be made with *les hommes*—and as too many liaisons sound pedantic and ugly, we have given only those which are necessary.

The transcription does not, as we have said, show the length of the vowels, nor does it attempt to show intonation and syllabic stress, as this would all complicate the user's task : we show in as simple a way as possible the bare bones of pronunciation.

One final word of advice : when practising the pronunciation always read the phonetic script ALOUD.

# A SKELETON OUTLINE OF FRENCH

## Nouns

All nouns are either masculine or feminine. This is shown by the articles and adjectives accompanying the noun, not by the noun itself. The gender has to be learnt by memory, e.g., by repeating aloud the noun with the article: *la fenêtre*, the window; *le livre*, the book.

The PLURAL of nouns is made by adding -*s* to the singular: *livre*, *livres* ; *fenêtre*, *fenêtres*.

If the sing. ends in -*s*, -*z*, -*x* no change is made : *fils*, son, *fils*, sons ; *nez*, nose, *nez*, noses ; *voix*, voice, *voix*, voices.

Nouns ending in -*au* and -*eu* add -*x* : *bureau*, desk, office, *bureaux*, desks, offices ; *lieu*, place, *lieux*, places.

Nouns ending in -*al* and a number in -*ail* change the ending into -*aux* : *animal*, *animaux* ; *travail*, work, *travaux*.

## The Articles

The Definite Article, " the ", is *le* for the masc. and *la* for the fem.: *le père*, the father; *la mère*, the mother; *le journal*, the newspaper; *la chaise*, the chair.

If the noun commences with a vowel or *h* mute, *l'* is used for both genders : *l'homme*, the man ; *l'encre*, the ink.

The plural is *les* for both genders : *les hommes*, the men ; *les femmes*, the women. If the noun commences with a vowel or *h* mute, the -*s* of *les* is pronounced : *les hommes* = [lezɔm].

*De* combines with the article *le* to form *du* : *la maison du professeur*, the master's house. *De* combines with *les* to form *des* : *les maisons des professeurs*, the masters' houses.

Thus the full forms with *de* are : masc. *du*, *de l'* ; fem. *de la*, *de l'* ; plural *des*.

*A* combines with the article *le* to form *au* : *au commencement*, at the beginning ; and with *les* to form *aux* : *aux*

*armes*, to arms.　Thus the full forms of the article with *à* are:
masc. *au, à l'*; fem. *à la, à l'*; plural *aux*.

The indefinite article is: masc. *un*; fem. *une*.　If *un* precedes a masc. noun commencing with a vowel or *h* mute, the
-*n* of *un* is pronounced: *un homme* = [œ̃nɔm].

The partitive article is used to indicate " a certain amount ",
and its forms are those of the def. art. with *de*: *du, de l', de
la, de l', des*.　*Donnez-moi du vin*, give me some wine; *avez-
vous de la bière?* have you any beer?; *j'ai vu des soldats*, I
have seen some soldiers.　After a negative *de* is used: *je n'ai
pas de vin*, I have no wine; *il n'y a pas de bière*, there is no
beer; *je n'ai pas vu de soldats*, I haven't seen any soldiers.
*De* is also used when an adj. precedes the noun in the plural:
*j'ai de bons amis*, I have some good friends.

## Adjectives

The adj. agrees in gender and number with its noun: *le
petit livre*, the small book; *la petite maison*, the small house;
*les petits livres, les petites maisons*.

The fem. is formed by adding -*e* to the masc.: *grand*, big,
*grande*; *fermé*, closed, *fermée*.

If the masc. ends in -*e* there is no change for the fem.: *un
homme raisonnable*; *une femme raisonnable*.

A number of adjs. double the last consonant: *bon, bonne*,
good; *sujet, sujette*, subject; *épais, épaisse*, thick.

Adjs. ending in -*f* change it into -*ve*: *furtif, furtive*, furtive;
those ending in -*x* change this into -*se*: *peureux, peureuse*,
timid; those in -*er* change this into -*ère*: *premier, première*,
first; -*et* often changes into -*ète*: *discret, discrète*, discreet.

The following do not conform to rule: *blanc, blanche*, white;
*long, longue*, long; *sec, sèche*, dry; *frais, fraîche*, fresh; *public,
publique*, public; *grec, grecque*, Greek; *doux, douce*, sweet,
gentle; *beau, belle*, beautiful (masc. singular before a vowel *bel*:
*un bel homme*, a handsome man); *nouveau, nouvelle*, new (masc.
singular before a vowel *nouvel*); *vieux, vieille*, old (masc. singular before a vowel *vieil*); *fou, folle*, mad (masc. singular before
a vowel *fol*).

The plurals of adjs. follow the rule for nouns : they add -*s* to the singular : *petits, petites*; but if ending in -*s* or -*x* they do not change ; if they end in *au* they add -*x* in the masc.: *beau, beaux*; if they end in -*al* they change this into -*aux* : *vertical, verticaux*, but there are a few exceptions—*naval* makes *navals*.

The Comparative is formed by *plus* : *plus petit que*, smaller than ; *plus intelligent que*, more intelligent than. Equality is expressed by *aussi* : *aussi petit que*, as small as ; inferiority is expressed by *moins* : *moins petit que*, less small than, not so small as.

Irregular comparisons are : *bon, meilleur*, good, better ; *mauvais, pire*, bad, worse ; and *petit, moindre*, little, lesser (smaller) (but also, as above, *plus petit*).

The Superlative is formed by putting the definite article before the Comparative : *le plus doux*, the sweetest, *la plus douce, les plus doux, les plus douces*.

The adj. generally follows the noun it qualifies, but a number of very common short adjs. precede it : *un bon livre*, a good book ; *un grand homme*, a great man ; *un jeune homme*, a young man ; *un mauvais conseil*, bad advice.

## The Demonstrative Adjective

" This " or " that " are expressed by : masc. *ce* (*cet* before a vowel or *h* mute) ; fem. *cette*; plural *ces* : *ce petit garçon est malade*, this little boy is ill ; *cet homme est vieux*, this man is old ; *cette dame est vieille*, this lady is old ; *ces enfants sont jolis*, these children are pretty.

In order to distinguish clearly between " this " and " that ", French uses -*ci* and -*là* : *ce garçon-ci est petit, ce garçon-là est grand* ; *cette dame-ci est vieille, cette dame-là est jeune*, this lady is old, that lady is young.

## The Demonstrative Pronouns

Corresponding to the adjs., we have the pronouns : masc. sing. *celui*, plural *ceux* ; fem. sing. *celle*, plural *celles*. They are used as follows :

*Voici deux livres, celui-ci est ouvert, celui-là est fermé*, here are two books, this (one) is open, that (one) is closed.

*Voici des papiers, ceux-ci sont à moi, ceux-là sont à vous*, here are papers, these are mine, those are yours.

*Voici deux roses, celle-ci est jaune, celle-là est blanche*, here are two roses, this (one) is yellow, that (one) is white.

*Voici des roses, celles-ci sont jaunes, celles-là sont blanches*, here are roses, these are yellow, those are white.

*Regardez ces hommes, celui qui écrit est mon ami, celui qui lit est un étranger*, look at those men, the one who is writing is my friend, the one who is reading is a stranger.

*Regardez ces femmes, celle qui écrit est mon amie, celle qui lit est une étrangère.*

In the same way in the plural masc. *ceux qui écrivent . . . ceux qui lisent*; and fem. *celles qui écrivent . . . celles qui lisent.*

*J'ai mon livre et celui de mon frère*, I have my book and my brother's (that of my brother); *j'ai mes livres et ceux de mon frère*, I have my books and my brother's (those of my brother).

*J'ai ma plume et celle de mon frère*, I have my pen and my brother's (that of my brother); *j'ai mes plumes et celles de mon frère*, I have my pens and my brother's (those of my brother).

*Celui qui dit cela ment*, he who says that is lying.

*Ceci* and *cela* are neuter and refer to something indefinite : *Donnez-moi ceci pas cela*, give me this, not that. *Cela* is also found as *ça*.

## Possessive Adjectives

" My " is masc. *mon*, fem. *ma* (but *mon* before a vowel or *h* mute), plural *mes* for both genders : *mon père, ma mère* (but *mon habitude*, my custom), *mes livres, mes roses.*

" Thy "—still used in French for close intimates—is in the same way masc. *ton*, fem. *ta* (*ton* before a vowel or *h* mute), plural *tes*.

" His " and " her "—no distinction is made in French—are : masc. *son*, fem. *sa* (or *son* as above), plural *ses*. " Its " is, of course, also *son*, *sa*, *ses*.

" Our " is *notre* for the masc. and fem. sing., and *nos* for the plural of both genders.

" Your " is *votre* for the masc. and fem. sing., and *vos* for the plural of both genders.

" Their " is *leur* for the masc. and fem. sing., and *leurs* for the plural of both genders.

## Possessive Pronouns

The pronouns corresponding to the above are :

" Mine " :  masc. sing. *le mien*, plural *les miens*.
             fem. sing. *la mienne*, plural *les miennes*.

" Thine " :  masc. sing. *le tien*, plural *les tiens*.
             fem. sing. *la tienne*, plural *les tiennes*.

" His " ⎫  masc. sing. *le sien*, plural *les siens*.
" Hers " ⎭  fem. sing. *la sienne*, plural *les siennes*.

" Ours " :  masc. sing. *le nôtre*, plural *les nôtres*.
             fem. sing. *la nôtre*, plural *les nôtres*.

" Yours " :  masc. sing. *le vôtre*, plural *les vôtres*.
             fem. sing. *la vôtre*, plural *les vôtres*.

" Theirs " :  masc. sing. *le leur*, plural *les leurs*.
             fem. sing. *la leur*, plural *les leurs*.

## Personal Pronouns

The following Table sets out the Personal Pronouns. Col. 1 gives the Disjunctive form, i.e., the form which is used apart from the verb, emphatically or after a preposition or in some cases with the Imperative : *moi, j'ai dit cela, I* said that ; *c'est pour moi*, it is for me ; *regardez-moi*, look at me. Col. 2 is the Nominative form or the subject of the verb : *je regarde le professeur*, I am looking at the teacher. Col. 3 is the Reflexive form : *je me lave*, I wash myself. Col. 4 is the Accusative or the direct object of the verb : *il me voit*, he sees me. Col. 5 is the Dative form or the indirect object of the verb : *il me donne un cadeau*, he gives me a present, he gives a present to me.

| Col. 1. Disj. | Col. 2. Nom. | Col. 3. Reflex. | Col. 4. Acc. | Col. 5. Dat. |
|---|---|---|---|---|
| *moi* | *je* | *me* | *me* | *me* |
| *toi* | *tu* | *te* | *te* | *te* |
| *lui* | *il* | *se* | *le* | *lui* |
| *elle* | *elle* | *se* | *la* | *lui* |
| *nous* | *nous* | *nous* | *nous* | *nous* |
| *vous* | *vous* | *vous* | *vous* | *vous* |
| *eux* | *ils* | *se* | *les* | *leur* |
| *elles* | *elles* | *se* | *les* | *leur* |

It will be helpful to give you some examples of the use of the above, arranged under the columns.

Col. 1. *Moi, je ne veux pas le faire, I* won't do it. *Venez avec moi*, come with me. *Toi, tu es trop jeune, you* are too young. *C'est pour toi*, it's for you. *Lui, il travaille dur, he* works hard. *Je pars sans lui*, I am going without him. *Elle, elle écrit bien, she* writes well. *Il est assis à côté d'elle*, he is sitting beside her. The other persons are similar but care must be taken with the third person plural : *eux, ils disent ça, they* say that; *il n'y a rien pour eux*, there's nothing for them —masculine. The feminine is : *elles, elles sont belles, they* are lovely; *j'ai quelque chose pour elles*, I've something for them.

Col. 2. The use of the Nom., *je, tu, il, elle, nous, vous, ils, elles*, as subject of a verb needs no examples.

Col. 3. The reflexives, *me, te, se, nous, vous, se*, are simple since there is no difference between the Acc. and Dat. (direct and indirect objects) : *je me lave*, I wash myself; *je me dis que c'est impossible*, I say to myself it is impossible.

Cols. 4 and 5. It will make things clearer if we take these

together, as the Dat. differs from the Acc. only in the third persons. I advise you to learn the following by heart :

| | | | | |
|---|---|---|---|---|
| *il me voit* | he sees me | *il me donne ça* | he gives me that | |
| *il te voit* | ,, you | *il te donne ça* | ,, you | ,, |
| *il le voit* | ,, him | *il lui donne ça* | ,, him | ,, |
| *il la voit* | ,, her | *il lui donne ça* | ,, her | ,, |
| *il nous voit* | ,, us | *il nous donne ça* | ,, us | ,, |
| *il vous voit* | ,, you | *il vous donne ça* | ,, you | ,, |
| *il les voit* | ,, them | *il leur donne ça* | ,, them | ,, |

*Imperative.*—This is the most difficult part, as in the affirmative the first and second persons sing. take the form in Col. 1—*moi* and *toi*—and all the persons follow the verb, whereas in the negative all the persons have the normal form and the normal position before the verb. The following examples are worth while learning by heart :

### Accusative

| Affirmative. | | Negative. |
|---|---|---|
| *regardez-moi* | look at me | *ne me regardez pas* |
| *regarde-toi** | ,, yourself | *ne te regarde pas** |
| *regardez-le* | ,, him | *ne le regardez pas* |
| *regardez-la* | ,, her | *ne la regardez pas* |
| *regardez-nous* | ,, us | *ne nous regardez pas* |
| *regardez-vous** | ,, yourself | *ne vous regardez pas** |
| *regardez-les* | ,, them | *ne les regardez pas* |

### Dative

| Affirmative. | | Negative. |
|---|---|---|
| *donnez-moi ça* | give me that | *ne me donnez pas ça* |
| *donne-toi ça** | ,, yourself that | *ne te donne pas ça** |
| *donnez-lui ça* | ,, him ,, | *ne lui donnez pas ça* |
| *donnez-lui ça* | ,, her ,, | *ne lui donnez pas ça* |
| *donnez-nous ça* | ,, us ,, | *ne nous donnez pas ça* |
| *donnez-vous ça** | ,, yourself ,, | *ne vous donnez pas ça** |
| *donnez-leur ça* | ,, them ,, | *ne leur donnez pas ça* |

* These are reflexive.

Further, the disjunctives in Col. 1 are used when the verb is not expressed : *Qui a fait ça ? Moi*, who did that ? I (did). *Qui a-t-on envoyé ? Lui*, whom did they send ? Him.

To sum up : *me, te, nous, vous, le, lui, la, lui, les, leur* precede the verb except in the affirmative of the Imperative, where *me* and *te* become *moi* and *toi* and follow the verb, the others retaining their original form but following the verb. In the negative of the Imperative the order and form are normal.

The indefinite pronoun *on*, " one ", is largely used in French : *ici on parle français*, French is spoken here ; *où peut-on acheter ça ?* where can I buy that ? The Reflexive is *se* : *on se lève tard ici*, people get up late here. *Soi* is its disjunctive : *on n'a pas de place pour soi*, one has no room for one's self. *Chacun pour soi*, everybody for himself.

*Tu* is used with close relatives, intimate friends and animals.


## The Pronominal Adverbs

These are *y* and *en*. *Y* is used with the meaning of " there " : *Allez-vous au théâtre ? Oui, j'y vais*, are you going to the theatre ? Yes, I am (going there). *A quelle heure êtes-vous arrivé à la maison ? J'y suis arrivé à cinq heures*, at what time did you get home ? I got there at five.

*En* is used of place in cases such as : *Êtes-vous sorti de la maison ? Oui, j'en suis sorti*, did you go out of the house ? Yes, I went out of it. *En* is always associated with *de*, and is especially used to indicate a quantity, a certain number, like the partitive article : *Avez-vous des livres ? Oui, j'en ai*, have you any books ? Yes, I have some. *Combien de livres avez-vous ? J'en ai dix*, how many books have you ? I have ten (of them). *Voulez-vous me donner des timbres ? Oui, je vous en donnerai vingt*, will you give me some stamps ? Yes, I'll give you twenty (of them).

## Relative Order of the Personal Pronouns

The order of the personal pronouns in the oblique cases is as follows :

1. The first and second persons precede the third : *il me le donne*, he gives it to me; *il te le donne*, he gives it to thee; *il nous les donne*, he gives them to us; *il vous les donne*, he gives them to you.

2. When two third persons are together the accusative precedes the dative : *il le lui donne*, he gives it to him (her) ; *nous les leur donnons*, we give them to them.

3. With the affirmative Imperative the third person precedes the first and second : *donnez-le-moi*, give it to me; *donnez-les-nous*, give them to us; but the rule for two third persons holds good : *donnez-le-lui*, give it to him (her) ; *donnez-les-leur*, give them to them; in the negative Imperative the order becomes normal in all cases : *ne me le donnez pas ; ne nous les donnez pas ; ne le lui donnez pas ; ne les leur donnez pas*.

4. *y* and *en* come after all other personal pronouns and in that order : *Avez-vous vu mon frère au théâtre ? Oui, je l'y ai vu*, did you see my brother at the theatre ? Yes, I saw him there. *Avez-vous envoyé des fleurs à ma tante ? Oui, je lui en ai envoyé*, did you send some flowers to my aunt ? Yes, I sent her some. *Allez-y ; n'y allez pas*, go there; don't go there. *Donnez-m'en ; ne m'en donnez pas*, give me some; don't give me any. *Donnez-lui-en, ne lui en donnez pas*, give him some; don't give him any.

## Relative Pronouns

Nominative : *qui*    *Le monsieur qui traverse la rue*, the gentleman who is crossing the road ;

*La porte qui est ouverte*, the door which is open.

Accusative : *que*

*Le monsieur que je vois*, the gentleman I see ;

*La porte que je vois*, the door I see.

Genitive : *dont*

*Le monsieur dont je connais le fils*, the gentleman whose son I know ;

*La dame dont les filles sont mariées*, the lady whose daughters are married ;

*Le monsieur dont il parle*, the gentleman of whom he speaks ;

*La pièce de théâtre dont il parle*, the play he is speaking of.

BUT—

*Le monsieur au fils duquel j'ai donné la lettre*, the gentleman to whose son I gave the letter (this is used when " whose " is preceded in English by a preposition).

With preps. : *qui*

*Le monsieur à qui j'ai envoyé la lettre*, the gentleman to whom I sent the letter.

*lequel*, etc. *Le bureau auquel j'ai envoyé la lettre*, the office to which I sent the letter.

*Qui* is used for persons ; for things, and occasionally for persons, *lequel, laquelle, lesquels, lesquelles* are used, being treated as if they consisted of the def. art. plus *quel, quelle*, etc.

*Note.*—The Relative cannot be omitted in French. The man I see = *L'homme QUE je vois.*

## Interrogative Adjectives and Pronouns

The Adjectives " which? " and " what? " are : *quel, quels,* masc. and *quelle, quelles,* fem. : *Quel journal lisez-vous?* which (what) newspaper do you read? *Quelles fleurs préférez-vous?* which (what) flowers do you prefer?

The corresponding pronouns are : *lequel, lesquels,* masc. and *laquelle, lesquelles,* fem. : *Lequel (lesquels) de ces journaux lisez-vous?* which of these papers are you reading? *Laquelle (lesquelles) de ces fleurs préférez-vous?* which of these flowers do you prefer?

" Who? " and " what? " are as follows :

### Persons

| | | |
|---|---|---|
| Nom. | *Qui ?* who ? | *Qui parle ?* Who is speaking ? |
| | *Qui est-ce qui ?* | *Qui est-ce qui parle ?* Who is speaking ? |
| Acc. | *Qui ?* whom ? | *Qui voyez-vous ?* Whom do you see ? |
| | *Qui est-ce que ?* | *Qui est-ce que vous voyez ?* Whom do you see ? |
| With preps. | | *A qui donnez-vous la clé ?* To whom do you give the key ? |

### Things

| | | |
|---|---|---|
| Nom. | *Qu'est-ce qui ?* what ? | *Qu'est-ce qui est arrivé ?* What has happened ? |
| Acc. | *Que ?* what ? | *Que voyez-vous ?* What do you see ? |
| | *Qu'est-ce que ?* | *Qu'est-ce que vous voyez ?* What do you see ? |
| With preps. | | *Avec quoi écrivez-vous ?* With what are you writing ? |

*Quoi* is also used apart from the verb : *Je sais quelque chose. Quoi ?* I know something. What? It is also used exclamatorily : *Quoi ! vous avez dit cela ?* What ! you said that ?

The " condensed relative " " what ", as in " I know what you want ", is expanded into its component parts in French : *Je sais ce que vous voulez.* Similarly with : He came late, which angered me, *Il est venu en retard, ce qui* (or *chose qui*) *m'a fâché.*

" Whose ?" is rendered as follows : Whose hat is this ? *A qui est ce chapeau ?* Whose book did you borrow ? *Quel livre avez-vous emprunté ?* Whose son is he ? *De qui est-il le fils ?*

## Adverbs

A large number of adverbs are formed from the fem. of the adj. by adding -*ment* : *heureux, heureuse, heureusement,* fortunately ; *premier, première, premièrement,* firstly.

If the adj. ends in -*ant* or -*ent* the ending changes into -*amment* or -*emment* : *galant, galamment ; ardent, ardemment. Lent,* slow, makes *lentement,* and *présent* makes *présentement,* now, at the present time.

Adjs. ending in a vowel add -*ment* to the masc. : *joli, joliment,* prettily ; *vrai, vraiment,* truly, but *gai* makes *gaiement* or *gaîment.*

Irregular forms are : *bon,* good, *bien,* well ; *mauvais,* bad, *mal,* badly ; *gentil,* nice, kind, *gentiment ; aveugle,* blind, makes *aveuglément,* and *profond,* deep, *profondément,* together with a few others of this type.

Adverbs of quantity are : *combien, beaucoup, bien, assez, peu, trop.* Like all expressions of quantity, they are followed by *de* : *beaucoup de courage,* much courage (but *bien du courage*) ; *assez d'argent,* enough money ; *peu de temps,* little time ; *trop de travail,* too much work.

Adverbs are compared like adjs. : *rarement, plus rarement que, le plus rarement ; souvent, plus souvent que, le plus souvent.* Irregular comparisons are : *bien, mieux, le mieux,* well, better, best ; *mal, pis, le pis,* badly, worse, the worst ; *peu, moins, le moins,* little, less, least.

Affirmation and negation involve the use of adverbs. *Non*

is the neg. adverb: *Êtes-vous content ? Non, monsieur.* Are you satisfied? No. The emphatic neg. is *mais non* or *que non* : *Vous êtes content, n'est-ce pas ? Mais non !* You are satisfied, aren't you? No, I'm not.

When used with a verb the negative is *ne*, together with a word further defining the negation, as follows :

| | |
|---|---|
| *ne . . . pas*, not : | *il ne le voit pas*, he doesn't see it. |
| *ne . . . point*, not (at all) : | *je ne vois point pourquoi . . .* I don't see why . . . |
| *ne . . . jamais*, never : | *je n'y vais jamais*, I never go there. |
| *ne . . . guère*, scarcely : | *je n'ai guère le temps*, I have scarcely time. |
| *ne . . . plus*, no more, no longer : | *je ne le vois plus*, I no longer see him. |
| *ne . . . personne*, nobody : | *je ne rencontre personne*, I meet nobody. |
| | But *Qui est là ? Personne*, who is there? Nobody. |
| *ne . . . que*, only : | *je n'ai qu'un bras*, I have only one arm. |
| *ne . . . rien*, nothing : | *je ne vois rien*, I see nothing. |
| | But *Que voyez-vous ? Rien*, what do you see? Nothing. |

The affirmative adverb is *oui*, yes, with the emphatic form *si*. *Êtes-vous heureux ? Oui, monsieur.* Are you happy? Yes. *Vous n'êtes pas heureux ? Si, monsieur.* You aren't happy? Yes, I am.

Note that *monsieur, madame, mademoiselle* should be used in French where the title is generally omitted in English, and note especially that *Oui, mademoiselle* does not correspond to the English " Yes, miss."

## The Verb

The infinitive of the verb is a noun, and is still in some cases used as a pure noun with the article : *le pouvoir*, power; *le savoir*, knowledge. It can be used exclamatorily : *Moi dire ça !* I say that ! and in orders : *Ne pas se pencher au dehors !* Do not lean out.

The infin. ends in *-er*, *-ir*, *-re* or *-oir*, and is used after all prepositions except *en* : *pour payer*, in order to pay ; *j'hésite à vous suivre*, I hesitate to follow you ; *je suis obligé de le dire*, I am obliged to say it, etc. *En* forms the gerundive with the present part. : *en arrivant*, *nous avons trouvé la maison vide*, on arriving we found the house empty.

The present participle always ends in *-ant*; it is adjectival, and may be used as a pure adjective: *une mère aimante*, a loving mother, when it agrees with its noun. In *une mère aimant ses enfants*, a mother loving her children, it is verbal and does not agree.

The past participle is also adjectival, as in *une porte fermée*, a closed door ; *la porte est fermée*, the door is closed. It agrees with the subject when the auxiliary verb is *être*, as in *la porte est fermée*, and with the preceding object if the auxiliary verb is *avoir*. In *j'ai fermé la porte* it does not agree because the object *porte* follows the verb ; in *la porte que j'ai fermée* and in *La porte ? je l'ai fermée*, it does agree because the objects precede the verbs.

The verb has three Moods : the Indicative, which reports facts; the Subjunctive, which reports non-facts, imaginations, possibilities, contingencies, concessions; and the Imperative, which states commands.

It has two Voices : the Active, which reports the doer of the action as performing it ; the Passive, which reports the object of the action as suffering the action by the doer—e.g., He strikes the iron, and The iron is struck by him: *il frappe le fer*, *le fer est frappé par lui*. The Passive is little used in French.

The Verb has Tenses which show the time of the action, its relationship to another action, or the quality of the action —e.g., continuous, incipient, etc. The PRESENT TENSE, as in *il chante*, refers to an action now going on—he is singing— or repeated—he often sings—or stated emphatically—he does sing—French having only the one form for all of these. He is singing may be paraphrased by *il est en train de chanter*. The PERFECT (or *Passé Composé*) refers to an action that is completed now and is no longer going on : *j'ai écrit une lettre*. It also reports an action which took place in an unspecified past time : *Rome n'a pas été bâtie en un jour*, Rome was not built in a day. Finally it is used in the spoken language in place of the Historic Past (*Passé Simple*) : *Mon père est mort en* 1917, my father died in 1917, instead of the " paper " tense, *Mon père mourut en* 1917.

The FUTURE is formed from the infin. by adding *-ai, -as, -a, -ons, -ez, -ont*, but dropping the *-e* in *-re* verbs : *chanter, je chanterai; finir, je finirai; vendre, je vendrai*; the *-oir* verbs are irregular : *recevoir, je recevrai*. In the spoken language this formal future is often replaced by the present of *aller* plus the infin. : *Je vais vous dire ce que j'en pense*, I'll tell you what I think of it. The Present is often used with a Future meaning : *Alors on se voit lundi prochain?* so we'll see each other next Monday? The CONDITIONAL is also formed in the same way from the infin. by adding the endings of the Imperfect, *-ais, -ais, -ait, -ions, iez, -aient* : *chanter, je chanterais*, etc., I should sing.

The IMPERFECT is formed from the pres. part. by changing *-ant* into *-ais, -ais, -ait, -ions, -iez, -aient*. It is used for a repeated or habitual action : *Pendant les vacances nous faisions de longues promenades*, during the holidays we used to go for long walks. It is also used for an action which was already going on when another action started : *Il descendait la rue quand il rencontra son ami*, he was going down the street when he met his friend.

The PAST HISTORIC (*Passé Simple*) is used in written French, or in solemn, formal speech, to report an action at a definite time in the past and of definite duration : *Louis XIV naquit en* 1638 *et mourut en* 1715, Louis XIV was born in 1638 and died in 1715. It is the tense of narration by means of which the action is carried on step by step, the Imperfect halting the narrative in order to describe the circumstances : *Jean*

*Chabot, les coudes sur la table, repoussa son assiette et garda le regard rivé à la petite cour qu'on apercevait à travers les rideaux et dont le badigeon blanc ruisselait au soleil,* Jean Chabot, with his elbows on the table, pushed his plate away and kept his eyes fixed on the little yard which was visible through the curtains, the whitewash blazing in the sunshine. The tale moves on with *repoussa* and *garda,* and then is held up by the description of the courtyard.

The other compound tenses besides the Perfect are the Pluperfect, *j'avais chanté,* I had sung, the Future Perfect, *j'aurai chanté,* I shall have sung, and the Conditional Perfect, *j'aurais chanté,* I should have sung. The others—*j'eus chanté* and *j'ai eu chanté*—are of little practical importance.

The SUBJUNCTIVE has a present tense which ends in *-e, -es, -e, -ions, -iez, -ent,* and can be formed from the 3rd pers. plur. of the Pres. Indic. by dropping the *-nt* : *chantent, je chante ; finissent, je finisse ; vendent, je vende.* The Imperfect Subjunctive is a " paper " tense which is not used in the spoken language except in solemn and studied speech and is used in the written language almost exclusively in the 3rd pers. sing. It is formed from the 2nd pers. sing. of the Past Historic by adding *-se, -ses, ât, -ssions, -ssiez, -ssent* : *tu chantas, je chantasse, tu chantasses, il chantât, nous chantassions, vous chantassiez, ils chantassent ; tu finis, je finisse, tu finisses, il finît,* etc. ; *tu reçus, je reçusses, tu reçusses, il reçût,* etc.

The Subj. is used in the principal clause to express a wish : *Vive le roi !* long live the King ; *Dieu soit loué !* God be praised. It may also express a command, as in the 3rd pers. of the Imperative : *qu'il vienne,* let him come.

In a subordinate clause it is used when the principal verb expresses an emotion, a movement of the mind—fear, anger, surprise, regret, satisfaction, dissatisfaction, desire, fear, etc. To put it round the other way, the Subj. is used in the subordinate clause when that clause deals with what is not a fact but only a conception of the mind, or with a fact which is viewed as being merely the cause of a state of mind. The following examples will make this clearer :

*Je désire qu'elle vienne*, I wish her to come—" her coming " is not a fact.

*Je veux qu'elle obéisse*, I want her to obey—" her obeying " is not a fact.

*J'ordonne qu'elle s'en aille*, I order her to go away—" her going away " is not a fact.

*Je défends qu'elle écrive*, I forbid her to write—" her writing " is not a fact.

*Il faut que vous lisiez cela*, you must read that—" your reading " is not a fact.

*Il est possible que tu réussisses*, it is possible you may succeed —" your success " is not a fact.

*Je doute qu'il vienne*, I doubt whether he will come—" his coming " is not a fact.

*J'ai peur qu'elle ne meure*, I am afraid lest she die—" her dying " is not a fact.

*Je regrette qu'elle ait dit cela*, I regret she has said that—" her saying that " is a fact, but is considered merely as the cause of my regret.

*Je suis fâché qu'il ait échoué*, I am sorry he has failed—" his failure " is a fact, but is considered merely as the cause of my being sorry.

*Je suis étonné qu'elle soit malade*, I am astonished she is ill— " her illness " is a fact, but is considered merely as the cause of my astonishment.

*Je suis content que vous soyez venu*, I am glad you have come —" your coming " is a fact, but is considered merely as the cause of my gladness.

*Ce n'est pas que je sois malade* . . ., it is not that I am ill— " my illness " is evidently not a fact, since it is denied This use of the Subj. is common after a negative of this sort.

The two following examples of relative clauses show clearly the contrast between fact (Indic.) and non-fact (Subj.) : *J'ai trouvé une maison qui a un beau jardin*, I have found a house which has a nice garden ; *Je cherche une maison qui ait un beau jardin,* I am looking for a house which has (shall have) a nice garden.

After a superlative the Subj. is used to soften the affirmation : *C'est la plus belle femme que j'aie jamais vue,* she is the most beautiful woman I have ever seen.

The following conjunctions, amongst others, require the Subj. : *avant que,* before ; *bien que,* although ; *quoique,* although ; *pour que* and *afin que,* in order that ; *de peur que,* for fear lest.

The COMPOUND TENSES of the verb are formed with the auxiliary verbs *avoir* and *être.* All transitive verbs are conjugated with *avoir,* and also most intransitives.

All reflexive verbs and a number indicating change of state or motion are conjugated with *être.* Those always taking *être* are : *aller,* to go ; *arriver,* to arrive ; *entrer,* to enter ; *naître,* to be born ; *mourir,* to die ; *devenir,* to become ; *partir,* to set out, leave ; *sortir,* to go out ; *venir,* to come. To these may be added *accourir,* to hasten up ; *descendre,* to descend ; *monter,* to go up ; *tomber,* to fall, which are generally found with *être* but may be used with *avoir.* Examples are : *je me suis lavé,* I washed myself ; *elle est allée en ville,* she went to town ; *il est entré dans la salle à manger,* he came into the dining-room, etc.

Verbs which indicate merely a bodily activity are conjugated with *avoir* : *marcher,* to walk ; *courir,* to run ; *sauter,* to jump, etc.

Impersonal verbs are used only in the 3rd pers. sing. : *il pleut,* it is raining ; *il faut,* it is necessary ; *il tonne,* it is thundering.

French uses reflexive verbs more readily than English, and especially when it is a true reflexive : I wash at 7 o'clock = *Je me lave à 7 heures.* The reflexive is frequently used in French where we use a Passive : That is not done, *cela ne se fait pas.*

## CONJUGATION OF THE VERBS

### Avoir and être

Pres. part. : ayant, étant.   Past part. : eu, été

| Pres. Indic. | | Future. | | Conditional. | | Imperfect. | |
|---|---|---|---|---|---|---|---|
| ai | suis | aurai | serai | aurais | serais | avais | étais |
| as | es | auras | seras | aurais | serais | avais | étais |
| a | est | aura | sera | aurait | serait | avait | était |
| avons | sommes | aurons | serons | aurions | serions | avions | étions |
| avez | êtes | aurez | serez | auriez | seriez | aviez | étiez |
| ont | sont | auront | seront | auraient | seraient | avaient | étaient |

| Past Historic. | | Perfect. | | Pluperfect. | |
|---|---|---|---|---|---|
| eus | fus | ai eu | ai été | avais eu | avais été |
| eus | fus | as eu | as été | avais eu | avais été |
| eut | fut | a eu | a été | avait eu | avait été |
| eûmes | fûmes | avons eu | avons été | avions eu | avions été |
| eûtes | fûtes | avez eu | avez été | aviez eu | aviez été |
| eurent | furent | ont eu | ont été | avaient eu | avaient été |

| Subjunctive. | | | | | | Imperative. | |
|---|---|---|---|---|---|---|---|
| Present. | | Imperfect. | | Perfect. | | | |
| aie | sois | eusse | fusse | aie eu | aie été | — | — |
| aies | sois | eusses | fusses | aies eu | aies été | aie | sois |
| ait | soit | eût | fût | ait eu | ait été | — | — |
| ayons | soyons | eussions | fussions | ayons eu | ayons été | ayons | soyons |
| ayez | soyez | eussiez | fussiez | ayez eu | ayez été | ayez | soyez |
| aient | soient | eussent | fussent | aient eu | aient été | — | — |

## Endings of the Three Regular Conjugations in (1) -er, (2) -ir, (3) -re

In the following table the hyphen represents the stem of the verb—e.g., chant(er), fin(ir), vend(re).   No compound tenses are given, as they can be made up with the Past Part. plus the appropriate tense of *avoir* or *être*.

|  | Infinitive : | (1) -er ; | (2) -ir ; | (3) -re. |
|---|---|---|---|---|
|  | Pres. part. : | -ant ; | -issant ; | -ant. |
|  | Past part. : | -é ; | -i ; | -u. |

## Indicative

| Present. | | | Future. | | Conditional. | | Imperfect. | |
|---|---|---|---|---|---|---|---|---|
| -e | -is | -s | | ⌠ -ai | | ⌠ -ais | | ⌠ -ais |
| -es | -is | -s | | ⎪ -as | | ⎪ -ais | | ⎪ -ais |
| -e | -it | -(t) | chanter | ⎪ -a | chanter | ⎨ -ait | chant | ⎨ -ait |
| -ons | -issons | -ons | finir | ⎬ -ons | finir | ⎪ -ions | finiss | ⎪ -ions |
| -ez | -issez | -ez | vendr | ⎪ -ez | vendr | ⎪ -iez | vend | ⎪ -iez |
| -ent | -issent | -ent | | ⌡ -ont | | ⌡ -aient | | ⌡ -aient |

| Past Historic. | | | Imperative Mood. | | |
|---|---|---|---|---|---|
| -ai | -is | -is | -e | -is | -s |
| -as | -is | -is | -ons | -issons | -ons |
| -a | -it | -it | -ez | -issez | -ez |
| -âmes | -îmes | -îmes | | | |
| -âtes | -îtes | -îtes | | | |
| -èrent | -irent | -irent | | | |

## Subjunctive

| Present. | | | Imperfect. | | |
|---|---|---|---|---|---|
| -e | -isse | -e | -asse | -isse | -isse |
| -es | -isses | -es | -asses | -isses | -isses |
| -e | -isse | -e | -ât | -ît | -ît |
| -ions | -issions | -ions | -assions | -issions | -issions |
| -iez | -issiez | -iez | -assiez | -issiez | -issiez |
| -ent | -issent | -ent | -assent | -issent | -issent |

## The Reflexive Verb

To show the position of the reflexive pronouns we give below the conjugation of the Present Tense of *se laver*, to wash oneself, in the affirmative, negative and interrogative, followed by the Imperative in the affirmative and negative.

## Present Tense

| Affirmative. | Negative. | Interrogative. |
|---|---|---|
| je me lave | je ne me lave pas | *est-ce que je me lave? |
| tu te laves | tu ne te laves pas | te laves-tu? |
| il se lave | il ne se lave pas | se lave-t-il? |
| elle se lave | elle ne se lave pas | se lave-t-elle? |
| nous nous lavons | nous ne nous lavons pas | nous lavons-nous? |
| vous vous lavez | vous ne vous lavez pas | vous lavez-vous? |
| ils se lavent | ils ne se lavent pas | se lavent-ils? |
| elles se lavent | elles ne se lavent pas | se lavent-elles? |

## Imperative

| Affirmative. | Negative. |
|---|---|
| lave-toi | ne te lave pas |
| lavons-nous | ne nous lavons pas |
| lavez-vous | ne vous lavez pas |

### *Notes on the Conjugation of the Regular Verbs*

1. When followed by -*e* or -*i*, *c* is pronounced soft [= s]; when followed by -*a*, -*o*, or -*u*, *c* is pronounced hard [= k]; *ç* is always pronounced soft. Hence if a verb ends in -*cer*, the *c* must have the cedilla when it is followed by -*a* or -*o* or -*u*: *je commence, nous commençons, je commençais*. With verbs in -*cevoir* similarly : *je reçois, j'ai reçu*.

2. In the same way, -*ge* is pronounced [ʒə] and -*gi* [ʒi], but -*go*, -*ga*, -*gu* are pronounced [go, ga, gy]. Hence verbs in -*ger* must insert an -*e* after the *g* so as to keep it soft when followed by -*a*, -*o*, -*u* : *j'engage, nous engageons, j'engageais*.

3. Verbs with the stem vowel *é* [= e] change this to the open vowel *è* [= ɛ] when the stress falls on it : *protéger, je protège, tu protèges, il protège, nous protégeons, vous protégez, ils protègent; je protégerai*.

4. Verbs with the stem vowel in " *e* mute " [= ə] change this into the " open *e* " [= ɛ] when the stress falls on it or when it is followed by a mute syllable.

* In the 1st pers. sing. the interrogative is not formed by inversion as in the other persons but by prefixing *est-ce que*.

The " open *e* " [= ɛ] is spelt " *è* " in most verbs of this type : *je lève, tu lèves, il lève, nous levons, vous levez, ils lèvent*. A number of verbs in *-eler* and *-eter*, however, spell the " open *e* " by doubling the consonant : *j'appelle, tu appelles, il appelle, nous appelons, vous appelez, ils appellent ; je jette, nous jetons*, etc.

5. Verbs in *-ayer*, *-oyer*, *-uyer* keep the *y* only before a sounded vowel : *essayer, j'essaie, tu essaies, il essaie, nous essayons, vous essayez, ils essaient, j'ai essayé, essayant*, etc. Verbs in *-ayer* may keep the *y* in all positions : *payer, je paie* or *je paye*.

## The Interrogative

The Interrogative is formed : (1) by inversion when the subject is a pronoun : *vous voyez ; voyez-vous ?* With the 1st pers. sing. inversion is replaced by the periphrastic form *est-ce que* : *est-ce que je vois ?* With *-er* verbs (in literary usage only) inversion is used and for the sake of euphony the " mute *e* " becomes *é* : *je chante; chanté-je ?* (2) When the subject is a noun the corresponding pronoun is used to form the interrogative : *la femme chante ; la femme chante-t-elle ?* This *-t-* is inserted in all inversions of the 3rd pers. sing. of the Present of *-er* verbs. (3) In all cases *est-ce que* may be used to form the interrogative : *est-ce que vous venez ? est-ce que la femme chante ?* (4) The interrogative is often made by rising intonation : *vous voyez ?*

The use of " do " in the interrogative and negative is peculiar to English, and must not be imitated in French : Do I take it ? = *Est-ce que je le prends ?* I don't take it = *Je ne le prends pas*.

## LIST OF THE COMMON IRREGULAR VERBS

The List below gives : in Col. 1 the Infin. ; the Pres. Part. ; the Past Part. in the form of the 3rd pers. sing. of the Perfect, thus showing whether the auxiliary is *avoir* or *être*. This is followed by the Future if it is not formed regularly from the Infin. Col. 2 gives the Pres. Indic., and shows by an asterisk the 2nd pers. sing. and the 1st and 2nd pers. plural if they are used as the Imperative. Col. 3 gives the Pres. Subj. if it is not formed regularly from the 3rd pers. plural of the Pres. Indic. Col. 4 gives the Imperative if it is not shown by asterisks in Col. 2. Col. 5 gives the 1st pers. sing. of the Past Historic.

| Col. 1. Infin., Pres. Part., Perf., Fut. | Col. 2. Pres. Indic. and Imperative. | | Col. 3. Pres. Subj. | | Col. 4. Imperative. | Col. 5. Past Hist. |
|---|---|---|---|---|---|---|
| abattre, fell, *see* battre | | | | | | |
| admettre, admit, *see* mettre | | | | | | |
| aller, go | vais | allons | aille | allions | va (vas-y) | j'allai |
| allant | vas | allez | ailles | alliez | allons | |
| il est allé | va | vont | aille | aillent | allez | |
| j'irai | | | | | | |
| apercevoir, perceive, *see* recevoir | | | | | | |
| apprendre, learn, *see* prendre | | | | | | |
| asseoir, seat | assieds | asseyons* | | | | j'assis |
| asseyant | *assieds | asseyez* | | | | |
| il a assis | assied | asseyent | | | | |
| (il s'est assis) | | | | | | |
| j'assiérai or j'assoirai | | | | | | |

| Col. 1. Infin., Pres. Part., Perf., Fut. | Col. 2. Pres. Indic. and Imperative. | | Col. 3. Pres. Subj. | | Col. 4. Imperative. | Col. 5. Past Hist. |
|---|---|---|---|---|---|---|
| battre, **beat** | bats | battons* | | | | je battis |
| battant | *bats | battez* | | | | |
| il a battu | bat | battent | | | | |
| boire, **drink** | bois | buvons* | boive | buvions | | je bus |
| bûvant | *bois | buvez* | boives | buviez | | |
| il a bu | boit | boivent | boive | boivent | | |
| combattre, **fight,** *see* battre | | | | | | |
| commettre, **commit,** *see* mettre | | | | | | |
| comprendre, **understand,** *see* prendre | | | | | | |
| connaître, **know** | connais | connaissons* | | | | je connus |
| connaissant | *connais | connaissez* | | | | |
| il a connu | connaît | connaissent | | | | |
| construire, **construct** | construis | construisons* | | | | je construisis |
| construisant | *construis | construisez* | | | | |
| il a construit | construit | construisent | | | | |
| courir, **run** | cours | courons* | | | | je courus |
| courant | *cours | courez* | | | | |
| il a couru | court | courent | | | | |
| je courrai | | | | | | |
| couvrir, **cover,** *see* ouvrir | | | | | | |
| craindre, **fear** | crains | craignons* | | | | je craignis |
| craignant | *crains | craignez* | | | | |
| il a craint | craint | craignent | | | | |
| croire, **believe** | crois | croyons* | croie | croyions | | je crus |
| croyant | *crois | croyez* | croies | croyiez | | |
| il a cru | croit | croient | croie | croient | | |

| Col. 1.<br>Infin., Pres.<br>Part., Perf., Fut. | Col. 2.<br>Pres. Indic. and<br>Imperative. | | Col. 3.<br>Pres. Subj. | | Col. 4.<br>Im-<br>perative. | Col. 5.<br>Past<br>Hist. |
|---|---|---|---|---|---|---|
| décrire, de-<br>scribe, *see*<br>écrire | | | | | | |
| détruire, de-<br>stroy, *see*<br>construire | | | | | | |
| devoir, owe,<br>must<br>devant<br>il a dû (fem. due)<br>je devrai | dois<br>*dois<br>doit | devons*<br>devez*<br>doivent | doive<br>doives<br>doive | devions<br>deviez<br>doivent | | je dus |
| dire, say<br>disant<br>il a dit | dis<br>*dis<br>dit | disons*<br>dites*<br>disent | | | | je dis |
| dormir, sleep<br>dormant<br>il a dormi | dors<br>*dors<br>dort | dormons*<br>dormez*<br>dorment | | | | je dormis |
| écrire, write<br>écrivant<br>il a écrit | écris<br>*écris<br>écrit | écrivons*<br>écrivez*<br>écrivent | | | | j'écrivis |
| envoyer, send<br>envoyant<br>il a envoyé<br>j'enverrai | envoie<br>envoies<br>envoie | envoyons<br>envoyez<br>envoient | | | envoie<br>envoyons<br>envoyez | j'envoyai |
| faire, make<br>faisant<br>il a fait<br>je ferai | fais<br>*fais<br>fait | faisons*<br>faites*<br>font | fasse<br>fasses<br>fasse | fassions<br>fassiez<br>fassent | | je fis |
| faillir, fail<br>(none)<br>il a failli<br>(none) | (Le cœur me faut =<br>My heart fails me) | | | | | je faillis |
| falloir, be<br>necessary<br>(none)<br>il a fallu<br>il faudra | il faut | | il faille | | (none) | il fallut |

| Col. 1. Infin., Pres. Part., Perf., Fut. | Col. 2. Pres. Indic. and Imperative. | | Col. 3. Pres. Subj. | Col. 4. Im- perative. | Col. 5. Past Hist. |
|---|---|---|---|---|---|
| introduire, in- troduce, see construire | | | | | |
| lire, **read** | lis | lisons* | | | je lus |
| lisant | *lis | lisez* | | | |
| il a lu | lit | lisent | | | |
| luire, **shine** | luis | luisons* | | | je luisis |
| luisant | *luis | luisez* | | | |
| il a lui | luit | luisent | | | |
| mentir, **lie** | mens | mentons* | | | je mentis |
| mentant | *mens | mentez* | | | |
| il a menti | ment | mentent | | | |
| mettre, **put** | mets | mettons* | | | je mis |
| mettant | *mets | mettez* | | | |
| il a mis | met | mettent | | | |
| mourir, **die** | meurs | mourons* | meure | mourions | je mourus |
| mourant | *meurs | mourez* | meures | mouriez | |
| il est mort | meurt | meurent | meure | meurent | |
| je mourrai | | | | | |
| naître, **to be born** | nais | naissons* | | | je naquis |
| | *nais | naissez* | | | |
| naissant | naît | naissent | | | |
| il est né | | | | | |
| offrir, **offer,** see ouvrir | | | | | |
| ouvrir, **open** | ouvre | ouvrons | | ouvre | j'ouvris |
| ouvrant | ouvres | ouvrez | | ouvrons | |
| il a ouvert | ouvre | ouvrent | | ouvrez | |
| paraître, ap- pear, see con- naître | | | | | |
| partir, **set out,** see mentir | | | | | |
| peindre, **paint,** see craindre | | | | | |
| plaindre, **pity,** see craindre | | | | | |

| Col. 1.<br>Infin., Pres.<br>Part., Perf., Fut. | Col. 2.<br>Pres. Indic. and<br>Imperative. | | Col. 3.<br>Pres. Subj. | Col. 4.<br>Im-<br>perative. | Col. 5.<br>Past<br>Hist. |
|---|---|---|---|---|---|
| plaire, **please**<br>plaisant<br>il a plu | plais<br>*plais<br>plaît | plaisons*<br>plaisez*<br>plaisent | | | je plus |
| pleuvoir, **rain**<br>pleuvant<br>il a plu<br>il pleuvra | il pleut | | il pleuve | (none) | il plut |
| pouvoir, **be able**<br>pouvant<br> a pu<br>je pourrai | peux<br>peux<br>peut | pouvons<br>pouvez<br>peuvent | puisse puissions<br>puisses puissiez<br>puisse puissent | (none) | je pus |
| prendre, **take**<br>prenant<br>il a pris | prends<br>*prends<br>prend | prenons*<br>prenez*<br>prennent | | | je pris |
| produire, **pro-<br>duce**, *see* con-<br>struire | | | | | |
| recevoir, **receive**<br>recevant<br>il a reçu<br>je recevrai | reçois<br>*reçois<br>reçoit | recevons*<br>recevez*<br>reçoivent | reçoive recevions<br>reçoives receviez<br>reçoive reçoivent | | je reçus |
| rire, **laugh**<br>riant<br>il a ri | ris<br>*ris<br>rit | rions*<br>riez*<br>rient | | | je ris |
| savoir, **know**<br>sachant<br>il a su<br>je saurai<br>Imperfect:<br>je savais | sais<br>sais<br>sait | savons<br>savez<br>savent | sache sachions sache<br>saches sachiez sachons<br>sache sachent sachez | | je sus |
| sentir, **feel**, *see*<br>mentir | | | | | |
| servir, **serve**,<br>*see* mentir | | | | | |
| sortir, **go out**,<br>*see* mentir | | | | | |
| souffrir, **suffer**,<br>*see* ouvrir | | | | | |

| Col. 1.<br>Infin., Pres.<br>Part., Perf., Fut. | Col. 2.<br>Pres. Indic. and<br>Imperative. | Col. 3.<br>Pres. Subj. | Col. 4.<br>Im-<br>perative. | Col. 5.<br>Past<br>Hist. |
|---|---|---|---|---|
| suivre, follow | suis | suivons* | | | je suivis |
| suivant | *suis | suivez* | | | |
| il a suivi | suit | suivent | | | |
| taire, keep<br>silent | tais<br>*tais | taisons*<br>taisez* | | | je tus |
| taisant | tait | taisent | | | |
| il a tu | | | | | |
| tenir, hold | tiens | tenons* | tienne | tenions | je tins |
| tenant | *tiens | tenez* | tiennes | teniez | |
| il a tenu | tient | tiennent | tienne | tiennent | |
| je tiendrai | | | | | |
| vaincre, van-<br>quish | vaincs<br>*vaincs | vainquons*<br>vainquez* | | | je vain-<br>quis |
| vainquant | vainc | vainquent | | | |
| il a vaincu | | | | | |
| valoir, be<br>worth | vaux<br>*vaux | valons*<br>valez* | vaille<br>vailles | valions<br>valiez | je valus |
| valant | vaut | valent | vaille | vaillent | |
| il a valu | | | | | |
| je vaudrai | | | | | |
| venir, come,<br>see tenir | | | | | |
| il est venu | | | | | |
| vivre, live | vis | vivons* | | | je vécus |
| vivant | *vis | vivez* | | | |
| il a vécu | vit | vivent | | | |
| voir, see | vois | voyons* | voie | voyions | je vis |
| voyant | *vois | voyez* | voies | voyiez | |
| il a vu | voit | voient | voie | voient | |
| je verrai | | | | | |
| vouloir, wish | veux | voulons* | veuille | voulions † | je voulus |
| voulant | *veux | voulez* | veuilles | vouliez | |
| il a voulu | veut | veulent | veuille | veuillent | |
| je voudrai | | | | | |

† *Veux, voulons, voulez* are used in the sense of " use your will-power "
—e.g., *voulez que ça se fasse et ça se fera* = wish that it shall be done and
it will be done. *Veuille* and *veuillez* are used with a dependent infin.
and *bien* for " please ": *veuillez bien vous asseoir*, please take a seat.

# PASSPORT FORMALITIES

## Vocabulary

| English. | | Pronunciation. |
|---|---|---|
| The passport | **Le passeport** | lə pɑspɔr |
| The passport examination | **Le contrôle des passeports** | lə kɔ̃trol de pɑspɔr |
| The visa | **Le visa** | lə viza |
| The permit to stay | **Le permis de séjour** | lə pɛrmitseʒur |
| The stay | **Le séjour** | lə seʒur |
| The purpose | **Le but** | lə by(t) |
| The fee | **Le droit** | lə drwa |

## Phrases

| | | |
|---|---|---|
| Do I need a visa? | **Ai-je besoin d'un visa?** | ɛʒ bəzwɛ̃ dœ̃ viza? |
| I am going as a tourist | **Je voyage comme touriste** | ʒvwajaʒ kɔm turist |
| I wish to seek employment | **Je veux chercher un emploi** | ʒvøʃɛrʃe œ̃nɑ̃plwa |
| I am travelling through France | **Je vais traverser la France** | ʒvɛ travɛrse la frɑ̃s |
| I wish to break the journey | **Je veux m'arrêter en route** | ʒvø marɛte ɑ̃ rut |
| How long may I stay in the country? | **Combien de temps puis-je séjourner dans le pays?** | kɔ̃bjɛ̃ttɑ̃ pɥiʒ seʒurne dɑ̃lpei? |
| Do I report to the police? | **Dois-je déclarer mon arrivée à la police?** | dwaʒ deklare mɔ̃narive alapɔlis? |

49

| English. | | Pronunciation. |
|---|---|---|
| How much does the visa cost ? | Combien le visa coûte-t-il ? | kɔ̃bjɛ̃ lviza kuttil ? |
| Must I get a permit to stay (to take up work) ? | Dois-je me procurer un permis de séjour (permis de travail) ? | dwaʒ mə prɔkyre œ̃ pɛrmitseʒur (pɛrmittravaj) ? |
| You must have your passport renewed | Il vous faut faire renouveler votre passeport | il vu fo fɛr rnuvle vɔt paspɔr |
| Where is the British Consulate ? | Où se trouve le Consulat britannique ? | ustruv lə kɔ̃syla britanik ? |

## CUSTOMS

### Vocabulary

| The duty | Le droit de douane | le drwaddwan |
|---|---|---|
| The custom-house | (Le bureau de) la douane | lə byro dla dwan |
| The custom-house officer | Le douanier | lə dwanje |
| The luggage | Les bagages | le bagaʒ |
| The tobacco | Le tabac | lə taba |
| The cigars | Les cigares | le sigar |
| The perfume | Le parfum | lə parfœ̃ |
| The camera | L'appareil (de prise de vues) | laparɛj (də priz də vy) |
| The dutiable articles | Les articles soumis aux droits de douane | lezartiklə sumizo drwaddwan |

### Phrases

| Where is the custom-house ? | Où se trouve la douane ? | ustruv la dwan ? |
|---|---|---|
| Here is my luggage. | Voici mes bagages | vwasi me bagaʒ |

| English. | | Pronunciation. |
|---|---|---|
| Will you examine my luggage, please? | Voulez-vous visiter mes bagages, s'il vous plaît? | vulevu visite me bagaʒ, sivuplɛ? |
| Have you anything to declare? | Avez-vous quelque chose à déclarer? | avevu kɛlkəʃoz a deklare? |
| Have you any of the articles on this list? | Avez-vous des articles qui se trouvent sur cette liste? | avevu dezartikl ki struv syr sɛt list? |
| Have you any spirits or tobacco? | Avez-vous des spiritueux ou du tabac? | avevu de spiritɥø u dy taba? |
| I have this small bottle of perfume. | J'ai ce petit flacon de parfum | ʒe sə pti flakɔ̃ də parfœ̃ |
| That is free of duty. | Ça, c'est exempt de droits de douane | sa sɛtɛgzɑ̃ də drwaddwan |
| Is that all? | Est-ce tout? | ɛs tu? |
| Is my luggage passed? | Est-ce que mes bagages ont passé la douane? | ɛskə me bagaʒ ɔ̃ pɑse la dwan? |
| Will you take this luggage to a taxi? | Voulez-vous porter ces bagages à un taxi? | vulevu pɔrte se bagaʒ a œ̃ taksi? |

## TRAVELLING BY RAIL[1]
### Vocabulary

| | | |
|---|---|---|
| The transport | Le transport | lə trɑ̃spɔr |
| The railway | Le chemin de fer | lə ʃmɛ̃tfɛr |
| The station | La gare | la gar |
| The train | Le train | lə trɛ̃ |
| The enquiry office | Le bureau de renseignements | lə byro drɑ̃sɛɲəmɑ̃ |

[1] Apply to French Railways Ltd., 179 Piccadilly, London, W.1, for particulars of Tourist Tickets, Combined Rail–Road Tickets, Family Tickets, Party Tickets, Students' Tickets. You may be entitled to considerable reductions on the ordinary fare.

| English. | | Pronunciation. |
|---|---|---|
| The booking-office | Le guichet (des billets) | lə giʃɛ (de bijɛ) |
| The fare | Le prix du voyage | lə pri dy vwajaʒ |
| The ticket | Le billet | lə bijɛ |
| The platform | Le quai | lə ke |
| The express train | Le train express (l'express, le rapide) | lə trɛ̃ ɛkspres (lɛkspres, lə rapid) |
| The slow train | Le train omnibus | lə trɛ̃ ɔmnibys |
| The coach, carriage | La voiture (le wagon) | la vwatyr (lə vagɔ̃) |
| The compartment | Le compartiment | lə kɔ̃partimɑ̃ |
| The seat | La place | la plas |
| The corner seat | La place de coin | la plas də kwɛ̃ |
| To reserve a seat | Retenir une place | rətnir yn plas |
| The lavatory | La toilette | la twalɛt |
| The passenger | Le voyageur (la voyageuse) | lə vwajaʒœr (la vwajaʒøz) |
| The luggage | Les bagages | le bagaʒ |
| The cloak-room | La consigne | la kɔ̃siɲ |
| The arrival | L'arrivée | larive |
| The departure | Le départ | lə depar |
| The barrier | La barrière | la barjɛr |

## Phrases

| | | |
|---|---|---|
| Where do I get a ticket ? | Où peut-on prendre son billet ? | u pøtɔ̃ prɑ̃dr sɔ̃ bijɛ ? |
| Is the booking-office open ? | Est-ce que le guichet (des billets) est ouvert ? | ɛskə lgiʃɛ (de bijɛ) ɛtuvɛr ? |
| One second return Paris, and a platform ticket | Un aller et retour, deuxième classe, pour Paris et un billet de quai | œ̃nale e rtur døzjɛm klas pur pari e œ̃ bijɛtke. |

| English. | | Pronunciation. |
|---|---|---|
| Are you travelling via Dieppe or Boulogne? | Voyagez-vous par Dieppe ou par Boulogne? | vwajaʒevu par djɛp u par buloɲ? |
| Which is the shortest way? | Quel est le trajet le plus court? | kɛl ɛ ltraʒe lə ply kur? |
| What is the fare to Paris? | Quel est le prix du billet pour Paris? | kɛl ɛ lpri dy bijɛ pur pari? |
| You have to pay a surcharge on this ticket | Il vous faut payer un supplément sur ce billet | il vu fo pɛje œ̃ syplemã syr sə bijɛ |
| Have your change ready | Veuillez faire l'appoint | vœje fɛr lapwɛ̃ |
| Can I break the journey? | Puis-je m'arrêter en route? | pɥiʒ marɛte ã rut? |
| Shall I get the connection? | Vais-je attraper la correspondance? | vɛʒ atrape la korɛspɔ̃dãs? |
| Where must I change? | Où faut-il changer de train? | u fotil ʃãʒe də trɛ̃? |
| Will the train be late? | Est-ce que le train aura du retard? | ɛskəltrɛ̃ ɔra dy rtar? |
| Porter, please register this luggage to Bordeaux | Porteur, faites enregistrer ces bagages jusqu'à Bordeaux, s'il vous plaît | pɔrtœr, fɛtzãrəʒistre se bagaʒ ʒyska bɔrdo, sivuplɛ |
| You will have to pay excess luggage on this | Il vous faudra payer un excédent de bagages pour ceci | il vu fodra pɛje œ̃nɛksedãdbagaʒ pur səsi |
| Please bring me the registration slip to the 1st Class restaurant | Apportez-moi, s'il vous plaît, le billet de bagages au restaurant de première classe | apɔrtemwa, sivuplɛ, lə bijɛ dbagaʒ o rɛstɔrã də prəmjɛr klɑs |
| Please leave these suitcases in the cloakroom | Mettez ces mallettes à la consigne, s'il vous plaît | mɛte se malɛt ala kɔ̃siɲ, sivuplɛ |

| English. | | Pronunciation. |
|---|---|---|
| From which platform does the train start? | De quel quai le train part-il? | dəkɛl ke ltrɛ̃ partil? |
| Platform No. IV through the subway | Du quai numéro quatre. On y accède par le passage souterrain | dy ke nymero katr. ɔ̃ni aksɛd par lpasaʒ sutɛrɛ̃ |
| Please get me a corner seat, 1st Class, facing the engine, non-smoker | Marquez-moi, s'il vous plaît, une place de coin, première classe, face à la route, dans un compartiment non-fumeurs | marke mwa, sivuplɛ, yn plas dəkwɛ̃, prəmjɛr klɑs, fas ala rut, dɑ̃zœ̃ kɔ̃partimɑ̃ nɔ̃fymœr |
| Is there a restaurant car on the train? | Y a-t-il un wagon-restaurant dans le train? | jatil œ̃ vagɔ̃rɛstɔrɑ̃ dɑ̃ ltrɛ̃? |
| This train is entirely a sleeper | Ce train est composé entièrement de wagons-lits | sə trɛ̃ ɛ kɔ̃poze ɑ̃tjɛrmɑ̃ dvagɔ̃li |
| Have you a reserved seat? | Votre place est-elle retenue? | vɔt plas ɛtɛl rətny? |
| When does the train arrive? | A quelle heure le train arrive-t-il? | a kɛl œr ltrɛ̃ arivtil? |
| You will find the arrival and departure times of the trains in the railway guide | Vous trouverez dans l'indicateur les heures d'arrivée et de départ | vu truvre dɑ̃ lɛ̃dikatœr lezœr darive eddepar. |
| Here is the summer time-table | Voici l'horaire d'été. | vwasi lɔrɛr dete. |
| I bought my ticket at the travel agency | J'ai acheté mon billet à l'agence de tourisme | ʒe aʃte mɔ̃ bijɛ a laʒɑ̃s də turism |
| Have you insured your luggage? | Avez-vous fait assurer vos bagages? | avevu fɛtasyre vo bagaʒ? |

| English. | | Pronunciation. |
|---|---|---|
| Take your seats, please | En voiture, s'il vous plaît | ɑ̃ vwatyr, sivuplɛ |
| Your case is too large for this luggage rack | Votre valise est trop grande pour ce filet | vɔt valiz ɛ tro grɑ̃d pursfilɛ |
| Windows may only be opened with the permission of all fellow passengers | On ne peut baisser les glaces qu'avec le consentement de tous les voyageurs | ɔ̃npø bɛse le glas kavɛk lə kɔ̃sɑ̃tmɑ̃ də tu le vwajaʒœr |
| Do not lean out of the window | Ne vous penchez pas au dehors | nə vu pɑ̃ʃe pɑzodəɔr |
| Where is the emergency brake | Où est le signal d'alarme ? | wɛ lsiɲaldalarm ? |
| Which is the next station ? | Quelle est la prochaine gare ? | kɛl ɛ la prɔʃɛn gar ? |
| How long do we stop here ? | Combien d'arrêt ici ? | kɔ̃bjɛ̃ darɛ isi ? |
| You had better ask the ticket-collector when he checks the tickets | Vous feriez mieux de le demander au contrôleur quand il viendra contrôler les billets | vu fərje mjø dəl dəmɑ̃de o kɔ̃trolœr kɑ̃til vjɛ̃dra kɔ̃trole le bijɛ |
| Bordeaux ! All change here | Bordeaux ! Tout le monde descend ! | bɔrdo ! tulmɔ̃d dɛsɑ̃ ! |
| I have left my overcoat in the train. Where is the Lost Property Office ? | J'ai laissé mon pardessus dans le train. Où est le service des objets trouvés ? | ʒe lɛse mɔ̃ pardəsy dɑ̃ltrɛ̃. wɛlsɛrvis dezɔbʒe truve ? |
| Where is the station hotel ? | Où est l'hôtel de la gare ? | wɛ lotɛl dla gar ? |

## TRAVELLING BY CAR

### Vocabulary

| English. | | Pronunciation. |
|---|---|---|
| The motor-car | L'automobile | lotɔmɔbil |
| The motor bus (coach) | L'autobus (l'auto-car) | lotɔbys (lotɔkar) |
| The taxi(cab) | Le taxi | lə taksi |
| The motorist | L'automobiliste | lotɔmɔbilist |
| The chassis | Le châssis | lə ʃɑsi |
| The body | La carrosserie | la karɔsri |
| The bonnet | Le capot | lə kapo |
| The mudguard | Le garde-boue | lə gardəbu |
| The wheel | La roue | la ru |
| The tyre | Le pneu | lə pnø |
| The brake | Le frein | lə frɛ̃ |
| The gear-lever | Le levier des vi-tesses | lə ləvje de vitɛs |
| The gear-box | La boîte (de change-ments) de vitesses | la bwat (də ʃɑ̃mɑ̃) dvitɛs |
| The steering wheel | Le volant | lə vɔlɑ̃ |
| The exhaust | L'échappement | leʃapmɑ̃ |
| The battery | La batterie | la batri |
| The carburettor | Le carburateur | lə carbyratœr |
| The accelerator | L'accélérateur | lakseleratœr |
| The bumper | Le pare-choc(s) | lə parʃɔk |
| The motor-horn | Le klaxon | lə klaksɔ̃ |
| The windscreen | Le pare-brise | lə parbriz |
| The spare parts | Les pièces de re-change | le pjɛs dərʃɑ̃ʒ |
| The petrol-station | Le distributeur d'es-sence | lə distribytœr dɛsɑ̃s |
| The petrol | L'essence | lɛsɑ̃s |
| The clutch | L'embrayage | lɑ̃brejaʒ |

| English. | | Pronunciation. |
|---|---|---|
| The headlamp | Le phare | lə far |
| The spring | Le ressort | lə rəsɔr |
| The plug | La bougie | la buʒi |
| The steering | La direction | la dirɛksjɔ̃ |
| The starter | Le démarreur | lə demarœr |
| The garage (for repairs) | Le garage (pour les réparations) | lə garaʒ (pur le reparasjɔ̃) |
| To overtake | Doubler | duble |

## Phrases

| | | |
|---|---|---|
| Are you an owner-driver? | Êtes-vous conducteur-propriétaire? | ɛtvu kɔ̃dyktœr prɔprietɛr? |
| What is the horse-power of your car? | Quelle est la puissance en chevaux de votre auto? | kɛl ɛ la pɥisɑ̃s ɑ̃ ʃvo də vɔtroto? |
| I have a touring saloon (sports car) | J'ai une conduite-intérieure de tourisme (machine grand sport) | ʒe yn kɔ̃dɥitɛ̃terjœr də turism (maʃin grɑ̃spɔr) |
| My car is a two-seater | Ma voiture est une deux-places | ma vwatyr ɛt yn døplas |
| Who will drive to-day? | Qui va conduire aujourd'hui? | ki va kɔ̃dɥir oʒurdɥi? |
| Have you got your driving licence with you? | Avez-vous votre permis de conduire sur vous? | avevu vot pɛrmi-tkɔ̃dɥir syr vu? |
| Look out for the bends, otherwise we shall skid | Faites attention aux virages, autrement nous allons déraper | fɛtsatɑ̃sjɔ̃ o viraʒ, otrəmɑ̃ nuzalɔ̃ derape |
| Did you see the traffic lights? | Avez-vous vu les feux de signalisation? | avevu vy le fø də siɲalizasjɔ̃? |

| English. | | Pronunciation. |
|---|---|---|
| The traffic policeman took our number | L'agent de la circulation a noté le numéro de notre voiture | laʒɑ̃ dla sirkylasjɔ̃ a nɔte lnymero də not vwatyr |
| We shall have to pay a fine | Nous aurons une amende à payer | nuzɔrɔ̃zynamɑ̃d a pɛje |
| I have had a breakdown | Je suis resté en panne | ʒə sɥi rɛste ɑ̃ pan |
| It does not matter if we get a puncture, I have a spare wheel with me | Ça ne fait rien si nous avons une crevaison, j'ai une roue de secours | san fɛ rjɛ̃ si nuzavɔ̃zyn krəvɛzɔ̃, ʒe yn rutskur |
| Have you any spare parts with you? | Avez-vous des pièces de rechange avec vous? | avevu de pjɛs dərʃɑ̃ʒ avɛk vu? |
| Shall I press the self-starter? | Voulez-vous que j'appuie sur le démarreur? | vulevu kə ʒapɥi syr ldemarœr |
| Step on the gas | Mettez pleins gaz | mɛte plɛ̃ gɑz |
| You must switch on the head-lights | Il faut allumer les phares | il fotalyme le far |
| We are going downhill | Nous descendons une côte | nu dɛsɑ̃dɔ̃zyn kot |
| Shall I start the screen-wiper? | Voulez-vous que je mette l'essuie-glace en marche? | vulevu kə ʒmɛt lɛsɥiglas ɑ̃ marʃ? |
| I must change into second gear | Je dois mettre en deuxième vitesse | ʒdwamɛtr ɑ̃ døzjɛm vitɛs |
| Where can I park (my car)? | Où puis-je garer mon auto? | u pɥiʒ gare mɔ̃noto? |
| Where can I get this car repaired? I have had a collision | Où puis-je faire réparer cette auto? J'ai été tamponné | u pɥiʒ fɛr repare sɛt oto? ʒe ete tɑ̃pɔne |

| English. | | Pronunciation. |
|---|---|---|
| Where is the nearest petrol-station | Où se trouve le distributeur d'essence le plus proche ? | ustruv lə distribytœr dɛsɑ̃s lə ply prɔʃ ? |
| I must get my tank filled and have my tyres inflated | Je dois faire le plein d'essence et faire gonfler mes pneus | ʒdwa fɛr lə plɛ̃ dɛsɑ̃s e fɛr gɔ̃fle me pnø |
| Slow down | Ralentir ! | ralɑ̃tir ! |
| One-way road | Route (rue) à sens unique | rut (ry) a sɑ̃synik |
| Speed limit eighty kilometres | Vitesse maxima quatre-vingts kilomètres | vitɛs maksima katrəvɛ̃ kilɔmɛtr |
| Beware of the cross-roads | Croisement dangereux ! | krwazmɑ̃ dɑ̃ʒrø |
| Main road ahead | Route à grande circulation en avant ! | rut a grɑ̃d sirkylasjɔ̃ ɑ̃ avɑ̃ |
| Street repairs | Travaux de voirie | travo dvwari |
| Diversion | Déviation de route | devjasjɔ̃ drut |
| Level crossing | Passage à niveau | pasaʒ a nivo |

# TRAVELLING BY SEA

## Vocabulary

| | | |
|---|---|---|
| The port, harbour | Le port | lə pɔr |
| The steamship company | La compagnie de navigation | la kɔ̃paɲi də navigasjɔ̃ |
| The liner | Le transatlantique | lə trɑ̃satlɑ̃tik |
| The one-class liner | Le transatlantique à classe unique | lə trɑ̃satlɑ̃tik a klɑs ynik |
| First class | La première classe | la prəmjer klɑs |
| The steerage | L'entrepont (la troisième classe) | lɑ̃trəpɔ̃ (la trwazjem klɑs) |

| English. | | Pronunciation. |
|---|---|---|
| The passage, crossing | La traversée | la traverse |
| The hull | La coque | la kɔk |
| The bow | L'avant | lavã |
| The stern | L'arrière | larjɛr |
| The gangway | La passerelle de service | la pɑsrɛl də servis |
| The funnel | La cheminée | la ʃəmine |
| The porthole | Le hublot | lə yblo |
| The railings | Le bastingage | lə bastɛ̃gaʒ |
| The mast | Le mât | lə mɑ |
| The dining-saloon | La salle-à-manger | la salamãʒe |
| The smoking-room | Le fumoir | lə fymwar |
| The cabin | La cabine | la kabin |
| The deck | Le pont | lə pɔ̃ |
| The deck-chair | Le (fauteuil) transatlantique | lə (fotœj) trãsatlãtik |
| The life-boat | Le bateau de sauvetage | lə batotsovtaʒ |
| The life-belt | La ceinture de sauvetage | la sɛ̃tyrtsovtaʒ |
| The passenger | Le passager | lə pasaʒe |
| The seasickness | Le mal de mer | lə maldmɛr |
| The crew | L'équipage | lekipaʒ |
| The captain | Le capitaine | lə kapitɛn |
| The purser | Le commissaire | lə kɔmisɛr |
| To book the passage | Prendre passage sur un bateau | prãdr pasaʒ syr œ̃ bato |
| To embark | S'embarquer | sãbarke |
| To disembark | Débarquer | debarke |
| To roll | Rouler (avoir du roulis) | rule (avwar dy ruli) |
| To pitch | Tanguer | tãge |

## Phrases

| English. | | Pronunciation. |
|---|---|---|
| Have you taken your steamer-ticket? Have you booked your passage? | Avez-vous pris votre passage sur le bateau? | avevu pri vot pasaʒ syr lbato? |
| Which route are you travelling? | Quel est l'itinéraire de votre voyage? | kɛl ɛ litinerɛr də vɔt vwajaʒ? |
| When are you sailing? | Quand partez-vous? | kɑ̃ partevu? |
| I am travelling first class | Je vais voyager en première classe | ʒvɛ vwajaʒe ɑ̃ prə-mjer klɑs |
| This cargo boat (freighter) takes some passengers | Ce cargo prend quelques passagers | sə kargo prɑ̃ kɛlkə pasaʒe |
| How many knots does she do? | Combien de nœuds le bateau file-t-il? | kɔ̃bjɛ̃dnø lə bato filtil? |
| This steamer is not one of the fastest, but a very comfortable one | Ce vapeur n'est pas des plus rapides, mais il est bien confortable | sə vapœr nɛpɑ de ply rapid, mɛzilɛ bjɛ̃ kɔ̃fɔrtabl |
| Where does she stop on the voyage? | Où le bateau fait-il escale? | u lbato fɛtil ɛskal? |
| Where is my cabin? | Où se trouve ma cabine? | ustruv ma kabin? |
| I can't stand the noise of the propellers | Je ne peux pas supporter le bruit des hélices | ʒənpøpɑ sypɔrte lə brɥi dezelis |
| Where can I get a deck-chair? | Où puis-je me procurer un transatlantique? | u pɥiʒ mə prɔkyre œ̃ trɑ̃satlɑ̃tik? |
| Is there a doctor on board? | Y a-t-il un médecin à bord? | jatil œ̃ metsɛ̃ a bɔr? |

| English. | | Pronunciation. |
|---|---|---|
| My wife has been seasick for some days | Ma femme a le mal de mer depuis quelques jours | ma fam a lə maldmɛr dəpɥi kɛlkə ʒur |
| Are you a good sailor? | Avez-vous le pied marin? | avevu lpje marɛ̃? |
| We are having a rough passage | Nous faisons une mauvaise traversée | nufəzɔ̃z yn mɔvɛz travɛrse |
| The ship is rolling and pitching | Le bateau roule et tangue | lbato rul e tɑ̃g |
| The sea is very rough | La mer est très grosse | la mɛr ɛ trɛ gros |
| It is getting foggy | Le brouillard tombe | lə brujar tɔ̃b |
| Visibility is bad | La visibilité est mauvaise | la vizibilite ɛ mɔvɛz |
| The fog-horn is sounding | La sirène sonne | la sirɛn sɔn |
| Where can I send a wireless telegram? | Où puis-je envoyer un radiotélégramme? | u pɥiʒ ɑ̃vwaje œ̃ radjotelegram? |
| In the wireless-operator's cabin | Dans le poste de T.S.F. | dɑ̃ lpost də teɛsɛf |
| Get your passports and landing cards ready, the coast is in sight | Tenez prêts vos passeports et vos cartes de débarquement, la côte est en vue | tne prɛ vo paspɔr e vo kart də debarkəmɑ̃, la kot ɛt ɑ̃ vy |
| We shall soon be alongside | Nous allons bientôt aborder à quai (accoster) | nuzalɔ̃ bjɛ̃to abɔrde a ke (akɔste) |

# TRAVELLING BY AIR

## Vocabulary

| English. | | Pronunciation. |
|---|---|---|
| The air-transport | Le transport par avion | lə trãspɔr par avjɔ̃ |
| The aircraft | L'avion | lavjɔ̃ |
| The flying-boat | L'hydravion | lidravjɔ̃ |
| The engine | Le moteur | lə mɔtœr |
| The airscrew (pro-peller) | L'hélice | lelis |
| The cabin | La cabine des passagers | la kabin de pasaʒe |
| The cockpit | La carlingue | la karlɛ̃g |
| The wing | L'aile | lɛl |
| The undercarriage | Le train d'atterrissage | lə trɛ̃ datɛrisaʒ |
| The airways time-table | L'horaire des réseaux aériens | lɔrɛr de rezo aerjɛ̃ |
| The Continental airways | Les réseaux aériens (de l'Europe) | le rezo aerjɛ̃ dəl œrɔp |
| The passenger | Le passager | lə pasaʒe |
| The airport | L'aéroport | laerɔpɔr |
| The aerodrome | L'aérodrome | laerɔdrom |
| To take off | Décoller | dekɔle |
| To land | Atterrir | atɛrir |
| To fly | Voler | vɔle |

## Phrases

| | | |
|---|---|---|
| Which is the quickest way to the airport? | Quelle est la route la plus courte qui mène à l'aéroport? | kɛl ɛ la rut la ply kurt ki mɛn a laerɔpɔr? |
| When does the next plane leave for Vienna? | A quelle heure est le prochain départ d'avion pour Vienne? | a kɛl œr ɛ lə prɔʃɛ̃ depar davjɔ̃ pur vjɛn? |

| English. | | Pronunciation. |
|---|---|---|
| The time-table is in the hall | L'horaire se trouve dans le hall | lɔrɛr struv dã lə al |
| I should like to travel without breaking the journey (without intermediate landing) | Je voudrais voyager sans m'arrêter en route (sans atterrissage intermédiaire) | zvudrɛ vwajaʒe sã marɛte ã rut (sãz atɛrisaʒ ɛ̃tɛrmedjɛr) |
| How many passengers does this aircraft take? | Combien de passagers cet avion porte-t-il? | kɔ̃bjɛ̃tpasaʒe sɛt avjɔ̃ pɔrtətil? |
| This plane carries fifty passengers in the cabin and a crew of five | Cet avion peut porter cinquante passagers dans la cabine et un équipage de cinq hommes | sɛt avjɔ̃ pø pɔrte sɛ̃kãt pasaʒe dã la kabin e œ̃n ekipaʒ də sɛ̃k ɔm |
| Where will they put my luggage? | Où mettra-t-on mes bagages? | u mɛtratɔ̃ me bagaʒ? |
| In the luggage hold | Dans la soute aux bagages | dã la sut o bagaʒ |
| The plane is just taxi-ing out of the hangar | L'avion est en train de quitter le hangar en roulant sur le sol | lavjɔ̃ ɛt ã trɛ̃ də kite lə ãgar ã rulã syr lə sɔl |
| It is a four-engined plane | C'est un quadrimoteur | sɛt œ̃ kadrimɔtœr |
| Europe is served by a network of air-routes | L'Europe est desservie par un réseau de routes aériennes | lœrɔp ɛ desɛrvi par œ̃ rezo drut aerjɛn |
| The jet-propelled aircraft has a great range | L'avion à réaction a un grand rayon de vol | lavjɔ̃ a reaksjɔ̃ a œ̃ grã rejɔ̃ dvɔl |
| The load-capacity of an aircraft is limited | La charge utile d'un avion est limitée | la ʃarʒ ytil dœ̃navjɔ̃ ɛ limite |

# TRAVELLING BY BICYCLE

## Vocabulary

| English. | | Pronunciation. |
|---|---|---|
| The bicycle | La bicyclette | la bisiklɛt |
| The handle-bar | Le guidon | lə gidɔ̃ |
| The saddle | La selle | la sɛl |
| The pedal | La pédale | la pedal |
| The free-wheel | La roue libre | la ru libr |
| The chain | La chaîne | la ʃɛn |
| The bell | La sonnette | la sɔnɛt |
| The frame | Le cadre | lə kɑdr |
| The pump | La pompe à air | la pɔ̃paɛr |
| The tool-bag | La sacoche | la sakɔʃ |
| The back-pedalling brake | Le frein sur moyeu | lə frɛ̃ syr mwajø |
| The spokes | Les rayons | le rɛjɔ̃ |

## Phrases

| | | |
|---|---|---|
| I am fond of cycling | J'aime faire de la bicyclette | ʒɛm fɛr dla bisiklɛt |
| Is your brake in working order ? | Est-ce que votre frein fonctionne bien ? | ɛskə vɔt frɛ̃ fɔ̃ksjɔn bjɛ̃ ? |
| Yes, but the chain is a bit loose | Oui, mais la chaîne a pris du jeu | wi, mɛ la ʃɛn a pri dy ʒø |
| You are riding on the pavement, you will have to pay a fine | Vous pédalez sur le trottoir. Vous aurez à payer une amende | vu pedale syr ltrɔtwar. vuzɔrez a pɛje ynamɑ̃d |
| I shall have to push my bicycle up-hill | Il me faudra monter la côte en poussant ma bicyclette | il mə fodra mɔ̃te la kot ɑ̃ pusɑ̃ ma bisiklɛt |

| English. | | Pronunciation. |
|---|---|---|
| I must inflate the tyres | Je dois gonfler les pneus | ʒdwa gɔ̃fle lepnø |
| I have got a puncture in my back tyre and shall have to mend it | Mon pneu arrière a crevé et il va falloir le réparer | mɔ̃ pnø arjɛr a krəve e il va falwar lə repare |
| Put your bicycle into the shed | Garez votre bicyclette dans le hangar | gare vot bisiklɛt dɑ̃ lə ɑ̃gar |
| No cycling | Interdit aux cyclistes ! | ɛ̃tɛrdi o siklist ! |

# THE TOWN

## Vocabulary

| The town, city | La ville | la vil |
|---|---|---|
| The capital | La capitale | la kapital |
| The suburb | Le faubourg | lə fobur |
| The market-square | La place du marché | la plas dy marʃe |
| The street | La rue | la ry |
| The lane | Le passage (la ruelle) | lə pasaʒ (la rɥɛl) |
| The main street | La grand'rue | la grɑ̃ry |
| The side street | La rue latérale | la ry lateral |
| The street corner | Le coin de la rue | lə kwɛ̃ dla ry |
| The pedestrian crossing | Le passage pour piétons (passage clouté) | lə pasaʒ pur pjetɔ̃ (pasaʒ klute) |
| The roadway | La chaussée | la ʃose |
| The pavement | Le trottoir | lə trɔtwar |
| The gardens | Les jardins | le ʒardɛ̃ |
| The bridge | Le pont | lə pɔ̃ |
| The cemetery | Le cimetière | lə simtjɛr |

| English. | | Pronunciation. |
|---|---|---|
| The building | Le bâtiment | lə batimã |
| The hospital | L'hôpital | lɔpital |
| The town hall | La mairie | la mɛri |
| The post office | Le bureau de poste | lə byrotpɔst |
| The police station | Le bureau de police | lə byrotpɔlis |
| The policeman | L'agent de police | laʒãtpɔlis |
| The public library | La bibliothèque municipale | la bibliɔtɛk mynisipal |
| The school | L'école | lekɔl |
| The church | L'église | legliz |
| The university | L'université | lynivɛrsite |
| The cathedral | La cathédrale | la katedral |
| The fire station | Le poste d'incendie | lə pɔst dɛ̃sãdi |
| The block of flats | Le groupe de maisons de rapport | lə grup də mɛzɔ̃ drapɔr |
| The café | Le café | lə kafe |
| The restaurant | Le restaurant | lə rɛstɔrã |
| The shop | Le magasin | lə magazɛ̃ |
| The shop-window | La vitrine | la vitrin |
| The pedestrian | Le piéton | lə pjetɔ̃ |
| The tramcar | Le tramway | lə tramwe |
| The Underground | Le Métro | lə metro |
| The bus | L'autobus | lotobys |
| The lorry | Le camion | lə kamjɔ̃ |
| The stopping place | L'arrêt | larɛ |
| The terminus | Le terminus | lə tɛrminys |

## Phrases

| How far is it to the High Street? | Combien y a-t-il d'ici à la Grand' rue? | kɔ̃bjɛ̃ jatil disi ala grãry? |
|---|---|---|
| Which is the shortest way to the cathedral? | Quel est le chemin le plus court pour arriver à la cathédrale? | kɛl ɛ lə ʃmɛ̃ lə ply kur pur arive a la katedral? |

| English. | | Pronunciation. |
|---|---|---|
| Can you tell me the way to the theatre? | Pouvez-vous m'indiquer le chemin qui mène au théâtre? | puvevu mɛ̃dike lə ʃmɛ̃ ki mɛn o teɑtr? |
| Where is the post office? | Où se trouve le bureau de poste? | ustruv lə byrot-pɔst? |
| The second turning on the right | Prenez la deuxième rue à droite | prəne la døzjɛm ry a drwat |
| Don't cross the street before you see the green light | Ne traversez pas avant de voir le feu vert | nə travɛrse pazavɑ̃ dvwar lə fø vɛr |
| There are the traffic lights | Voilà les feux de signalisation | vwala le fø də siɲal-izasjɔ̃ |
| Don't step off the pavement | Ne descendez pas du trottoir | nə desɑ̃de pɑ dy trɔtwar |
| The traffic is very heavy | La circulation est intense | la sirkylasjɔ̃ et ɛ̃tɑ̃s |
| The streets are narrow | Les rues sont étroites | le ry sɔ̃t etrwat |
| I have lost my way | Je me suis égaré(e) | ʒəm sɥiz egare |
| Turn to the left | Prenez à gauche | prənez a goʃ |
| Straight on | Tout droit devant vous | tu drwa dvɑ̃ vu |
| Where is the main entrance to the hospital? | Où est l'entrée principale de l'hôpital? | wɛ lɑ̃tre prɛ̃sipal də lɔpital? |
| Where does Mr. Smith live? | Où M. Dupont demeure-t-il? | u məsjø dypɔ̃ dəmœrtil? |
| On the top floor | Au dernier étage | o dɛrnjɛretaʒ |
| They have a flat on the ground floor | Ils ont un appartement au rez-de-chaussée | ilzɔ̃t œ̃napartəmɑ̃ o retʃose |
| Can I get to the Palace Square by Underground? | Est-ce que je peux me rendre par le Métro à la Place du Palais? | ɛskə ʒpø mə rɑ̃dr par lmetro a la plas dy palɛ? |

| English. | | Pronunciation. |
|---|---|---|
| Take the escalator. Or do you prefer the stairs? | Prenez l'escalier (le trottoir) roulant. Ou préférez-vous l'escalier? | prəne leskalje (lə trotwar) rulɑ̃. u prefere vu leskalje? |
| You have to book a ticket | Il faut louer une place d'avance | il fo lwe yn plas davɑ̃s |
| Take your tickets from the machine | Prenez vos billets au distributeur automatique | prəne vo bijez o distribytœr otɔmatik |
| You can also take the bus | Vous pouvez aussi prendre l'autobus | vupuvez osi prɑ̃dr lotobys |
| Does this bus take me to the park? | Est-ce que cet autobus me mène au parc? | eskə set otobys mə men o park? |
| The buses are crowded | Les autobus sont bondés | lez otɔbys sɔ̃ bɔ̃de |
| We are full up. Take the next bus, please | L'autobus est au complet. Prenez le suivant, s'il vous plaît | lotɔbys et o kɔ̃ple. prəne lə sɥivɑ̃, sivuple |
| Standing-room only | Places debout seulement | plas dbu sœlmɑ̃ |
| Don't push | Ne poussez pas | npuse pɑ |
| Fares, please | Les places, s'il vous plaît | le plas, sivuple |
| Move up, please | Avancez, s'il vous plaît | avɑ̃se, sivuple |
| Keep a gangway | Laissez le passage libre | lese lpasaʒ libr |
| I have lost my ticket | J'ai perdu mon ticket | ʒe perdy mɔ̃ tike |
| A transfer to the Central Station, please | Une correspondance pour la Gare Centrale, s'il vous plaît | yn kɔrespɔ̃dɑ̃s pur la gar sɑ̃tral, sivuple |

| English. | | Pronunciation. |
|---|---|---|
| Don't alight when the vehicle is in motion | Ne descendez pas pendant que le véhicule est en marche | nə desɑ̃de pɑ pɑ̃dɑ̃ kəl veikyl ɛt ɑ̃ marʃ |
| When does the last tube train leave? | A quelle heure part le dernier Métro? | a kɛl œr par lə dɛrnje metro? |
| Sunday traffic is limited | Le dimanche la circulation est restreinte | lə dimɑ̃ʃ la sirkylasjɔ̃ ɛ rɛstrɛ̃t |
| Where do I get off? | Où dois-je descendre? | u dwaʒ desɑ̃dr? |
| No thoroughfare for vehicles | Interdiction de passage aux véhicules | ɛ̃tɛrdiksjɔ̃ də pasaʒ o veikyl |
| Closed to pedestrians | Passage interdit aux piétons | pasaʒ ɛ̃tɛrdito pjetɔ̃ |
| No admittance (private) | Entrée interdite au public | ɑ̃tre ɛ̃tɛrdit o pyblik |

# HOTELS

## Vocabulary

| | | |
|---|---|---|
| The inn, guest-house | L'auberge, la pension de famille | loberʒ, la pɑ̃sjɔ̃tfamij |
| The single room | La chambre pour une personne | la ʃɑ̃br pur yn pɛrsɔn |
| The double room | La chambre à deux lits | la ʃɑ̃br a dø li |
| The reception desk | La réception | la resɛpsjɔ̃ |
| The lounge | Le hall | lə al |
| The public rooms | Les salles | le sal |
| The dining-room | La salle-à-manger | la salamɑ̃ʒe |

| English. | | Pronunciation |
|---|---|---|
| The writing-room | La salle de correspondance | la sal də kɔrɛspɔ̃dɑ̃s |
| The gentlemen's cloak-room | Le vestiaire | lə vɛstjɛr |
| The ladies' cloak-room | " Dames " | dam |
| The bell | La sonnette | la sɔnɛt |
| The bell-boy (page) | Le chasseur (groom) | lə ʃasœr (grum) |
| The chambermaid | La femme de chambre | la famtʃɑ̃br |
| The boots | Le garçon d'étage | lə garsɔ̃detaʒ |
| The waiter | Le garçon | lə garsɔ̃ |
| The head-waiter | Le maître d'hôtel | lə mɛtrdotɛl |
| The waitress | La serveuse | la sɛrvøz |
| The porter | Le portier | lə pɔrtje |
| The manager | Le gérant | lə ʒerɑ̃ |
| The proprietor | Le propriétaire | lə prɔprietɛr |

## Phrases

| | | |
|---|---|---|
| At which hotel are you staying ? | A quel hôtel êtes-vous descendu ? | a kɛl otɛl ɛtvu desɑ̃dy ? |
| The service is good (bad) | Le service est bon (mauvais) | lə sɛrvis ɛ bɔ̃ (mɔvɛ) |
| Can I have a single room looking on to the park ? | Puis-je avoir une chambre à un lit donnant sur le parc ? | pɥiʒ avwar yn ʃɑ̃br aœ̃ li dɔnɑ̃ syr lpark ? |
| Is there central heating and hot and cold water in the rooms ? | Est-ce que le chauffage central est installé avec eau courante, chaude et froide, dans les chambres ? | ɛskə lə ʃofaʒ sɑ̃tral ɛt ɛ̃stale avɛk o curɑ̃t, ʃod e frwad, dɑ̃ le ʃɑ̃br ? |
| Here is the key to your room | Voici la clé de votre chambre | vwasi la kle dvɔt ʃɑ̃br |

| English. | | Pronunciation. |
|---|---|---|
| The lift-boy will take your luggage up | Le liftier montera vos bagages | lə liftje mɔ̃tra vo bagaʒ |
| Can I have breakfast in my room ? | Est-ce que je puis prendre le petit déjeuner dans ma chambre ? | ɛskə ʒpɥi prɑ̃dr lə pti deʒœne dɑ̃ ma ʃɑ̃br ? |
| Where is the bar ? | Où se trouve le bar ? | ustruv lə bar ? |
| Where is the bathroom, please ? | Où est la salle de bains, s.v.p. ? | wɛ la saldbɛ̃, sivuplɛ ? |
| Please enter your name and address in the visitors' book | Veuillez inscrire votre nom et adresse dans le livre des voyageurs | vœjez ɛ̃skrir vɔt nɔ̃ e adrɛs dɑ̃ lə livr de vwajaʒœr |
| How long do you intend to stay ? | Combien de temps comptez-vous rester ? | kɔ̃bjɛ̃tɑ̃ kɔ̃tevu rɛste ? |
| What are your inclusive terms ? | Quelles sont vos conditions, tout compris ? | kɛl sɔ̃ vo kɔ̃disjɔ̃, tu kɔ̃pri ? |
| I want to lodge a complaint with the manager | Je veux me plaindre au gérant | ʒvø mə plɛ̃dr o ʒerɑ̃ |
| How much is bed and breakfast ? | Quel est le prix de la chambre, y compris le petit déjeuner ? | kɛl ɛ lpri dla ʃɑ̃br, ikɔ̃pri lə pti deʒœne ? |
| I should like another blanket, or a quilt | Je voudrais bien avoir encore une couverture ou un édredon | ʒvudrɛ bjɛ̃ avwar ɑ̃kɔr yn kuvɛrtyr u œ̃n edrədɔ̃ |
| Please give me another towel | Donnez-moi, s'il vous plaît, encore un essuie-mains | dɔnemwa, sivuplɛ, ɑ̃kɔr œ̃n esɥimɛ̃ |

| English. | | Pronunciation. |
|---|---|---|
| Can you call me to-morrow at six o'clock? | Pouvez-vous m'éveiller demain à six heures? | puvevu meveje dmɛ̃ a sizœr? |
| I have ordered a room with bath | J'ai commandé une chambre avec salle de bain | ʒe kɔmãde yn ʃãbr avɛk sal də bɛ̃ |
| Have you reserved a room for me? | M'avez-vous réservé une chambre? | mavevu reserve yn ʃãbr? |
| Any letters for me? | Y a-t-il du courrier pour moi? | jatil dy kurje pur mwa? |
| Ring twice for the chambermaid | Sonnez deux fois pour la femme de chambre | sɔne dø fwɑ pur la famtʃãbr |
| Where did you put my comb and brush? | Où avez-vous mis mon peigne et ma brosse à cheveux? | u avevu mi mɔ̃pɛɲ e ma brɔsaʃvø? |
| When can you let me have my laundry? | Quand pouvez-vous me faire donner mon linge blanchi? | kã puvevu mə fɛr dɔne mɔ̃ lɛ̃ʒ blãʃi? |
| | | |
| LAUNDRY LIST: | La liste de blanchissage: | la list də blãʃisaʒ |
| Four white shirts | Quatre chemises blanches | kat ʃmiz blãʃ |
| Three coloured shirts | Trois chemises de couleur | trwɑ ʃmiz də kulœr |
| Six stiff collars | Six cols empesés | si kɔlzãpəze |
| Five soft collars | Cinq cols mous | sɛ̃ kɔl mu |
| Two vests | Deux maillots de corps | dø majo də kɔr |
| Two pairs of drawers (pants) | Deux paires de caleçons | dø pɛr dɔ kalsɔ̃ |
| One pair of pyjamas | Une paire de pyjamas | yn pɛr də piʒama |

| English. | | Pronunciation. |
|---|---|---|
| One night-gown (nightdress) | Une chemise de nuit | yn ʃmiz də nyi |
| Ten handkerchiefs | Dix mouchoirs | di muʃwar |
| Five pairs of socks (stockings) | Cinq paires de chaussettes (bas) | sɛ̃ pɛr də ʃosɛt (ba) |
| One slip | Un dessous de robe | œ̃ dsu də rɔb |
| Three cami-knickers | Trois combinaisons-culottes | trwa kɔ̃binɛzɔ̃ kylɔt |
| One blouse | Une blouse | yn bluz |
| One linen dress | Une robe de toile | yn rɔb də twal |
| One brassiere | Un soutien-gorge | œ̃ sutjɛ̃ gɔrʒ |
| One petticoat | Un jupon | œ̃ ʒypɔ̃ |

## Phrases

| | | |
|---|---|---|
| I have forgotten my razor | J'ai oublié mon rasoir | ʒe ublje mɔ̃ razwar |
| Is there a barber's shop in the hotel? | Y a-t-il un salon de coiffure dans l'hôtel? | jatil œ̃ salɔ̃ də kwafyr dɑ̃ lotɛl? |
| Can you have this suit pressed for me? | Pouvez-vous faire donner un coup de fer à ce complet (costume)? | puvevu fɛr dɔne œ̃ kutfɛr a skɔ̃plɛ (kɔstym)? |
| Let me have the bill, please | Donnez-moi la note, s.v.p. | dɔnemwa la nɔt, sivuplɛ |
| Do you like your boarding-house? | Êtes-vous content(e) de votre pension de famille? | ɛtvu kɔ̃tɑ̃(t) də vɔt pɑ̃sjɔ̃tfamij? |
| The food is good and plentiful | La nourriture est bonne et copieuse | la nurityr ɛ bɔn e kɔpjøz |
| The cooking is excellent | La cuisine est excellente | la kɥizin ɛteksɛlɑ̃t |
| Can I book rooms for August? | Puis-je retenir des chambres pour le mois d'août? | pɥiʒ rətnir de ʃɑ̃br pur lə mwadu? |

| English. | | | | Pronunciation. |
|---|---|---|---|---|
| Sorry, we are booked up till October | Je regrette, mais tout est pris jusqu'au mois d' octobre | | | ʒə rgrɛt, mɛ tut ɛ pri ʒysko mwɑ dɔktɔbr |

## RESTAURANTS AND MEALS

### Vocabulary

| The plate | L'assiette | lasjɛt |
|---|---|---|
| The dish | Le plat | lə pla |
| The knife | Le couteau | lə kuto |
| The fork | La fourchette | la furʃɛt |
| The spoon | La cuillère | la kɥijɛr |
| The cup | La tasse | la tɑs |
| The saucer | La soucoupe | la sukup |
| The glass | Le verre | lə vɛr |
| The tea-pot | La théière | la tejɛr |
| The coffee-pot | La cafetière | la kaftjɛr |
| The milk-jug | Le pot au lait | lə po o lɛ |
| The sugar-basin | Le sucrier | lə sykrie |
| The tray | Le plateau | lə plato |
| The breakfast | Le petit déjeuner | lə pti deʒœne |
| The lunch | Le déjeuner | lə deʒœne |
| The dinner | Le dîner | lə dine |
| The supper | Le souper | lə supe |
| The bill of fare | La carte du jour | la kart dy ʒur |
| The wine list | La liste des vins | la list devɛ̃ |
| The course | Le service (le plat) | lə sɛrvis (lə pla) |
| The cold dish | Le plat froid | lə pla frwa |
| The vegetarian dish | Le plat végétarien | lə pla veʒetarjɛ̃ |
| The meat dish | Le plat de viande | lə pla dvjɑ̃d |
| The salt | Le sel | lə sɛl |
| The pepper | Le poivre | lə pwavr |
| The mustard | La moutarde | la mutard |

| English. | | Pronunciation. |
|---|---|---|
| The vinegar | Le vinaigre | lə vinɛgr |
| The oil | L'huile | lɥil |
| The bread | Le pain | lə pɛ̃ |
| The roll | Le petit pain | lə pti pɛ̃ |
| The toast | Le pain grillé (le toast) | lə pɛ̃ grije (lə tost) |
| The butter | Le beurre | lə bœr |
| The porridge | La bouillie d'avoine | la bwiji davwan |
| The ham | Le jambon | lə ʒɑ̃bɔ̃ |
| The bacon | Le lard (le bacon) | lə lar (lə bakɔ̃) |
| The sausage | La saucisse (le saucisson) | la sosis (lə sosisɔ̃) |
| The egg | L'œuf, les œufs | lœf, lez ø |
| The scrambled eggs | Les œufs brouillés | lez ø bruje |
| The poached eggs | Les œufs pochés | lez ø poʃe |
| The hors d'œuvre | Les hors-d'œuvre | le ordœvr |
| The (thick) soup | La crème, la purée | la krɛm, la pyre |
| The clear soup | Le consommé | lə kɔ̃some |
| The entree | L'entrée | lɑ̃tre |
| The joint | Le rôti | lə roti |
| The fish | Le poisson | lə pwasɔ̃ |
| The vegetables | Les légumes | le legym |
| The potatoes | Les pommes de terre | le pom də tɛr |
| The sauce | La sauce | la sos |
| The salad, lettuce | La salade, la laitue | la salad, la lɛty |
| The dessert | Le dessert | lə desɛr |
| The sweet | L'entremets sucré | lɑ̃trəmɛ sykre |
| The ices | Les glaces | le glas |
| The fruit | Le fruit | lə frɥi |
| The stewed fruit | La compote de fruits | la kɔ̃pot də frɥi |
| The cheese | Le fromage | lə fromaʒ |
| The beverage, drink | La boisson | la bwasɔ̃ |
| The beer | La bière | la bjɛr |
| The wine | Le vin | lə vɛ̃ |

| English. | | Pronunciation. |
|---|---|---|
| The brandy | Le cognac, l'eau-de-vie | lə kɔɲak, lodvi |
| The liqueur | La liqueur | la likœr |
| The mineral-water | L'eau minérale | lo mineral |
| The lemonade (squash) | La limonade (la citronnade) | la limɔnad (la sitrɔnad) |
| The fruit juice | Le jus de fruit | lə ʒy d frɥi |
| The coffee | Le café | lə kafe |
| The tea | Le thé | lə te |
| The cocoa | Le cacao | lə kakao |
| The milk | Le lait | lə lɛ |
| The cream | La crème | la krɛm |
| The cake | Le gâteau (la pâtisserie) | lə gɑto (la pɑtisri) |
| The biscuits | Les biscuits | le biskɥi |
| The jam | Les confitures | le kɔ̃fityr |
| The marmalade | La confiture d'oranges | la kɔ̃fityr dɔrɑ̃ʒ |

## Phrases

| | | |
|---|---|---|
| Waiter, a table for four persons | Garçon, une table pour quatre personnes | garsɔ̃, yn tabl pur kat persɔn |
| Please let us have the bill of fare and the wine list | La carte du jour et la liste des vins, s.v.p. | la kart dy ʒur e la list de vɛ̃, sivuplɛ |
| Here is the menu : | Voici le menu : | vwasi lə mny |
| Hors d'Œuvre : | Hors-d'œuvre : | ɔrdœvr |
| Lobster Mayonnaise | Mayonnaise de homard | majɔnez də ɔmar |
| or | ou | u |
| Sardines with Salad | Sardines avec salade | sardin avɛk salad |
| or | ou | u |
| Dutch Oysters | Huîtres hollandaises | ɥitr ɔlɑ̃dez |

| English. | | Pronunciation. |
|---|---|---|
| Tomato Soup | Soupe purée de to-mates | sup pyretɔmat |
| or | ou | u |
| Clear Soup | Consommé | kɔ̃sɔme |
| Fish : | Poissons : | pwasɔ̃ : |
| Salmon with (fresh) Butter | Saumon au beurre (frais) | somɔ̃ o bœr (frɛ) |
| Fried or Boiled Sole | Soles frites ou bouillies | sɔl frit u bwiji |
| Meat Dishes : | Plats de viande : | pla dvjãd : |
| Chicken with Rice and Mush-rooms | Poulet au riz aux champignons | pulɛ o ri o ʃãpiɲɔ̃ |
| or | ou | u |
| Roast Lamb with Beans | Agneau rôti, hari-cots | aɲo roti, ariko |
| or | ou | u |
| Venison with Red Cabbage | Venaison, chou rouge | vənɛzɔ̃, ʃu ruʒ |
| Dessert : | Dessert : | desɛr : |
| Baked Apples | Pommes au beurre | pɔmzobœr |
| Ices : | Glaces : | glas : |
| Strawberry Ice | Glace aux fraises | glas o frɛz |
| Peach Melba | Pêche Melba | peʃ mɛlba |
| Cheeses : | Fromages : | frɔmaʒ : |
| Gruyère | Gruyère | gryjɛr |
| Dutch Cheese | Fromage de Hol-lande | frɔmaʒ də ɔlãd |
| Will you have your meal à la carte ? | Voulez-vous manger à la carte ? | vulevu mãʒe a la kart ? |
| I can recommend our fish : cod, haddock, turbot, pike, sole, carp and trout | Je peux vous re-commander notre poisson : morue, aigrefin, turbot, brochet, sole, carpe et truite | ʒpø vu rəkɔmãde nɔt pwasɔ̃ : mɔry, ɛgrəfɛ̃, tyrbo, brɔʃe, sɔl, karp e trɥit |

| English. | | Pronunciation. |
|---|---|---|
| Halibut with parsley sauce is our special dish to-day (plat du jour) | Le flétan sauce persil est notre plat du jour | lə fletɑ̃ sos pɛrsi ɛ nɔt pla dy ʒur |
| Do you prefer salt-water fish to fresh-water fish? | Préférez-vous le poisson de mer au poisson d'eau douce? | preferevu lə pwasɔ̃ dmɛr o pwasɔ̃ do dus? |
| What have you in the way of roast meat? | Qu'est-ce que vous avez comme rôti? | kɛskə vuzave kɔm roti? |
| Anything you like: pork, beef, mutton, veal | Tout ce que vous voudrez: porc, bœuf, mouton, veau | tuskə vu vudre: pɔr, bœf, mutɔ̃, vo |
| For poultry we have: turkey, goose, and young duck | Comme volaille nous avons: dinde, oie, caneton | kɔm vɔlaj nuz avɔ̃: dɛ̃d, wa, kantɔ̃ |
| There is a great variety of vegetables: spinach, cabbage, kale, in fact everything that is in season. Asparagus is over | Il y a un grand choix de légumes: épinards, chou, chou frisé, en fait tout ce qui est de saison. Les asperges sont finies maintenant | ilja œ̃ grɑ̃ ʃwa dlegym: epinar, ʃu, ʃu frize, ɑ̃ fɛ tuski ɛ də sezɔ̃. lez aspɛrʒ sɔ̃ fini mɛ̃tnɑ̃ |
| What can I order for you? | Qu'est-ce que je peux commander pour vous? | kɛskə ʒpø kɔmɑ̃de pur vu? |
| I should like a lamb-cutlet with peas and carrots | Je voudrais bien manger une côtelette d'agneau avec des petits pois et des carottes | ʒvudrɛ bjɛ̃ mɑ̃ʒe yn kotlɛt daɲo avɛk de pti pwɑ e de karɔt |

| English. | | Pronunciation. |
|---|---|---|
| Could I have some kidneys or liver with onions and cauliflower | Pourrais-je avoir des rognons ou du foie aux oignons avec du chou-fleur ? | purɛ̃ʒ avwar de rɔɲɔ̃ u dy fwɑ ozɔɲɔ̃ avɛk dy ʃuflœr ? |
| What have you chosen ? | Qu'est-ce que vous avez choisi ? | kɛskə vuzave ʃwazi |
| What would you like to follow ? | Que voudriez-vous pour suivre ? | kə vudrijevu pur sɥivr ? |
| Are there any sweets ? | Y a-t-il des entremets sucrés ? | jatil dez ɑ̃trəmɛ sykre ? |
| You can either have an ice or chocolate pudding or apple tart | Vous pouvez prendre une glace ou un entremets au chocolat ou une tarte aux pommes | vu puve prɑ̃dr yn glas u œ̃n ɑ̃trəmɛ o ʃɔkɔla u yn tart o pɔm |
| There are no more strawberries with whipped cream | Il n'y a plus de fraises à la crème fouettée | il nja ply də frɛz a la krɛm fwɛte |
| A glass of porter or stout | Un verre de porter ou de stout | œ̃ vɛr də pɔrtœr u də stut |
| A glass of pale ale | Un bock blonde | œ̃ bɔk blɔ̃d |
| I can recommend French claret and Burgundy | Je peux recommander le bordeaux et le bourgogne | ʒpø rəkɔmɑ̃de lə bɔrdo e lə burgɔɲ |
| How do you like this Moselle ? | Comment trouvez-vous ce moselle ? | kɔmɑ̃ truvevu sə mɔzel ? |
| The Rhine wine (hock) is not iced | Le vin du Rhin (le hochheimer) n'est pas frappé | lə vɛ̃ dyrɛ̃ (lə ɔkhɛmɛr) nepɑ frape |
| This wine is too sour for me, I like sweet wines (sherry, port, etc.) | Ce vin est trop acide pour moi, j'aime les vins doux (vin de Xérès, porto, etc.) | sə vɛ̃ ɛ tropasid pur mwa, ʒɛm le vɛ̃ du (vɛ̃ də kerɛs, pɔrto, etsetera) |

| English. | | Pronunciation. |
|---|---|---|
| Another glass of brandy? | Encore un verre de cognac? | ãkɔr œ̃ vɛr tkɔɲak? |
| Do you take sugar and cream (milk) with your coffee? | Prenez-vous du su- cre et de la crème (du lait) dans le café? | prənevu dy sykr e dla krɛm (dylɛ) dã lkafe? |
| Have a cigarette? | Puis-je vous offrir une cigarette? | pɥiʒ vuz ɔfrir yn sigarɛt? |
| May I smoke a pipe? | Puis-je fumer la pipe? | pɥiʒ fyme la pip? |
| Where are my matches? | Où sont mes allu- mettes? | u sɔ̃ mez alymɛt? |
| Here is a lighter | Voici un briquet | vwasi œ̃ brikɛ |
| Pass the ashtray, please | Passez-moi le cen- drier, s.v.p. | pasemwa lsãdrije, sivuplɛ |
| Let me have the bill, please | Donnez-moi l'addi- tion, s.v.p. | dɔnemwa ladisjɔ̃, sivuplɛ |
| Pay at the desk, please | Veuillez payer à la caisse | vœje pɛje ala kɛs |
| Shall we have tea now? | Allons-nous prendre le thé maintenant? | alɔ̃nu prãdr lə te mɛ̃tnã? |
| The tea is too strong (weak) | Le thé est trop fort (faible) | lə te ɛ tro fɔr (fɛbl) |
| Would you rather have toast or cake? | Qu'est-ce que vous préférez, du pain grillé ou une pâtisserie? | kɛskə vu prefere, dy pɛ̃ grije u yn patisri? |
| Come and have a simple supper with us | Venez prendre un petit souper avec nous (chez nous) | vne prãdr œ̃ pti supe avɛk nu (ʃe nu) |
| You'll have to put up with pot-luck | Il faudra vous con- tenter de manger à la bonne fran- quette | il fodra vu kɔ̃tãte də mãʒe ala bɔn frãkɛt |
| A heavy meal does not agree with me | Un repas copieux ne me va pas | œ̃ rpa kɔpjø nə mvapa |

| English. | | Pronunciation. |
|---|---|---|
| You can have sandwiches, celery and radishes | Vous pouvez avoir des sandwichs, du céleri et des radis | vu puvez avwar de sɑ̃dwiʃ, dy selri et de radi |
| Help yourself | Servez-vous | sɛrvevu |
| What would you like for breakfast? | Qu'est-ce que vous aimeriez pour le petit déjeuner? | kɛskə vuzɛmərje pur lə pti deʒœne? |
| Porridge, a boiled or fried egg with bacon and marmalade, if possible | De la bouillie d'avoine, un œuf à la coque ou sur le plat avec du bacon et de la confiture d'oranges, si possible | dla bwiji davwan, œ̃n œf ala kɔk u syr lpla avɛk dy bakɔ̃ e dla kɔ̃fityr dɔrɑ̃ʒ, si pɔsibl |
| A hot meal | Un repas chaud | œ̃ rpa ʃo |
| A hot drink | Une boisson chaude | yn bwasɔ̃ ʃod |
| The mustard sauce is very hot | La sauce moutarde vous emporte la bouche | la sos mutard vuz ɑ̃pɔrt la buʃ |
| I am thirsty | J'ai soif | ʒe swaf |
| I am hungry | J'ai faim | ʒe fɛ̃ |
| Here's luck | A votre santé! | a vɔt sɑ̃te! |
| He is a hearty eater | C'est un gros mangeur | sɛtœ̃ gro mɑ̃ʒœr |
| I have no appetite | Je n'ai pas d'appétit | ʒənepɑ dapeti |
| No gratuities | Service compris | sɛrvis kɔ̃pri |
| Where is the toilet? | Où sont les toilettes? | u sɔ̃ le twalɛt |

## SHOPPING

### Vocabulary

| | | |
|---|---|---|
| The shop | Le magasin | lə magazɛ̃ |
| The stores | Le grand magasin | lə grɑ̃ magazɛ̃ |
| The baker's (shop) | La boulangerie (chez le boulanger) | la bulɑ̃ʒri (ʃe lə bulɑ̃ʒe) |

| English. | | Pronunciation. |
|---|---|---|
| The pastry-cook's | La pâtisserie (chez le pâtissier) | la pɑtisri (ʃe lə pɑ̃tisje) |
| The confectioner's | La confiserie (chez le confiseur) | la kɔ̃fizri (ʃe lə kɔ̃fizœr) |
| The butcher's | La boucherie (chez le boucher) | la buʃri (ʃe lə buʃe) |
| The fishmonger's | La poissonnerie (chez le marchand de poisson) | la pwasɔnri (ʃe lə marʃɑ̃tpwasɔ̃) |
| The grocer's | L'épicerie (chez l'épicier) | lepisri (ʃe lepisje) |
| The greengrocer's | La boutique du marchand de légumes, la fruiterie | la butik dy marʃɑ̃ dlegym, la frɥitri |
| The stationer's | La papeterie (chez le papetier) | la paptri (ʃe lə paptje) |
| The men's outfitter's | Chez le marchand de confections et le chemisier | ʃe lə marʃɑ̃ də kɔ̃fɛksjɔ̃ e lə ʃmizje |
| The haberdasher's | La mercerie (la chemiserie) | la mɛrsri (la ʃmizri) |
| The cleaner's and dyer's | Chez le teinturier dégraisseur | ʃe lə tɛ̃tyrje degrɛsœr |
| The tobacconist's | Le débit de tabac | lə debittaba |
| The chemist's or drug store | La pharmacie (chez le pharmacien) | la farmasi (ʃe lə farmasjɛ̃) |
| The bookseller's | La librairie (chez le libraire) | la librɛri (ʃe lə librɛr) |
| The shop assistant | L'employé (la demoiselle) de magasin | lɑ̃plwaje (la dmwazɛl) də magazɛ̃ |
| The customer | Le client, la cliente | lə klijɑ̃, la klijɑ̃t |
| To buy | Acheter | aʃte |
| To sell | Vendre | vɑ̃dr |
| To choose, select | Choisir | ʃwazir |

| English. | | Pronunciation. |
|---|---|---|
| To order | Commander | kɔmãde |
| To cancel | Annuler, contre-mander | anyle, kɔ̃trəmãde |
| To exchange | Échanger | eʃãʒe |
| To deliver | Livrer | livre |
| To fetch | Aller chercher | ale ʃɛrʃe |
| To wrap up | Envelopper | ãvlɔpe |

## Phrases

| | | |
|---|---|---|
| At the baker's: | Chez le boulanger: | ʃe lə bulãʒe: |
| What can I do for you? | Qu'y a-t-il pour votre service? | kjatil pur vɔt sɛrvis? |
| Are you being served? | Est-ce qu'on vous sert? | ɛskɔ̃ vu sɛr? |
| A new white loaf and half a loaf of brown bread (rye bread), please | Un pain blanc frais et un demi pain bis (pain de seigle), s.v.p. | œ̃ pɛ̃ blã frɛ e œ̃ dmi pɛ̃ bi (pɛ̃-sɛgl), sivuplɛ |
| Six rolls, four crescents, some fruit cake and an apple tart, please | Six petits pains, quatre croissants, du gâteau anglais et une tarte aux pommes, s.v.p. | sipti pɛ̃, katkrwasã, dy gɑto ãglɛ e yn tart o pɔm, sivuplɛ |
| At the greengrocer's and fruiterer's: | Chez le marchand de légumes et de fruits: | ʃe lə marʃã də legym e də frɥi: |
| Have you any eating apples? | Avez-vous des pommes de dessert? | avevu de pɔm də dɛsɛr? |
| I should like three pounds of pears, please | Je voudrais trois livres de poires, s.v.p. | ʒvudrɛ trwa livr də pwar, sivuplɛ |
| Can I have five pounds of potatoes, please? | Puis-je avoir cinq livres de pommes de terre, s.v.p.? | pɥiʒ avwar sɛ̃(k) livr də pɔmdətɛr, sivuplɛ? |

| English. | | Pronunciation. |
|---|---|---|
| Could you send me some spinach, lemons, and bananas? | Pouvez-vous me faire envoyer des épinards, des citrons, et des bananes? | puvevu mfɛr ɑ̃vwaje dez epinar, de sitrɔ̃, e de banan? |
| The nuts are too dear | Les noisettes (noix) sont trop chères | le nwazet (nwɑ) sɔ̃ tro ʃɛr |
| The tomatoes and radishes are cheap and quite fresh | Les tomates et les radis sont bon marché et bien frais | le tɔmat e le radi sɔ̃ bɔ̃marʃe e bjɛ̃ frɛ |
| Strawberries are out of season, madam/sir | Les fraises sont hors de saison, madame/monsieur | lefrɛz sɔ̃ ɔrtsɛzɔ̃, madam/msjø |
| Have you any gooseberries or red or black currants? | Avez-vous des groseilles à maquereau, des groseilles rouges ou des cassis? | avɛvu de grɔzej a makro, de grɔzej ruʒ u de kasi? |
| Will you be having any cherries in to-morrow? | Est-ce que vous aurez des cerises demain? | ɛskə vuzɔre de sriz dmɛ̃? |
| Shall I keep some for you, madam/sir? | Voulez-vous que je vous en réserve, madame / monsieur? | vulevu kə ʒvuzɑ̃ rezɛrv, madam/msjø? |
| At the grocer's: | Chez l'épicier: | ʃe lepisje: |
| Half a pound of ground coffee and a quarter of a pound of tea, please | Une demi-livre de café moulu et un quart de livre de thé, s.v.p. | yn dmilivr də kafe muly e œ̃ kardlivr də te, sivuplɛ |
| Will you have granulated or lump sugar? | Voulez-vous du sucre cristallisé ou en morceaux? | vulevu dy sykr kristalize u ɑ̃ mɔrso? |

| English. | | Pronunciation. |
|---|---|---|
| Let me have a pint of vinegar, please | Donnez-moi un demi-litre de vinaigre, s.v.p. | dɔnemwa œ̃ dmi litr də vinɛgr, si-vuplɛ |
| I want half a pound of cooking fat, three pounds of flour, a packet of baking-powder, and a pound of raisins | Je veux une demi-livre de graisse, trois livres de farine, un paquet de poudre à lever et une livre de raisins secs | ʒvøz yn dmilivr də grɛs, trwɑ livr də farin, œ̃ pakɛ də pudr a ləve e yn livr də rɛzɛ̃ sɛk |
| Have you any tinned fruit (vegetables) ? | Avez-vous des conserves de fruits (légumes) en boîtes ? | avevu de kɔ̃sɛrv də frɥi (legym) ɑ̃ bwat ? |
| At the stores : | Dans un grand magasin : | dɑ̃z œ̃ grɑ̃ magazɛ̃ : |
| There is a sale on at the stores | C'est le moment des soldes au grand magasin | sɛ lmɔmɑ̃ desɔld o grɑ̃ magazɛ̃ |
| What sort of woollen material have you in stock ? | Quelles étoffes de laine avez-vous en magasin (en stock) ? | kɛlz etɔf də lɛn avevuz ɑ̃ magazɛ̃ (ɑ̃ stɔk) ? |
| Can you show me your latest designs in silks ? | Pouvez-vous me faire voir les derniers modèles en soierie ? | puvevu mfɛr vwar le dɛrnje mɔdɛlzɑ̃ swari ? |
| We have a large selection | Nous en avons un grand assortiment | nuzɑ̃ avɔ̃z œ̃ grɑ̃ta-sɔrtimɑ̃ |
| Four metres of red velvet | Quatre mètres de velours rouge | kat mɛtr də vlur ruʒ |
| That will do | Ça fera mon affaire | sa fra mɔ̃n afɛr |
| A reel of black cotton | Une bobine de coton noir | yn bɔbin də kɔtɔ̃ nwar |

| English. | | Pronunciation. |
|---|---|---|
| Three metres of that white elastic | Trois mètres de cet élastique blanc | trwɑ mɛtr də sɛt elastik blɑ̃ |
| I also want a zip-fastener | Je désire aussi une fermeture glissière | ʒə dezir osi yn fɛrmətyr glisjɛr |
| Do you stock small sewing-boxes, with scissors, a thimble, darning material, tape and buttons? | Avez-vous en magasin des petits nécessaires de couture contenant des ciseaux, un dé, de la laine et du coton à repriser, du ruban de coton et des boutons? | avevuz ɑ̃ magazɛ̃ de pti nesɛser də kutyr kɔ̃tnɑ̃ de sizo, œ̃ de, dla lɛn e dy kɔtɔ̃ a rprize, dy rybɑ̃tkɔtɔ̃ e de butɔ̃? |
| I want a plain blue tie and a coloured handkerchief to match | Je désire un nœud bleu uni et un mouchoir de couleur assortie | ʒə dezir œ̃ nø blø yni e œ̃ muʃwar də kulœr asɔrti |
| Does this material wash well? | Cette étoffe se lave-t-elle bien? | sɛt etɔf slavtɛl bjɛ̃? |
| It does not lose colour in the wash | Elle ne déteint pas au lavage | ɛl ndetɛ̃ paz o lavaʒ |
| At the cleaner's: | Chez le dégraisseur: | ʃe lə degrɛsœr: |
| I want this suit cleaned | Je veux faire nettoyer ce costume | ʒvø fɛr nɛtwaje skɔstym |
| When can I call for it? | Quand puis-je venir le chercher? | kɑ̃ pɥiʒ vnir lə ʃɛrʃe? |
| Can this coat be dyed brown? | Peut-on faire teindre ce veston (cette jaquette) en brun? | pøtɔ̃ fɛr tɛ̃dr sə vɛstɔ̃ (sɛt ʒakɛt) ɑ̃ brœ̃? |
| Do you do invisible mending? | Faites-vous du stoppage? | fɛtvu dy stɔpaʒ? |

| English. | | Pronunciation. |
|---|---|---|
| At the chemist's : | Chez le pharmacien: | ʃe lə farmasjɛ̃ : |
| Have you a safety-razor and some blades ?* | Avez-vous un rasoir de sûreté et des lames ? | avevuz ɶ̃ razwar də syrte e de lam ? |
| I want a shaving-brush and a stick of shaving-soap * | Je veux un blaireau et un savon à barbe | ʒvøz ɶ̃ blɛro e ɶ̃ savɔ̃nabarb |
| How much will that be altogether ? | Combien est-ce que cela fait en tout ? | kɔ̃bjɛ̃ ɛskə sla fɛ ɑ̃tu ? |
| I want a tube of tooth-paste and a tooth-brush | Je veux un tube de pâte dentifrice et une brosse à dents | ʒvøz ɶ̃ tyb də pɑt dɑ̃tifris e yn brɔsadɑ̃ |
| Have you anything for headaches ? | Avez-vous un remède contre les maux de tête ? | avevuz ɶ̃ rmɛd kɔ̃tr le modtɛt ? |
| Can you recommend a gargle ? | Pouvez-vous me recommander un gargarisme ? | puvevu mə rəkɔmɑ̃de ɶ̃ gargarism ? |
| A bottle of peroxide and some adhesive plaster, please | Une bouteille d'eau oxygénée et du taffetas d'Angleterre, s.v.p. | ynbutɛj do oksiʒene e dy tafta dɑ̃glətɛr, sivuplɛ |
| A box of cough lozenges | Une boîte de pastilles pectorales | yn bwɑtpastij pɛktɔral |
| A big packet of cotton-wool, please | Un grand paquet de coton hydrophile, s.v.p. | ɶ̃ grɑ̃ pakɛtkɔtɔ̃ idrofil, sivuplɛ |
| Please have this prescription made up for me | Veuillez faire préparer cette ordonnance, s.v.p. | vœje fɛr prepare sɛt ɔrdɔnɑ̃s, sivu- plɛ |
| I want a good tonic | Je désire un bon tonique | ʒə dezir ɶ̃ bɔ̃ tɔnik |
| At the tobacconist's : | Chez le débitant de tabac : | ʃe lə debitɑ̃taba : |

* In France these articles are not generally sold by chemists but by hair-dressers.

| English. | | Pronunciation. |
|---|---|---|
| Can you recommend a mild cigar? | Pouvez-vous me recommander un cigare doux? | puvevu mə rəkɔmãde œ̃ sigar du? |
| What brands of cigarettes do you stock? | Quelles marques de cigarettes avez-vous en stock? | kɛl mark də sigarɛt avevuz ã stɔk? |
| Have you any flints (wicks, petrol) for my lighter? | Avez-vous des pierres à feu (de la mèche, de l'essence) pour mon briquet? | avevu de pjɛrza fø (dla mɛʃ, dəlesãs) pur mɔ̃ brikɛ? |
| Sorry, we are sold out of everything | Je regrette, mais nous sommes démunis de tout | ʒə rgrɛt, mɛnu sɔm demyni dətu |
| Don't touch goods displayed on the counter | Ne touchez pas aux marchandises en montre sur le comptoir | ne tuʃe pɑzo marʃãdiz ã mɔ̃tr syr lə kɔ̃twar |
| Can you change a 10-franc note? | Pouvez-vous changer un billet de dix francs? | puvevu ʃãʒe œ̃ bijɛ də dis frã |
| Can you give me change for 10 francs? | Pouvez-vous me donner la monnaie d'un billet de dix francs? | puvevu mɑ̃ne la mɔnɛ dœ̃ bijɛ də dis frã? |
| Will you please send these things to my flat? | Voulez-vous faire envoyer ces articles à mon appartement, s.v.p.? | vulevu fɛr ãvwaje sezartikl a mɔ̃n apartəmã, sivuplɛ? |
| Our delivery-van calls in your neighbourhood to-morrow | Nos livreuses passent demain dans votre quartier | no livrøz pɑs dəmɛ̃ dã vɔtr kartje |

## POST OFFICE

### Vocabulary

| English. | | Pronunciation. |
|---|---|---|
| The letter-box, pillar-box | La boîte aux lettres, la boîte-borne | la bwatolɛtr, la bwatbɔrn |
| The letter | La lettre | la lɛtr |
| The postcard | La carte postale | la kartpɔstal |
| The printed matter | L'imprimé | lɛ̃prime |
| The registered letter | La lettre recommandée | la lɛtr rəkɔmɑ̃de |
| The express letter | La lettre express | la lɛtr ɛksprɛs |
| The telegram | Le télégramme, la dépêche | lə telegram, la depɛʃ |
| The parcel | Le colis | lə kɔli |
| The address | L'adresse | ladrɛs |
| The addressee | Le destinataire | lə dɛstinatɛr |
| The sender | L'expéditeur | lɛkspeditœr |
| The counter | Le guichet | lə giʃɛ |
| The post-office official | L'employé(e) des postes | lɑ̃plwaje depɔst |
| The postman | Le facteur | lə faktœr |
| The fee | Le droit, la taxe | lə drwa, la taks |
| Post-free | Franc (franche) de port | frɑ̃ (frɑ̃ʃ) də pɔr |
| The postage | Le port, l'affranchissement | lə pɔr, lafrɑ̃ʃismɑ̃ |
| The stamp | Le timbre-poste | lə tɛ̃brəpost |
| The wrapper | La bande | la bɑ̃d |
| The sample | L'échantillon | leʃɑ̃tijɔ̃ |
| Poste restante | Poste restante | post restɑ̃t |

### Phrases

| | | |
|---|---|---|
| Has the postman been ? | Est-ce que le facteur est passé ? | ɛskə lfaktœr ɛ pɑse ? |

| English. | | Pronunciation. |
|---|---|---|
| Letters are delivered three times a day | Les lettres sont distribuées trois fois par jour | le lɛt sɔ̃ distribɥe trwɑ fwɑ par ʒur |
| He delivered two letters and a postcard this morning | Il a distribué deux lettres et une carte postale ce matin | il a distribɥe dø lɛt e yn kartpɔstal smatɛ̃ |
| Take this letter to the nearest pillar-box | Portez cette lettre à la boîte aux lettres la plus proche | pɔrte sɛt lɛtrala bwatolɛtr la ply prɔʃ |
| The next collection is at six | La prochaine levée est à six heures | la prɔʃɛn lve ɛta siz œr |
| You must pay excess postage | Il vous faut payer le port supplémentaire (la surtaxe) | il vu fo peje lpɔr syplemɑ̃tɛr (la syrtaks) |
| Return to sender, address not known | Retour à l'expéditeur, adresse inconnue | rtur alɛkspeditœr, adrɛs ɛ̃kɔny |
| Please forward | Prière de faire suivre | prier də fɛr sɥivr |
| What is the postage for an airmail letter to England? | A combien doit-on affranchir une lettre par avion pour l'Angleterre? | a kɔ̃bjɛ̃ dwatɔ̃ afrɑ̃ʃir yn lɛtr par avjɔ̃ pur lɑ̃glətɛr? |
| Where can I enquire for poste restante letters? | Où peut-on se renseigner sur les lettres " poste restante "? | u pøtɔ̃ srɑ̃seɲe syr le lɛtr pɔstrestɑ̃t? |
| Where do I get postage stamps? | Où peut-on acheter les timbres-poste? | u pøtɔ̃ aʃte le tɛ̃brəpɔst? |
| Two sixpenny stamps, please | Deux timbres à trente francs, s.v.p. | dø tɛ̃br a trɑ̃t frɑ̃, sivuplɛ |

| English. | | Pronunciation. |
|---|---|---|
| Three letter-cards | Trois cartes-lettres | trwɑ kartlɛtr |
| Please send me this book, cash on delivery | Veuillez m'envoyer ce livre contre remboursement | vœje mãvwaje slivr kõtr rãbursəmã |
| Can I register this letter ? | Puis-je faire recommander cette lettre ? | pɥiʒ fɛr rəkɔmãde sɛt lɛtr ? |
| Do you want to register this parcel ? | Voulez-vous faire recommander ce colis ? | vulevu fɛr rəkɔmãde skɔli ? |
| You must complete the special form that has to accompany the parcel | Il vous faut remplir la formule spéciale qui accompagne le colis | il vu fo rãplir la formyl spesial ki akõpaɲ ləkɔli |
| Please let me have an international money-order form | Donnez-moi, s'il vous plaît, une formule de mandat-poste international | dɔnemwa, sivuplɛ, yn fɔrmyl də mãdapɔst ɛ̃ternasjɔnal |
| You have not completed it properly | Vous ne l'avez pas remplie correctement | vunlave pɑ rãpli kɔrɛktəmã |
| You must seal a registered parcel | Il faut cacheter un colis recommandé | il fo kaʃte œ̃ kɔli rəkɔmãde |
| I want to send a telegram | Je veux expédier un télégramme | ʒvøz ekspedje œ̃ telegram |
| Don't forget the name and address of sender | N'oubliez pas de mettre le nom et l'adresse de l'expéditeur | nublie pɑ dmɛtr lə nõ e l'adrɛs dələkspeditœr |
| In case it cannot be delivered, it will be returned | Au cas où il ne pourra pas être distribué, il sera renvoyé à l'expéditeur | o ka u il npura pɑz ɛtr distribɥe, il sra rãvwaje alekspeditœr |

| English. | | Pronunciation. |
|---|---|---|
| A telegram with pre-paid reply | Un télégramme réponse payée | œ̃ telegram repɔ̃s peje |
| What is the telegram rate to England? | Quel est le tarif télégraphique pour l'Angleterre? | kɛl ɛ ltarif telegrafik pur lɑ̃glətɛr? |
| Does the prefix count as a word? | Le préfixe compte-t-il comme un mot? | lə prefiks kɔ̃til kɔm œ̃ mo? |

## TELEPHONE

### Vocabulary

| The telephone | Le téléphone | lə telefɔn |
|---|---|---|
| The public telephone | La cabine téléphonique | la kabin telefɔnik |
| The receiver | Le récepteur | lə resɛptœr |
| The rest | L'étrier | letrije |
| The exchange | Le central | lə sɑ̃tral |
| The automatic exchange | Le central automatique | lə sɑ̃tral otomatik |
| The extension | La ligne supplémentaire | la liɲ syplemɑ̃tɛr |
| The operator | L'opérateur (opératrice) | lɔperatœr (operatris) |
| The subscriber | L'abonné(e) | labone |
| The directory | L'annuaire téléphonique | lanɥɛr telefɔnik |
| The call | L'appel | lapɛl |
| The caller | Le demandeur (la demandeuse) | lə dmɑ̃dœr (la dmɑ̃døz) |
| The night call | L'appel de nuit | lapɛl də nɥi |
| The local call | La communication locale | la komynikasjɔ̃ lokal |

| English. | | Pronunciation. |
|---|---|---|
| The trunk call | La communication interurbaine | la kɔmynikasjɔ̃ ɛ̃tɛryrbɛn |
| The connection | La communication | la kɔmynikasjɔ̃ |
| Engaged | Pas libre (ligne occupée) | pa libr (liɲ ɔkype) |
| To connect | Mettre en communication | mɛtrã kɔmynikasjɔ̃ |
| To dial | Composer un numéro (sur le disque d'appel) | kɔ̃poze œ̃ nymero (syr ldiskdapɛl) |
| To ring up, phone | téléphoner à, donner un coup de téléphone | telefɔne a, dɔne œ̃ kutelefɔn |

## Phrases

| | | |
|---|---|---|
| Are you on the phone? | Avez-vous le téléphone? | avevu ltelefɔn ? |
| Please give me a ring to-morrow evening | Donnez-moi un coup de téléphone demain soir, s.v.p. | dɔnemwa œ̃ kutelefɔn dmɛ̃ swar, sivuplɛ |
| How do I dial? | Comment est-ce qu'on compose le numéro? | kɔmãt ɛskɔ kɔ̃poz lə nymero ? |
| Lift the receiver | Décrochez le récepteur | dekrɔʃe lresɛptœr |
| Then dial the number required | Ensuite composez le numéro désiré | ãsɥit kɔ̃poze lə nymero dezire |
| Number, please? | Qui demandez-vous? ; j'écoute | ki dmãdevu ; ʒekut |
| Please give me Wagram 98–69 | Donnez-moi Wagram 98–69, s.v.p. | dɔnemwa vagram katrvɛ̃dizɥit-swasãtnœf |
| Number engaged | Pas libre (ligne occupée) | pa libr (liɲ ɔkype) |

| English. | | Pronunciation. |
|---|---|---|
| Put the receiver on the rest and repeat the call | Raccrochez et répétez l'appel | rakroʃe e repete lapɛl |
| I can't get through | Je ne peux pas obtenir la communication | ʒənpøpaz ɔbtənir la kɔmynikasjɔ̃ |
| Enquiries, please | Les renseignements, s.v.p. | le rɑ̃sɛɲəmɑ̃, sivuplɛ |
| Can you give me the number of Mr. Dupont, 10 Park Street? | Pouvez-vous me dire le numéro de M. Dupont, rue du Parc, numéro dix? | puvevu mdir lə nymero dməsjø dypɔ̃, ry dy park, nymero dis? |
| Can you connect me with 2968? | Pouvez-vous me mettre en communication avec le numéro 29–68? | puvevu mə mɛtr ɑ̃ kɔmynikasjɔ̃ avɛk lnymero vɛ̃tnœf – swasɑ̃tɥit? |
| There is no reply | (Ne) répond pas | (n)repɔ̃pa |
| Is that the Travel Bureau? | Est-ce là l'Agence de Tourisme? | ɛsla laʒɑ̃s də turism? |
| Extension four, please | La ligne supplémentaire quatre, s.v.p. | la liɲ syplemɑ̃tɛr katr, sivuplɛ |
| Just a minute, hold the line, please | Un moment, s'il vous plaît, ne quittez pas! | œ̃ mɔmɑ̃, sivuplɛ, nkitepa! |
| What's your number? | Quel est votre numéro? | kɛl ɛ vɔt nymero? |
| Sorry, wrong number | Je regrette, faux numéro d'appel | ʒə rgrɛt, fo nymero dapɛl |
| Sorry, we were cut off | Je regrette, on nous avait coupé la communication | ʒə rgrɛt, ɔ̃ nuz avɛ kupe la kɔmynikasjɔ̃ |
| The telephone is out of order | Le téléphone est détraqué | lə telefɔn ɛ detrake |

| English. | | Pronunciation. |
|---|---|---|
| You're through | Vous avez la communication | vuzave la kɔmynikasjɔ̃ |
| Telegrams, please | Télégrammes téléphonés, s.v.p. | telegram telefɔne, sivuplɛ |
| Where is there a public call office ? | Où y a-t-il une cabine téléphonique ? | ujatil yn kabin telefɔnik ? |
| Please insert the metal disk in slot when the operator tells you to do so | Veuillez introduire le jeton dans la fente quand l'opératrice vous dira de le faire | vœjez ɛ̃trɔdɥir lə ʒətɔ̃ dɑ̃ la fɑ̃t kɑ̃ lɔperatris vu dira dəl fɛr |
| Trunk call, please | Interurbain, s.v.p. | ɛ̃teryrbɛ̃, sivuplɛ |
| Can I speak to Mr. White ? | Puis-je parler avec M. Leblanc ? | pɥiʒ parle avɛk məsjø lblɑ̃ ? |
| Will you please give him a message ? | Voulez-vous lui dire un mot de ma part ? | vulevu lɥi dir œ̃ mo dma par ? |
| You are wanted on the phone | On vous demande au téléphone | ɔ̃vudmɑ̃d o telefɔn |
| We can make an appointment by telephone | Nous pouvons nous donner rendez-vous téléphoniquement | nu puvɔ̃ nu dɔne rɑ̃devu telefɔnikmɑ̃ |

# CORRESPONDENCE

## Vocabulary

| The letter | La lettre | la lɛtr |
|---|---|---|
| The business letter | La lettre de commerce | la lɛtr də kɔmɛrs |
| The letter of congratulation | La lettre de félicitations | la lɛtr də felisitasjɔ̃ |
| The letter of condolence | La lettre de condoléances | la lɛtr də kɔ̃dɔleɑ̃s |

| English. | | Pronunciation. |
|---|---|---|
| The postcard | La carte postale | la kart pɔstal |
| The picture post-card | La carte postale illustrée | la kart pɔstal ilystre |
| The letter-card | La carte-lettre | la kartlɛtr |
| The handwriting | L'écriture | lekrityr |
| The pen, nib | La plume | la plym |
| The penholder | Le porte-plume | lə pɔrtəplym |
| The fountain-pen | Le stylo, le porte-plume réservoir | lə stilo, lə pɔrtəplym rezɛrvwar |
| The ball-point pen | Le stylo à bille | lə stilo a bij |
| The pencil | Le crayon | lə krɛjɔ |
| The copying ink pencil | Le crayon-encre | lə krɛjɔ̃nɑ̃kr |
| The coloured pencil | Le crayon de couleur | lə krɛjɔ̃ də kulœr |
| The rubber | La gomme | la gɔm |
| The gum, glue | La colle | la kɔl |
| The letter-file | Le classeur | lə klasœr |
| The card-index | Le fichier | lə fiʃje |
| The paper | Le papier | lə papje |
| The notepaper | Le papier à lettres | lə papje a lɛtr |
| The envelope | L'enveloppe | lɑ̃vlɔp |
| The writing pad | Le sous-main | lə sumɛ̃ |
| The blotting paper | Le papier buvard | lə papje byvar |
| The blotting pad | Le (bloc) buvard | lə (blɔk) byvar |
| The ink | L'encre | lɑ̃kr |
| The inkstand | L'encrier | lɑ̃krie |
| The sealing wax | La cire à cacheter | la sir a kaʃte |
| The stationer's | La papeterie | la paptri |
| The writing desk | Le bureau, le pupitre | lə byro, lə pypitr |
| The shorthand | La sténographie | la stenɔgrafi |
| The typewriter | La machine à écrire | la maʃinaekrir |
| The carbon-paper | Le (papier) carbone | lə (papje) karbɔn |
| The sender | L'expéditeur | lekspeditœr |
| The addressee | Le destinataire | lə dɛstinatœr |
| The address | L'adresse | ladrɛs |
| The heading | L'en-tête | lɑ̃tɛt |

| English. | | Pronunciation. |
|---|---|---|
| The signature | La signature | la siɲatyr |
| The clerk | Le commis (de bureau) | lə kɔmi (də byro) |
| The typist | La dactylographe, la dactylo | la daktilɔgraf, la daktilo |
| The bookkeeper | Le comptable | lə kɔ̃tabl |
| The partner | L'associé | lasɔsje |
| The owner | Le propriétaire | lə prɔprietɛr |
| To write | Écrire | ekrir |
| To copy | Copier | kɔpje |
| To answer | Répondre à | repɔ̃dr a |
| To stick | Coller | kɔle |
| To seal | Cacheter | kaʃte |
| To send | Envoyer, expédier | ɑ̃vwaje, ekspedje |

## Phrases

| | | |
|---|---|---|
| Where is the writing room ? | Où est la salle de correspondance ? | wɛ la sal də kɔrɛspɔ̃dɑ̃s ? |
| There are envelopes and notepaper on the writing desk | Il y a des enveloppes et du papier à lettres sur le bureau | ilja dez ɑ̃vlɔp e dy papje a lɛtr syr lə byro |
| I have to write an urgent letter | J'ai une lettre urgente à écrire | ʒe yn lɛtr yrʒɑ̃t a ekrir |
| Shall I type it ? | Dois-je taper la lettre à la machine ? | dwaʒ tape la lɛtr ala maʃin ? |
| I am expecting important news | J'attends des nouvelles importantes | ʒatɑ̃ de nuvɛlz ɛ̃pɔrtɑ̃t |
| I have to answer some letters | Je dois répondre à quelques lettres | ʒdwa repɔ̃dr a kɛlkə lɛtr |
| There is no ink in the inkstand | Il n'y a pas d'encre dans l'encrier | ilnja pɑ dɑ̃kr dɑ̃ lɑ̃krie |
| Take my fountain pen | Prenez mon stylo | prəne mɔ̃ stilo |

| English. | | Pronunciation. |
|---|---|---|
| My fountain pen is broken. Where can I get it repaired? | Mon stylo est cassé. Où puis-je le faire réparer? | mɔ̃ stilo ɛ kase. u pɥiʒ lə fɛr repare? |
| He writes a very clear hand | Il a une main très lisible | ila yn mɛ̃ trɛ lizibl |
| Take this letter down in short-hand | Prenez cette lettre en sténo | prəne sɛt lɛtr ɑ̃ steno |
| Make two carbon copies of it | Faites-en deux copies au carbone | fɛtzɑ̃ dø kɔpi o karbɔn |
| Get the letter done quickly, we must catch the evening post | Dépêchez-vous de finir la lettre, il faut attraper le courrier du soir | depeʃevu də finir la lɛtr, il fot atrape lkurje dy swar |
| Have you filed the letters? | Avez-vous classé les lettres? | avevu klase le lɛtr? |
| You have not answered my letter | Vous n'avez pas répondu à ma lettre | vu nave pɑ repɔ̃dy a ma lɛtr |
| I told you all about it in my letter | Je vous ai tout raconté dans ma lettre | ʒvuze tu rakɔ̃te dɑ̃ ma lɛtr |
| I had great pleasure in reading your letter | J'ai pris beaucoup de plaisir à vous lire | ʒe pri bokutplɛzir a vu lir |
| My sincere congratulations | Toutes mes félicitations | tut me felisitasjɔ̃ |
| Many happy returns of the day | Mes meilleurs vœux pour votre anniversaire | me mɛjœr vø pur vɔtr anivɛrsɛr |
| I was very pleased to receive the news of your engagement (marriage) | J'ai été très heureux de recevoir la nouvelle de vos fiançailles (de votre mariage) | ʒe ete trɛz œrø də rsəvwar la nuvɛl dvo fjɑ̃saj (də vɔt marjaʒ) |
| My sincere condolences | Mes sincères condoléances | me sɛ̃sɛr kɔ̃dɔleɑ̃s |

| English. | | Pronunciation. |
|---|---|---|
| Please accept my deep sympathy | Veuillez agréer mes plus sincères condoléances | vœejez agree me ply sɛ̃sɛr kɔ̃dɔleɑ̃s |
| In reply to your favour . . . | En réponse à votre honorée . . . | ɑ̃ repɔ̃s a vɔtr ɔnɔre |
| I have received your letter of June 6th | J'ai bien reçu votre lettre du 6 juin | ʒe bjɛ̃ rsy vɔt lɛtr dy sis ʒɥɛ̃ |
| In receipt of your favour I beg to inform you that . . . | En possession de votre honorée, j'ai l'honneur de vous faire savoir que . . . | ɑ̃ pɔsesjɔ̃ də vɔtr ɔnɔre, ʒe lɔnœr də vu fɛr savwar kə . . . |
| I herewith acknowledge the receipt of your favour | Par la présente je vous accuse réception de votre honorée | par la prezɑ̃t ʒvuzakyz resɛpsjɔ̃ də vɔtr ɔnɔre |
| My dear father | Mon cher père | mɔ̃ ʃɛr pɛr |
| Dear Robert | Cher Robert | ʃɛr rɔbɛr |
| Dearest Margaret | Très chère Marguerite | trɛ ʃɛr margərit |
| Dear Professor (Doctor, Captain) | Mon cher Professeur (Docteur, Capitaine) or Cher Monsieur without the title | mɔ̃ ʃɛr prɔfɛsœr (dɔktœr, kapitɛn) or ʃɛr məsjø |
| (Dear) Madam | (Chère) Madame | (ʃɛr) madam |
| Dear Mr. Brown | Cher Monsieur (Cher Monsieur Dupont is frowned upon) | ʃɛr məsjø |
| Dear Mrs. Smith | Chère Madame | ʃɛr madam |
| Messrs. John Miller & Co., Ltd., Manchester | MM. John Miller et Cie, S.A., Manchester | məsjø . . . e kɔ̃paɲi, sɔsjete anɔnim . . . |
| Gentlemen/Dear Sirs | Messieurs | məsjø |

| English. | | Pronunciation. |
|---|---|---|
| Yours faithfully | Agréez, Monsieur/ Messieurs, nos (mes) meilleures salutations | agree, məsjø/mɛsjø, no (me) mɛjœr salytasjɔ̃ |
| Yours sincerely | Recevez, Monsieur/ Messieurs, l'assurance de mes sentiments distingués | rəsve, məsjø/mɛsjø, lasyrɑ̃s də me sɑ̃timɑ̃ distɛ̃ge |
| I remain, Yours sincerely | Je demeure avec mes sentiments cordiaux | ʒə dmœr avɛk me sɑ̃timɑ̃ kɔrdjo |
| With respectful greetings | Avec mes salutations respectueuses | avɛk me salytasjɔ̃ rɛspɛktɥøz |
| With kind regards from . . . | Avec les sincères amitiés de . . . | avɛk le sɛ̃sɛrz amitje də . . . |
| With all good wishes, Yours affectionately, Robert | Avec mes meilleurs vœux, bien affectueusement le vôtre, Robert | avɛk me mɛjœr vø, bjɛ̃ afɛktɥøzmɑ̃ lə votr, rɔbɛr |
| Your affectionate son | Ton fils affectionné | tɔ̃ fis afɛksjɔne |
| Much love from Joan | Jeanne vous envoie son affectueux souvenir | ʒɑn vuz ɑ̃vwa sɔ̃ afɛktɥø suvnir |
| A personal letter : | Une lettre personnelle : | yn lɛtr pɛrsɔnɛl: |
| Rouen, 4th May, '66 | Rouen, le 4 mai, 1966 | Rwɑ̃, lə katme diznøsɑ̃ sɛ̃kɑ̃tsis |
| Dear Madam (Mrs. Smith), | Chère Madame, | ʃɛr madam, |
| Many thanks for your kind invita- | Je vous remercie infiniment de votre | ʒə vu rəmɛrsi ɛ̃finimɑ̃ də votr |

| English. | | Pronunciation. |
|---|---|---|

tion to dinner. I am sorry to say I shall be away this week-end. But I shall be very pleased to spend one evening next week with you if convenient.

With kind regards,

Yours sincerely,

aimable invitation à dîner, mais à mon vif regret il me sera impossible de m'y rendre, car je serai absent de chez moi pendant la fin de semaine. J'aurai pourtant grand plaisir à passer une soirée chez vous la semaine prochaine, si ce projet vous convient.

Je vous prie d'agréer, chère Madame, mes amitiés sincères.

ɛmabl ɛ̃vitasjɔ̃ a dine, mɛz a mɔ̃ vif rəgrɛ il mə sra ɛ̃pɔsibl də mi rɑ̃dr, kar ʒəsre absɑ̃ də ʃemwa pɑ̃dɑ̃ la fɛ̃tsmɛn. ʒɔre purtɑ̃ grɑ̃ plɛzir a pɑse yn sware ʃevu la smɛn prɔʃɛn, si sə prɔʒe vu kɔ̃vjɛ̃.

ʒə vu pri dagree, ʃɛr madam, mɛz amitje sɛ̃sɛr.

---

A short business note :

Rue Royale 6, Nevers, 8th June, 1966.
The Manager, Municipal Electricity Works.
Dear Sir,

I beg to inform you that our electric meter is not working. Please send some one to attend to it.

Yours faithfully, B. Robert.

Une petite lettre de commerce :

Rue Royale 6, Nevers, le 8 juin, 1966.
M. le Gérant, Centrale Electrique Municipale.
Monsieur,

Je me permets de vous faire savoir que notre compteur d'électricité ne fonctionne pas. Veuillez avoir l'obligeance d'envoyer quelqu'un pour l'examiner.

yn ptit lɛtr də kɔmɛrs :

ry rwajal sis, nəvɛr, lə ɥit ʒɥɛ̃, 1966. məsjø lə ʒerɑ̃. sɑ̃tral elɛktrik mynisipal. məsjø,

ʒɑ̃mpɛrmɛ də vu fɛr savwar kə nɔtr kɔ̃tœr delɛktrisite nə fɔ̃ksjɔn pɑ. vœjez avwar lɔbliʒɑ̃s dɑ̃vwaje kɛlkœ̃ pur lɛgzamine.

| English. | | Pronunciation. |
|---|---|---|
| | Agréez, Monsieur, mes sentiments distingués, B. Robert. | agree, məsjø, me sãtimã distẽge, be rɔbɛr. |

| A business letter : | Une lettre de commerce : | yn lɛtr də kɔmɛrs : |
|---|---|---|
| Messrs. Fastré & Cie, Bruxelles. Gentlemen, | MM. Fastré et Cie, Bruxelles. Messieurs, | mɛsjø fastre e kɔ̃paɲi, brysɛl. mɛsjø, |

Enclosed I have pleasure in sending you invoice for two hundred pairs of best quality men's shoes bought for your account and to be shipped on the 22nd inst.

J'ai le plaisir de vous remettre ci-inclus la facture aux deux cents paires de chaussures d'hommes, première qualité, achetées pour votre compte et qui sont à embarquer le 22 courant.

ʒe lə plɛzir də vu rəmɛtr siẽkly la faktyr o dø sã pɛr də ʃosyr dɔm, prəmjɛr kalite, aʃte pur votr kɔ̃t e ki sɔ̃t a ãbarke lə vẽdø kurã.

The sizes you specified were in stock and I hope you will be pleased with the goods, as the make is strong and serviceable, and the manufacturers guarantee the goods to stand any climate.

Les pointures prescrites par vous étaient en magasin et j'espère que vous serez satisfaits de cette marchandise, car cette marque est bien solide et durable. Les fabricants garantissent que ces marchandises peuvent résister à tous les climats.

le pwẽtyr prɛskrit par vu etɛtã magazẽ e ʒɛspɛr kə vu sre satisfɛ də sɛt marʃãdiz, kar sɛt mark ɛ bjẽ sɔlid e dyrabl. Le fabrikã garãtis kə se marʃãdiz pœv reziste a tu le klima.

You will see by the invoice that I have been able to obtain a special cash discount of five per cent., making

Vous remarquerez en lisant la facture que j'ai pu obtenir

vu rəmarkre ã lizã la faktyr kə ʒe py ɔbtənir œ̃n ɛskɔ̃t

| English. | | Pronunciation. |
|---|---|---|
| the total amount £800, for which please send me your remittance. | un escompte au comptant de 5 pour cent, le total s'élevant à £800 que je vous prie de me remettre. | o kɔ̃tɑ̃ də sɛk pur sɑ̃, lə tɔtal selvɑ̃ a ɥi sɑ̃ livr kə ʒə vu pri də mə rəmɛtr. |
| I remain with compliments, Yours faithfully, | Veuillez agréer, Messieurs, l'expression de mes sentiments distingués. | vœjez agree, mɛsjø, lɛkspresjɔ̃ də me sɑ̃timɑ̃ distɛ̃ge. |
| Addresses on envelopes : | La suscription de l'enveloppe : | la syskripsjɔ̃ dəlɑ̃vlɔp : |
| G. B. Smith, Esq., 45 Oxford Street, London, W. 1. | Monsieur G. B. Dupont, Rue d'Amsterdam 45, Paris (9ᵉ). | məsjø ʒe be dypɔ̃, ry damstɛrdam karɑ̃tsɛk, pari (nœvjɛm arɔ̃dismɑ̃). |
| Professor W. Roberts c/o L. Black, Esq., 5 Broad Street, Kingswood, Surrey. | Monsieur le Professeur Robert, aux bons soins de Monsieur L. Lenoir, Rue de la Grosse [Horloge, Rouen. | məsjø lə prɔfesœr rɔbɛr, o bɔ̃ swɛ̃ də məsjø ɛl lənwar, ry dla gros ɔrlɔʒ, rwɑ̃. |
| Please forward | Prière de faire suivre | priɛr də fɛr sɥivrə |
| Messrs. K. M. Brown & Co., Ltd., 72 Westbourne Grove, London, W.11. | MM. F. Delage et Cie, Boulevard des Capucines 3, Paris (2ᵉ). · | məsjø ɛf dəlaʒ e kɔ̃paɲi, bulvar de kapysin trwa, pari (døzjɛm arɔ̃dismɑ̃). |

# BANKING

## Vocabulary

| English. | | Pronunciation. |
|---|---|---|
| The bank | La banque | la bɑ̃k |
| The account | Le compte de banque | lə kɔ̃t də bɑ̃k |
| The deposit account | Le compte de dépôts à terme | lə kɔ̃t də depoz a term |
| The current account | Le compte courant | lə kɔ̃t kurɑ̃ |
| The cheque | Le chèque | lə ʃɛk |
| The crossed cheque | Le chèque barré | lə ʃɛk bare |
| The bank manager | Le gérant | lə ʒerɑ̃ |
| The cashier | Le caissier | lə kɛsje |
| The bearer | Le porteur | lə pɔrtœr |
| The stockbroker | L'agent de change | laʒɑ̃ də ʃɑ̃ʒ |
| The money market | Le marché de l'argent | lə marʃe dəlarʒɑ̃ |
| The bill of exchange | La traite/l'effet de commerce | la trɛt/lɛfɛ də kɔmɛrs |
| The I.O.U. | La reconnaissance de dette | la rəkɔnɛsɑ̃s də dɛt |
| The Exchange | La Bourse | la burs |
| The share | L'action | laksjɔ̃ |
| The shareholder | L'actionnaire | laksjɔnɛr |
| The security | Le titre/la valeur/l'effet | lə titr/la valœr/lɛfɛ |
| The bonds | Les obligations/les titres | lez ɔbligasjɔ̃/le titr |
| The interest | L'intérêt | lɛ̃terɛ |
| The profit | Le bénéfice | lə benefis |
| The net profit | Le bénéfice net | lə benefis nɛt |
| The loss | La perte | la pɛrt |
| The advance deposit | L'acompte | lakɔ̃t |

| English. | | Pronunciation. |
|---|---|---|
| The debitor | Le débiteur | lə debitœr |
| The creditor | Le créancier | lə kreãsje |
| To cash a cheque | Encaisser / toucher un chèque | ãkɛse/tuʃe œ̃ ʃɛk |
| To make out (write) a cheque | Établir /tirer un chèque | etablir/tire œ̃ ʃɛk |
| To sign | Signer | siɲe |
| To endorse | Endosser | ãdɔse |
| To overdraw | Mettre à découvert | mɛtr a dekuvɛr |
| To open (close) an account | Ouvrir (fermer) un compte | uvrir (fɛrme) œ̃ kɔ̃t |
| To pay by cheque | Payer par chèque | pɛje par ʃɛk |
| To borrow | Emprunter | ãprœ̃te |
| To lend | Prêter | prɛte |

## Phrases

| | | |
|---|---|---|
| Have you a banking account ? | Avez-vous un compte de banque ? | avevuz œ̃ kɔ̃t də bãk ? |
| I should like to pay this into my account | Je voudrais verser ceci dans mon compte | ʒvudrɛ vɛrse səsi dã mɔ̃ kɔ̃t |
| Can I deposit securities and valuables here ? | Puis-je déposer des valeurs et des objets de valeur ? | pɥiʒ depoze de valœr e dez obʒɛ də valœr ? |
| Can you let me have my pass book ? | Pouvez-vous me donner mon carnet de compte ? | puvevu mə dɔne mɔ̃ karnɛtkɔ̃t ? |
| What is my balance ? | A combien s'élève mon compte en banque ? | a kɔ̃bjɛ̃ selɛv mɔ̃ kɔ̃t ã bãk ? |
| You have overdrawn your account | Vous avez mis votre compte à découvert | vuzave mi vɔt kɔ̃t a dekuvɛr |
| I can't grant you any credit | Je ne peux pas vous accorder un crédit | ʒə npø pa vuz akɔrde œ̃ kredi |

| English. | | Pronunciation. |
|---|---|---|
| Can you cash this cheque for me? | Pouvez-vous me verser le montant de ce chèque? | puvevu mə vɛrse lə mõtã də sə ʃɛk? |
| You have forgotten your signature | Vous avez oublié de signer | vuzavez ublie də siɲe |
| Please let me have some notes and silver | Donnez-moi, s'il vous plaît, des billets de banque et de la monnaie d'argent | dɔnemwa, sivuplɛ, de bijɛ də bãk e dla mɔnɛ darʒã |
| Please pay my current bills | Veuillez régler mes traites courantes | vœje regle me trɛt kurã |
| Has this bill of exchange been honoured? | A-t-on fait honneur à cette traite? | atõ fɛt ɔnœr a sɛt trɛt? |
| When was this bill of exchange due? | Quand cette traite était-elle échéable? | kã sɛt trɛt etɛtɛl eʃeabl? |
| You get a discount if you meet the bill before it is due | Vous recevrez un escompte si vous faites face à la traite avant l'échéance | vu rəsvrez œn ɛskõt si vu fɛt fas ala trɛt avã leʃeãs |
| We only sell for cash | Nous ne vendons qu'au comptant | nu nvãdõ ko kõtã |
| Does the bank pay interest? | La banque paie-t-elle des intérêts? | la bãk pɛtɛl dez ɛ̃tere? |
| Only for deposit accounts | Seulement sur les comptes de dépôt | sœlmã syr lekõt də depo |
| Which shares pay a high rate of interest? | Quelles actions rapportent un taux d'intérêt élevé? | kɛlz aksjõ rapɔrt œ̃ to dɛ̃tere elve? |
| I do not speculate in industrial shares | Je ne spécule pas sur les valeurs industrielles | ʒə nspekyl pɑ syr le valœr ɛ̃dystrjɛl |

| English. | | Pronunciation. |
|---|---|---|
| Do you deposit your money in a savings-bank ? | Est-ce que vous déposez votre argent à la caisse d'épargne ? | ɛskə vu depoze vɔtr arʒɑ̃t ala kɛs deparɲ ? |
| I invest my money in real estate | Je place mon argent en biens immeubles | ʒə plas mɔ̃n arʒɑ̃t ɑ̃ bjɛ̃z imœbl |
| Please buy some shipping shares for me | Achetez pour moi, s'il vous plaît, des valeurs de navigation | aʃte pur mwa, sivuplɛ, de valœr də navigasjɔ̃ |
| The stock exchange is dull | La Bourse est inactive | la burs ɛt inaktiv |
| Shares are looking up | Les titres s'améliorent | letitr sameljɔr |
| There was a lively turnover in the money market | Il y avait sur le marché d'argent un courant d'affaires animé | iljavɛ syr lə marʃedarʒɑ̃ œ̃ kurɑ̃ dafɛr anime |
| Bonds are rising (falling) | Les valeurs montent (baissent) | le valœr mɔ̃t (bɛs) |
| Have you any gilt-edged securities ? | Avez-vous des valeurs de père de famille ? | avevu de valœr də pɛrtfamij ? |
| I have some Government loans | J'ai quelques emprunts publics | ʒe kɛlkəz ɑ̃prœ̃ pyblik |
| I must sell my shares to settle with my creditors | Je dois vendre mes titres pour régler les comptes de mes créanciers | ʒdwa vɑ̃dr me titr pur regle le kɔ̃t də me kreɑ̃sje |
| The firm is bankrupt | La maison a fait faillite | la mɛzɔ̃ a fɛ fajit |
| The debts exceed the assets | Le passif excède l'actif | lə pasif ɛksɛd laktif |
| He is a trustworthy business man | C'est un homme d'affaires digne de confiance | sɛt œ̃nɔm dafɛr diɲ də kɔ̃fjɑ̃s |

| English. | | Pronunciation. |
|---|---|---|
| He is in arrears with his interest | Il est en arrière pour ses intérêts | il ɛt ãnarjer pur sez ẽterɛ |
| The cheque is payable to bearer | Le chèque est payable au porteur | lə ʃɛk ɛ pɛjabl o pɔrtœr |

I.O.U. :
  London,
      10th Jan.,
      1966.
Mr. A. Brown.
  I.O.U. £40.
    F. G. Black.

Reconnaissance de dette:
  Je, soussigné, A. Lebrun, reconnais devoir à M. F. G. Lenoir la somme de 520 francs
  Fait à Londres, le 10 janvier, 1966.
  Bon pour la somme de 520 francs
    A. Lebrun.

rəkɔnɛsãs də dɛt :
  ʒə, susiɲe, a ləbrœ̃, rəkɔnɛ dəvwar a məsjø ɛf ʒe lənwar la sɔm də sɛk sã vẽ frã.
  fɛt a lɔ̃dr, le dis ʒɑ̃vje mil nœf sã swasã:tsis.
  bɔ̃ pur la sɔm də sɛk sã vẽ frã.
    a ləbrœ̃.

Bill of Exchange:
  Bristol,
      15th August,
      1966.
£250
  Three months after date pay to Messrs. Smith or order the sum of two hundred and fifty pounds for value received.
(signed)
  Thomas Brown.
Mr. Paul Miller,
  London.

A Monsieur Paul Miller, Londres.
A trois mois de date veuillez payer à MM. Smith. . . . (*address and profession*) ou à leur ordre, la somme de trois mille deux cent cinquante francs, valeur reçue.
  Bon pour 3250 francs.
    (signé)
  Thomas Lebrun,
    Bristol.

a məsjø pɔl milɛr, lɔ̃dr.
a trwa mwa də dat vœje pɛje a məsjø smit (. . .) u a lœr ɔrdr la sɔm də trwa mil dø sã sɛkã:t frã valœr rəsy.
  bɔ̃ pur trwa mil dø sã sɛkã:t frã.
  (siɲe) tɔma ləbrœ̃, bristɔl.

## NUMERALS

### Vocabulary

| English. Cardinals : | Les nombres cardinaux : | Pronunciation. le nɔ̃brə kardino : |
|---|---|---|
| nil, nought | zéro | zero |
| one | un(e) | œ̃ (yn) |
| two | deux | dø |
| three | trois | trwɑ |
| four | quatre | katr |
| five | cinq | sɛ̃k |
| six | six | sis |
| seven | sept | sɛt |
| eight | huit | ɥit |
| nine | neuf | nœf |
| ten | dix | dis |
| eleven | onze | ɔ̃z |
| twelve | douze | duz |
| thirteen | treize | trɛz |
| fourteen | quatorze | katɔrz |
| fifteen | quinze | kɛ̃z |
| sixteen | seize | sɛz |
| seventeen | dix-sept | disɛt |
| eighteen | dix-huit | dizɥit |
| nineteen | dix-neuf | diznœf |
| twenty | vingt | vɛ̃ |
| twenty-one | vingt et un | vɛ̃teœ̃ |
| twenty-two | vingt-deux | vɛ̃tdø |
| thirty | trente | trɑ̃t |
| thirty-one | trente et un | trɑ̃teœ̃ |
| thirty-two | trente-deux | trɑ̃tdø |
| forty | quarante | karɑ̃t |
| fifty | cinquante | sɛ̃kɑ̃t |
| sixty | soixante | swasɑ̃t |
| seventy | soixante-dix | swasɑ̃tdis |

| English. | | Pronunciation. |
|---|---|---|
| eighty | quatre-vingts | katrəvɛ̃ |
| ninety | quatre-vingt-dix | katrəvɛ̃dis |
| a hundred | cent | sɑ̃ |
| two hundred | deux cents | døsɑ̃ |
| three hundred | trois cents | trwɑ sɑ̃ |
| four hundred and thirty | quatre cent trente | kat sɑ̃ trɑ̃t |
| a thousand | mille | mil |
| one thousand four hundred and six | mille quatre cent six | mil kat sɑ̃ sis |
| two thousand | deux mille | dø mil |
| a million | un million | ɛ̃ miljɔ̃ |

| Ordinals : | Les nombres ordinaux : | le nɔ̃br ɔrdino : |
|---|---|---|
| the first | le premier, la première | lə prəmje, la prəmjer |
| the second | le (la) deuxième | lə (la) døzjɛm |
| the third | le (la) troisième | lə (la) trwɑzjɛm |
| the fourth | le (la) quatrième | lə (la) katrjɛm |
| the fifth | le (la) cinquième | lə (la) sɛ̃kjɛm |
| the sixth | le (la) sixième | lə (la) sizjɛm |
| the seventh | le (la) septième | lə (la) sɛtjɛm |
| the eighth | le (la) huitième | lə (la) ɥitjɛm |
| the ninth | le (la) neuvième | lə (la) nœvjɛm |
| the tenth | le (la) dixième | lə (la) dizjɛm |
| the twentieth | le (la) vingtième | lə (la) vɛ̃tjɛm |
| the twenty-fourth | le (la) vingt-quatrième | lə (la) vɛ̃katrjɛm |
| the thirtieth | le (la) trentième | lə (la) trɑ̃tjɛm |
| the hundredth | le (la) centième | lə (la) sɑ̃tjɛm |
| the thousandth | le (la) millième | lə (la) miljɛm |

| Fractions : | Les Fractions : | le fraksjɔ̃ : |
|---|---|---|
| a half | une moitié | yn mwatje |
| a third | un tiers | ɛ̃ tjer |

| English. | | Pronunciation. |
|---|---|---|
| a fourth | un quart | œ̃ kar |
| a fifth | un cinquième | œ̃ sɛ̃kjɛm |
| a sixth | un sixième | œ̃ sizjɛm |
| a twentieth | un vingtième | œ̃ vɛ̃tjɛm |
| a hundredth | un centième | œ̃ sãtjɛm |
| 3·5 | 3,5 = trois virgule cinq | trwɑ virgyl sɛ̃k |
| 4·75 | 4,75 = quatre virgule soixante-quinze | katr virgyl swa-sãtkɛz |
| Adverbs : | Adverbes : | adverb : |
| once | une fois | yn fwɑ |
| twice | deux fois | dø fwɑ |
| three times | trois fois | trwɑ fwɑ |
| The figure | Le chiffre | lə ʃifr |
| The number | Le nombre, le numéro | lə nɔ̃br, lə nymero |
| The mathematics | Les mathématiques | le matematik |
| The multiplication table | La table de multiplication | la tabdə myltiplikasjɔ̃ |
| The addition | L'addition | ladisjɔ̃ |
| The subtraction | La soustraction | la sustraksjɔ̃ |
| The multiplication | La multiplication | la myltiplikasjɔ̃ |
| The division | La division | la divizjɔ̃ |
| To add | Additionner | adisjɔne |
| To subtract | Soustraire | sustrɛr |
| To multiply | Multiplier | myltiplie |
| To divide | Diviser | divize |
| To calculate | Calculer | kalkyle |

## Phrases

| How long have you been waiting ? | Depuis combien de temps attendez-vous ? | dəpᴚi kɔ̃bjɛ̃tã atã-devu ? |

| English. | | Pronunciation. |
|---|---|---|
| Three quarters of an hour | Trois quarts d' heure | trwɑ kardœr |
| What are your office hours ? | Quelles sont vos heures de bureau? | kɛl sɔ̃ vozœr də byro ? |
| From nine till five | De neuf heures jusqu'à cinq heures | də nœvœr ʒyskɑ sɛ̃kœr |
| I had ten days leave | J'ai eu dix jours de congé | ʒe y di ʒur də kɔ̃ʒe |
| I spent eighteen months in France | J'ai passé dix-huit mois en France | ʒe pɑse dizɥi mwɑ ɑ̃ frɑ̃s |
| How far is it to Marseilles ? | Combien y a-t-il d'ici à Marseille ? | kɔ̃bjɛ̃ jatil disi a marsɛj ? |
| It is twenty-six km. from here | C'est à vingt-six kilomètres d'ici | sɛt a vɛ̃tsi kilɔmɛt disi |
| How long will it take me to get there ? | Combien de temps vais-je mettre à y arriver ? | kɔ̃bjɛ̃tɑ̃ veʒ mɛtr a iarive ? |
| About an hour and a half | A peu près une heure et demie | apøprɛ ynœr e dmi |
| The train will leave in thirty-five minutes | Le train partira dans trente-cinq minutes | lə trɛ̃ partira dɑ̃ trɑ̃tsɛ̃ minyt |
| The performance starts at eight-fifteen | La représentation (le spectacle) commencera à vingt heures quinze | la rəprezɑ̃tasjɔ̃ (lə spɛktakl) kɔmɑ̃sra a vɛ̃t œr kɛ̃z |
| My seat is number one hundred and six | Ma place est numéro cent six | ma plas ɛ nymero sɑ̃sis |
| The last day of my holidays | Le dernier jour de mes vacances | lə dɛrnje ʒur də me vakɑ̃s |
| In the second year of the war | Dans la deuxième année de la guerre | dɑ̃ la døzjɛm ane dla gɛr |
| He inherited a quarter of his father's fortune | Il a hérité d'un quart de la fortune de son père | il a erite dœ̃ kar dla fɔrtyn də sɔ̃ pɛr |

| English. | | Pronunciation. |
|---|---|---|
| Three-quarters of the book are uninteresting | Les trois quarts du livre sont ennuyeux | le trwa kar dy livr sõt ãnɥijø |
| He sold half of his property | Il a vendu la moitié de sa propriété | il a vãdy la mwatje də sa prɔpriete |
| A year and a half ago I was in hospital | Il y a un an et demi j'étais hospitalisé | ilja œ̃nã edmi ʒetɛz ɔspitalize |
| The child is six months old | L'enfant a six mois (est âgé(e) de six mois) | lãfã a si mwa (ɛt aʒe də si mwɑ) |
| He stayed abroad three years and a half | Il est resté trois ans et demi à l'étranger | il ɛ rɛste trwɑz ã edmi aletrãʒe |
| She took half a day off | Elle a pris un demi jour de congé | ɛl a pri œ̃ dmi ʒur də kõʒe |
| In nineteen hundred and fourteen | En mil neuf cent quatorze (dix-neuf cent quatorze) | ã mil nøsã katɔrz (diznøsã katɔrz) |

## COINAGE, WEIGHTS, MEASURES

### Vocabulary

| The money | L'argent | larʒã |
|---|---|---|
| The change | La petite monnaie | la ptitmɔnɛ |
| The note | Le billet de banque | lə bijɛdbãk |
| The franc | Le franc | lə frã |
| The fifty-franc piece | La pièce de cinquante francs | la pjɛs də sɛ̃kãt frã |
| The centimetre | Le centimètre | lə sãtimetr |

| English. | | Pronunciation. |
|---|---|---|
| The metre | Le mètre | lə mɛtr |
| The kilometre | Le kilomètre | lə kilɔmɛtr |
| The square metre (1·196 sq. yd.) | Le mètre carré | lə mɛtrə kare |
| The hectare | L'hectare | lɛktar |
| The cubic metre | Le mètre cube | lə mɛtrə kyb |
| The litre | Le litre | lə litr |
| The hectolitre (100 litres) | L'hectolitre (cent litres) | lɛktɔlitr (sã litr) |
| The kilogram (2·204 lbs.) | Le kilogramme | lə kilɔgram |
| 50 kilograms | Cinquante kilogrammes | sɛ̃kɑ̃t kilɔgram |
| 100 kilograms | Cent kilogrammes | sã kilɔgram |
| The ton (1000 kilograms) | La tonne (mille kilogrammes) | la tɔn (mil kilɔgram) |

## Phrases

| | | |
|---|---|---|
| I have no change on me | Je n'ai pas de petite monnaie sur moi | ʒə nepa də ptit mɔnɛ syr mwa |
| Can you lend me twenty francs? | Pouvez-vous me prêter vingt francs? | puvevu mprɛte vɛ̃ frã |
| Can I borrow a pound till to-morrow? | Puis-je vous emprunter une livre sterling jusqu'à demain? | pɥiʒ vuz aprœ̃te yn livr stɛrlɛ̃ ʒyska dmɛ̃? |
| I have only a little silver | Je n'ai que de la monnaie d'argent | ʒəne kə dla mɔnɛ darʒã |
| Put twenty francs in the slot | Introduisez une pièce de vingt francs dans la fente | ɛ̃trɔdɥize yn pjɛs də vɛ̃ frã dã la fãt |
| I have lost a thousand franc note | J'ai perdu un billet de mille francs | ʒe pɛrdy œ̃ bijɛ də mil frã |
| I have to pay 2000 francs | Je dois payer deux mille francs | ʒdwa pɛje dø mil frã |

| English. | | Pronunciation. |
|---|---|---|
| When can you repay me? | Quand pourrez-vous me rembourser? | kɑ̃ purevu mə rɑ̃burse? |
| May I defer paying till next month? | Puis-je remettre le paiement jusqu'au mois prochain? | pɥiʒ rəmɛtr lə pɛmɑ̃ ʒysko mwɑ prɔʃɛ̃? |
| He has run into debt | Il s'est endetté | il sɛt ɑ̃dete |
| What do I owe you? | Combien vous dois-je? | kɔ̃bjɛ̃ vudwaʒ? |
| Here is an advance payment of 30 francs | Voici un acompte de trente francs | vwasi œ̃nakɔ̃t də trɑ̃t frɑ̃ |
| I must pay my insurance policy | Je dois payer ma police d'assurance | ʒdwa pɛje ma pɔlis dasyrɑ̃s |
| Where can I exchange foreign money? | Où peut-on échanger de l'argent étranger? | u pøtɔ̃ eʃɑ̃ʒe də larʒɑ̃ etrɑ̃ʒe? |
| I have to earn my living | Il me faut gagner ma vie | il mə fo gɑɲe mavi |
| He receives a monthly allowance from his mother | Il reçoit une rente mensuelle de sa mère | il rəswa yn rɑ̃t mɑ̃sɥel də sa mɛr |
| He was a war profiteer and made his money on the black market | C'était un profiteur de guerre et il a fait sa fortune sur le marché noir | setɛt œ̃ prɔfitœr də gɛr et il a fɛ sa fɔrtyn syr lə marʃe nwar |
| Have you paid your income tax? | Avez-vous payé l'impôt sur le revenu? | avevu pɛje lɛ̃po syr lə rəvny? |
| It is deducted from my salary | On le retranche de mon salaire | ɔ̃ lə rətrɑ̃ʃ də mɔ̃ salɛr |
| How far is Paris from Lyons? | Quelle est la distance entre Paris et Lyon? | kɛl ɛ la distɑ̃s ɑ̃tr pari e ljɔ̃? |

| English. | | Pronunciation. |
|---|---|---|
| I drove at fifty kilometres an hour | J'ai roulé à cinquante kilomètres à l'heure | ʒe rule a sɛ̃kɑ̃t kilɔmɛtr alœr |
| Let me have three metres and forty centimetres of this ribbon | Donnez-moi trois mètres quarante de ce ruban | dɔnemwa trwɑ mɛtkarɑ̃t də srybɑ̃ |
| The garden is 35 m. long and 20 m. wide | Le jardin a trente-cinq mètres de long et vingt mètres de large | lə ʒardɛ̃ a trɑ̃tsɛ̃ mɛt də lɔ̃ e vɛ̃ mɛt də larʒ |
| Will you take my measurements for a suit ? | Voulez-vous prendre mes mesures pour un costume ? | vulevu prɑ̃dr me mzyr pur œ̃ kɔstym ? |
| These shoes are made to measure | Ces chaussures sont faites sur mesure | se ʃosyr sɔ̃ fɛt syr mzyr |
| A quarter litre of milk, please | Un quart de litre de lait, s.v.p. | œ̃ kar dlitr də lɛ, sivuplɛ |
| What is your weight ? | Combien pesez-vous ? | kɔ̃bjɛ̃ pəzevu ? |
| I weigh sixty kilograms | Je pèse soixante kilogrammes | ʒə pez swasɑ̃t kilɔgram |
| I have ordered ten hundredweight of coal and two cubic metres of wood | J'ai commandé une demi tonne de charbon et deux mètres cubes de bois | ʒe kɔmɑ̃de yn dmi tɔn də ʃarbɔ̃ e dø mɛtrə kyb də bwɑ |

## THE HUMAN BODY, HEALTH:
## AT THE DOCTOR'S, AT THE DENTIST'S

### Vocabulary

| English. | | Pronunciation. |
|---|---|---|
| The head | La tête | la tɛt |
| The face | La figure, le visage | la figyr, lə vizaʒ |
| The skull | Le crâne | lə krɑn |
| The forehead | Le front | lə frɔ̃ |
| The eye | L'œil (les yeux) | lœj (lezjø) |
| The eyelid | La paupière | la popjɛr |
| The eyebrow | Le sourcil | lə sursi |
| The ear | L'oreille | lɔrɛj |
| The nose | Le nez | lə ne |
| The mouth | La bouche | la buʃ |
| The lip | La lèvre | la lɛvr |
| The cheek | La joue | la ʒu |
| The chin | Le menton | lə mɑ̃tɔ̃ |
| The jaw | La mâchoire | la maʃwar |
| The tooth | La dent | la dɑ̃ |
| The gum | La gencive | la ʒɑ̃siv |
| The tongue | La langue | la lɑ̃g |
| The neck, throat | Le cou, la gorge | lə ku, la gɔrʒ |
| The tonsil | L'amygdale | lamigdal |
| The gland | La glande | la glɑ̃d |
| The hair | Le cheveu, les che-veux | lə ʃvø, le ʃvø |
| The skin | La peau | la po |
| The body | Le corps | lə kɔr |
| The trunk | Le tronc | lə trɔ̃ |
| The bone | L'os (les os) | lɔs (lezo) |
| The rib | La côte | la kot |
| The spine | L'épine dorsale | lepin dɔrsal |
| The chest | La poitrine | la pwatrin |

| English. | | Pronunciation. |
|---|---|---|
| The abdomen | L'abdomen | labdɔmen |
| The belly | Le ventre | lə vɑ̃tr |
| The lung | Le poumon | lə pumɔ̃ |
| The heart | Le cœur | lə kœr |
| The bowels | Les intestins | lez ɛ̃tɛstɛ̃ |
| The stomach | L'estomac | lɛstɔma |
| The shoulder | L'épaule | lepol |
| The arm | Le bras | lə bra |
| The elbow | Le coude | lə kud |
| The hand | La main | la mɛ̃ |
| The wrist | Le poignet | lə pwaɲɛ |
| The finger | Le doigt | lə dwa |
| The thumb | Le pouce | lə pus |
| The nail | L'ongle | lɔ̃gl |
| The leg | La jambe | la ʒɑ̃b |
| The thigh | La cuisse | la kɥis |
| The knee | Le genou | lə ʒnu |
| The ankle | La cheville | la ʃvij |
| The foot | Le pied | lə pje |
| The toe | Le doigt de pied | lə dwatpje |
| The blood | Le sang | lə sɑ̃ |
| The vein | La veine | la vɛn |
| The illness, disease | La maladie, le mal | la maladi, lə mal |
| The nutrition, feeding | La nutrition, l'alimentation | la nytrisjɔ̃, lalimɑ̃tasjɔ̃ |
| The food | La nourriture | la nurityr |
| The malnutrition | La sous-alimentation | la suzalimɑ̃tasjɔ̃ |
| The pain | La douleur | la dulœr |
| The headache | Le mal de tête | lə mal də tɛt |
| The sore throat | Le mal de gorge | lə mal də gɔrʒ |
| The cold | Le rhume | lə rym |
| The cold in the head | Le rhume de cerveau | lə rym də sɛrvo |
| The cough | La toux | la tu |
| The inflammation | L'inflammation | lɛ̃flamasjɔ̃ |

| English. | | Pronunciation. |
|---|---|---|
| The pneumonia | La pneumonie | la pnømɔni |
| The gastric trouble | L'embarras gastrique | lãbara gastrik |
| The tuberculosis | La tuberculose | la tybɛrkyloz |
| The medical examination | La visite médicale | la vizit medikal |
| The treatment | Le traitement | lə trɛtmã |
| The medicine | Le médicament, la médecine, le remède | lə medikamã, la metsin, lə rəmɛd |
| The prescription | L'ordonnance | lɔrdɔnãs |
| The adhesive plaster | Le taffetas d'Angleterre | lə tafta dãglətɛr |
| The cotton wool | Le coton hydrophile | lə kɔtɔ̃ idrɔfil |
| The sanitary towel | La serviette hygiénique | la servjɛt iʒenik |
| The ambulance | L'ambulance | lãbylãs |
| The nurse | La garde-malade, l'infirmière | la gardmalad, lɛ̃firmjɛr |
| The toothache | Le mal de dents | lə mal də dã |
| To extract | Arracher | araʃe |
| To stop | Plomber | plɔ̃be |
| To treat | Traiter, soigner | trɛte, swaɲe |
| To anæsthetize | Anesthésier, insensibiliser | anɛstezje, ɛ̃sãsibilize |
| To cure, heal | Guérir | gerir |

## Phrases

| | | |
|---|---|---|
| What are Dr. Baker's consultation hours? | Quelles sont les heures de consultation du Docteur Boulanger? | kɛl sɔ̃ lezœr də kɔ̃syltasjɔ̃ dy dɔktœr bulãʒe? |
| Send for the doctor | Envoyez chercher le médecin | ãvwaje ʃɛrʃe lə metsɛ̃ |
| Telephone for the doctor | Appelez le médecin téléphoniquement | aple lə metsɛ̃ telefɔnikmã |

| English. | | Pronunciation. |
|---|---|---|
| What is the matter with you ? | Qu'est-ce que vous avez ? | kɛskə vuzave ? |
| I don't feel well | Je ne me sens pas bien | ʒənməsã pɑ bjɛ̃ |
| I feel very ill | Je me sens très malade | ʒəmsã trɛ malad |
| I feel very sick (giddy) | J'ai des nausées (je suis pris de vertige) | ʒe de noze (ʒə sɥi pri dvɛrtiʒ) |
| I feel very weak | Je me sens très faible | ʒəmsã trɛ fɛbl |
| I've got a sore throat | J'ai mal à la gorge | ʒe mal ala gɔrʒ |
| You have inflammation of the throat | Vous avez une inflammation de la gorge | vuzavez yn ɛ̃flamasjɔ̃ dla gɔrʒ |
| Your tonsils are swollen | Vos amygdales sont enflées | voz amigdal sɔ̃t ãfle |
| I am hoarse | Je suis enroué(e) | ʒə sɥiz ãrue |
| I've caught a cold | Je me suis enrhumé(e) | ʒəmsɥiz ãryme |
| I keep sneezing and my nose runs | J'éternue tout le temps et mon nez coule | ʒetɛrny tultã e mɔ̃ ne kul |
| I cough all night | Je tousse toute la nuit | ʒə tus tut la nɥi |
| You must gargle and take a cough mixture | Il faut vous gargariser et prendre une potion béchique | il fo vu gargarize e prãdr yn pɔsjɔ̃ beʃik |
| Take the pills three times a day | Prenez les pilules trois fois par jour | prəne le pilyl trwɑ fwɑ par ʒur |
| I must take your temperature | Il me faut prendre votre température | il mə fo prãdr vɔt tãperatyr |
| You are feverish | Vous avez la fièvre | vuzave la fjɛvr |

| English. | | Pronunciation. |
|---|---|---|
| The temperature is going up (down) | La température monte (baisse) | la tãperatyr mõt (bɛs) |
| Your pulse is very irregular | Le pouls est très intermittent | lə pu ɛ trɛz ɛ̃termitã |
| My heart is very weak | Je suis cardiaque | ʒə sɥi kardjak |
| You have pneumonia | Vous êtes atteint(e) de pneumonie | vuzɛts atɛ̃ (atɛ̃t) də pnømɔni |
| She is suffering from pleurisy (measles, scarlet fever, typhoid) | Elle est atteinte d' une pleurésie (de la rougeole, de la fièvre scarlatine, de la typhoïde) | ɛl ɛt atɛ̃t dyn plœrezi (dla ruʒɔl, dla fjɛvr skarlatin, dla tifɔid) |
| Did he die of T.B. ? | Est-il mort de la tuberculose | ɛtil mɔr dla tyberkyloz ? |
| You must be moved into hospital | Il faut qu'on vous transporte à l' hôpital | il fo kõ vu trãspɔrt alɔpital |
| Keep warm | Tenez-vous au chaud | tənevu o ʃo |
| The patient must not be disturbed | Le malade ne doit pas être dérangé | lə malad nə dwa paz ɛt derãʒe |
| Must I have an operation ? | Dois-je me faire opérer ? | dwaʒ mə fɛr ɔpere ? |
| Have you been to a specialist ? | Avez-vous consulté un spécialiste ? | avevu kõsylte œ̃ spesjalist ? |
| You should consult my doctor | Vous devriez consulter mon médecin | vu dəvrie kõsylte mõ metsɛ̃ |
| What are his fees ? | Quels sont ses honoraires ? | kɛl sõ sez ɔnɔrɛr ? |
| I shall have to give you a thorough examination | Je vais vous faire subir un examen minutieux | ʒvɛ vu fɛr sybir œ̃n ɛgzamɛ̃ minysjø |
| We shall have to take an X-ray | Il va falloir prendre un radiogramme | il va falwar prãdr œ̃ radjɔgram |
| Is your digestion all right ? | Avez-vous la digestion facile ? | avevu la diʒɛstjõ fasil ? |

| English. | | Pronunciation. |
|---|---|---|
| The medicine was no good | Le médicament ne valait rien | lə medikamã nə valɛ rjɛ̃ |
| Shake the bottle | Agiter avant de s'en servir | aʒite avã də sã sɛrvir |
| For external use only | Pour l'usage externe | pur lyzaʒ ɛkstɛrn |
| Poison | Poison | pwazɔ̃ |
| You have broken your arm | Vous vous êtes cassé le bras | vuvuzɛt kɑse lə bra |
| He has fractured his skull | Il s'est fracturé le crâne | il sɛ fraktyre lə krɑn |
| I have had a bad concussion | J'ai eu une grave commotion cérébrale | ʒe y yn grav kɔmɔsjɔ̃ serebral |
| I am injured | Je suis blessé(e) | ʒə sɥi blɛse |
| Have you sprained your ankle ? | Vous êtes-vous foulé la cheville ? | vuzɛtvu fule la ʃvij ? |
| I must bandage your foot | Il me faut vous bander le pied | il mə fo vu bɑ̃de lə pje |
| You are badly bruised | Vous êtes gravement contusionné(e) | vuzɛt gravmã kɔ̃tyzjɔne |
| He is suffering from an internal ulcer | Il souffre d'un ulcère interne | il sufr dœ̃n ylsɛr ɛ̃tɛrn |
| The illness got worse (better) | La maladie a empiré (s'est améliorée) | la maladi a ɑ̃pire (sɛt ameljɔre) |
| Are you feeling better ? | Vous sentez-vous mieux ? | vusɑ̃tevu mjø ? |
| The cut is healed, but you can see the scar | La coupure (l'entaille) est guérie mais on peut voir la cicatrice | la kupyr (lɑ̃taj) ɛ geri mɛzɔ̃ pø vwar la sikatris |
| I must dress your wounds | Il me faut panser vos blessures | il mə fo pɑ̃se vo blɛsyr |
| I cannot hear well | Je n'entends pas bien | ʒə nɑ̃tɑ̃pa bjɛ̃ |

| English. | | Pronunciation. |
|---|---|---|
| I am deaf | Je suis sourd(e) | ʒə sɥi sur(d) |
| She is deaf and dumb | Elle est sourde-muette | ɛl ɛ surdmɥet |
| You must go to an ear-specialist | Il vous faut consulter un auriste | il vu fo kɔ̃sylte œ̃norist |
| Your middle-ear is inflamed | Vous avez l'oreille moyenne enflammée | vuzave lɔrɛj mwajɛn ɑ̃flame |
| Where does the oculist live? | Où l'oculiste demeure-t-il? | u lɔkylist dmœrtil? |
| I am short-sighted (long-sighted) | Je suis myope (presbyte) | ʒə sɥi mjɔp (presbit) |
| He is blind | Il est aveugle | il ɛt avøgl |
| I need a pair of spectacles | J'ai besoin de lunettes | ʒe bəzwɛ̃ də lynet |
| He squints a little | Il louche un peu | il luʃ œ̃ pø |
| At the dentist's: | Chez le dentiste: | ʃe ldɑ̃tist: |
| Please come into the surgery | Veuillez entrer dans le cabinet de consultation | vœjez ɑ̃tre dɑ̃ lə kabine də kɔ̃syltasjɔ̃ |
| This molar (incisor) hurts me | Cette molaire (incisive) me fait mal | set mɔlɛr (ɛ̃siziv) mə fɛ mal |
| It must be stopped | Il faut la faire plomber | il fo la fɛr plɔ̃be |
| The gums are bleeding | Les gencives saignent | le ʒɑ̃siv seɲ |
| The root is decayed | La racine est cariée | la rasin ɛ karje |
| Can you stop the drilling? | Pouvez-vous arrêter la fraise? | puvevuz arete la frɛz? |
| The tooth must be extracted | Il faut arracher la dent | il fot araʃe la dɑ̃ |
| I shall give you a local anæsthetic | Je vais pratiquer une anesthésie locale | ʒə vɛ pratike yn anestezi lɔkal |

| English. | | Pronunciation. |
|---|---|---|
| I have a gumboil | J'ai un abcès des gencives | ʒe œ̃n absɛ de ʒɑ̃siv |
| What sort of mouth-wash (tooth-paste) do you use? | De quelle eau dentifrice (pâte dentifrice) vous servez-vous? | də kɛl o dɑ̃tifris (pɑt dɑ̃tifris) vu-sɛrvevu? |
| I am afraid you must have dentures | Il vous faut un dentier, j'ai bien peur | il vu fot œ̃ datje, ʒe bjɛ̃ pœr |
| You must have a gold crown on your teeth | Il vous faut faire couronner vos dents en or | il vu fo fɛr kurɔne vo dɑ̃ ɑ̃nɔr |
| I shall have to get a new tooth-brush | Il va falloir m'acheter une nouvelle brosse à dents | il va falwar maʃte yn nuvɛl brɔsadɑ̃ |

## AT THE HAIRDRESSER'S

### Vocabulary

| The electric razor | Le rasoir électrique | lə razwar elɛktrik |
|---|---|---|
| The safety razor | Le rasoir de sûreté | lə razwar də syrte |
| The razor blade | La lame de rasoir | la lam də razwar |
| The permanent wave | L'ondulation permanente (la permanente) | lɔ̃dylasjɔ̃ pɛrmanɑ̃t (la pɛrmanɑ̃t) |
| The hair-net | Le filet à cheveux | lə filɛaʃvø |
| The hairpin | L'épingle à cheveux | lepɛ̃glaʃvø |
| The parting | La raie | la rɛ |
| The curl | La boucle | la bukl |
| The hair-curler | Le bigoudi | lə bigudi |
| The comb | Le peigne | lə pɛɲ |
| The brush | La brosse à cheveux | la brɔsaʃvø |
| To shave | (Se) raser | (sə) rɑze |
| To lather | Savonner | savɔne |

| English. | | Pronunciation. |
|---|---|---|
| To cut, trim | Couper, rafraîchir les cheveux | kupe, rafreʃir le ʃvø |
| To shampoo | Donner un shampooing | dɔne œ̃ ʃɑ̃pwɛ̃ |
| To set | Mettre les cheveux en plis | mɛtr le ʃvø ɑ̃ pli |

## Phrases

| | | |
|---|---|---|
| Is there a gentlemen's hairdresser near here ? | Y a-t-il un coiffeur pour messieurs près d'ici ? | jatil œ̃ kwafœr pur mesjø prɛ disi ? |
| Haircut, please | Les cheveux, s'il vous plaît | le ʃvø, sivuplɛ |
| Not too short, please | Pas trop court, s.v.p. | pɑ tro kur, sivuplɛ |
| I should like a shampoo | Je voudrais un shampooing | ʒvudrɛz œ̃ ʃɑ̃pwɛ̃ |
| Where do you have the parting ? | Où portez-vous la raie ? | u pɔrtevu la rɛ ? |
| You can give me a shave too | Vous pouvez me faire la barbe aussi | vupuve məfɛr la barb osi |
| You are getting bald (grey) | Vous devenez chauve (vous commencez à blanchir) | vu dəvne ʃov (vu kɔmɑ̃se a blɑ̃ʃir) |
| Have you got any good hair-oil ? | Avez-vous une bonne huile capillaire ? | avevuz yn bɔn ɥil kapilɛr ? |
| Have you got a hair-restorer ? | Avez-vous un régénérateur des cheveux ? | avevuz œ̃ reʒeneratœr de ʃvø ? |
| Can you recommend a ladies' hairdresser ? | Pouvez-vous me recommander un bon coiffeur pour dames ? | puvevu mə rəkɔmɑ̃de œ̃ bɔ̃ kwafœr pur dam ? |

| English. | | Pronunciation. |
|---|---|---|
| I want my hair shampooed and set | Je veux un shampooing et une mise en plis | ʒvøz œ̃ ʃɑ̃pwɛ̃ e yn miz ɑ̃ pli |
| Don't cut off too much, please | Ne coupez pas trop court, s.v.p. | nə kupe pɑ tro kur, sivuplɛ |
| Can I come for a perm to-morrow? | Puis-je venir demain pour une permanente? | pɥiʒ vnir dmɛ̃ pur yn pɛrmanɑ̃t? |
| How much will it be? | Combien est-ce que ça coûtera? | kɔ̃bjɛ̃ ɛskə sa kutra? |
| Will you have curls or a roll? | Voulez-vous en boucles ou en rouleau? | vulevuz ɑ̃ bukl u ɑ̃ rulo |
| I should like to try a new style of hairdressing | Je voudrais essayer un nouveau style de coiffure | ʒvudrɛz ɛsɛje œ̃ nuvo stil də kwafyr |
| You ought to have your hair dyed | Vous devriez vous faire teindre les cheveux | vu dəvrie vu fɛr tɛ̃dr le ʃvø |
| Would you like your hair bleached? | Aimeriez-vous vous faire blondir les cheveux? | ɛmərievu vu fɛr blɔ̃dir le ʃvø? |
| A packet of hairpins, please | Un paquet d'épingles à cheveux, s'il vous plaît | œ̃ pakɛ depɛ̃glaʃvø, sivuplɛ |
| My hair-net is torn | Mon filet à cheveux est déchiré | mɔ̃ filɛaʃvø ɛ deʃire |
| Do you sell lipsticks and nail-varnish? | Vendez-vous les bâtons de rouge et du vernis pour les ongles? | vɑ̃devu le batɔ̃ də ruʒ e dy vɛrni pur lez ɔ̃gl? |
| Some face powder and cream, please | De la poudre de riz et de la crème de beauté, s.v.p. | dla pudr də ri e dla krɛm də bote, sivuplɛ |
| Some scent, please | Du parfum, s.v.p. | dy parfœ̃, sivuplɛ |

| English. | | Pronunciation. |
|---|---|---|
| Have you anyone here for mani-cure and pedi-cure? | Avez-vous une manucure et une pédicure? | avevuz yn manykyr e yn pedikyr? |
| A cake of good toilet soap, please | Un bon savon de toilette, s.v.p. | œ̃ bɔ̃ savɔ̃ də twalɛt, sivuplɛ |

## CLOTHING
### Vocabulary

| MEN'S CLOTHES: | Les vêtements d' homme: | le vɛtmã dɔm |
|---|---|---|
| The pyjamas | Le pyjama | lə piʒama |
| The dressing-gown | La robe de chambre | la rɔb də ʃãbr |
| The slippers | Les pantoufles | le pãtufl |
| The socks | Les chaussettes | le ʃosɛt |
| The shoe | Le soulier, la chaus-sure | lə sulje, la ʃosyr |
| The suspenders, garter | Les jarretelles, la jarretière | le ʒartɛl, la ʒartjɛr |
| The drawers, pants | Le caleçon | lə kalsɔ̃ |
| The vest | Le maillot de corps | lə majo də kɔr |
| The shirt | La chemise | la ʃmiz |
| The braces | Les bretelles | le brətɛl |
| The belt | La ceinture | la sɛ̃tyr |
| The collar | Le col, le faux col | lə kɔl, lə fo kɔl |
| The stud | Le bouton de col | lə butɔ̃ də kɔl |
| The tie | La cravate, le nœud | la kravat, lə nø |
| The suit | Le complet, le cos-tume | lə kɔ̃plɛ, lə kɔstym |
| The jacket | Le veston | lə vɛstɔ̃ |
| The trousers | Le pantalon | lə pãtalɔ̃ |
| The waistcoat | Le gilet | lə ʒilɛ |
| The lounge-suit | Le complet veston | lə kɔple vɛstɔ̃ |
| The dinner-jacket | Le smoking | lə smɔkiɲ |
| The overcoat | Le pardessus | lə pardsy |
| The hat | Le chapeau | lə ʃapo |

| English. | | Pronunciation. |
|---|---|---|
| The cap | La casquette | la kaskɛt |
| The glove | Le gant | lə gɑ̃ |
| The stick | La canne | la kan |
| The umbrella | Le parapluie | lə paraplɥi |
| The scarf | Le foulard | lə fular |
| The handkerchief | Le mouchoir | lə muʃwar |
| The shorts | Le short | lə ʃɔrt |
| | | |
| WOMEN'S CLOTHES: | Les vêtements de femme : | le vɛtmɑ̃ də fɛm |
| The stocking | Le bas | lə bɑ |
| The underwear | Le linge de dessous | lə lɛ̃ʒ də dsu |
| The cami-knickers | La combinaison-culotte | la kɔ̃binɛzɔ̃ kylɔt |
| The slip | La combinaison | la kɔ̃binɛzɔ̃ |
| The dress, gown | La robe | la rɔb |
| The coat and skirt | Le (costume) tailleur | lə kɔstym tajœr |
| The blouse | La blouse | la bluz |
| The skirt | La jupe | la ʒyp |
| The night-dress | La robe de nuit | la rɔb də nɥi |
| The corsets | Le corset | lə kɔrsɛ |
| The girdle | La gaine | la gɛn |
| The brassiere | Le soutien-gorge | lə sutjɛ̃gɔrʒ |
| The fur coat | Le manteau de fourrure | lə mɑ̃to də furyr |
| The scarf | L'écharpe | leʃarp |
| The silk scarf | Le foulard | lə fular |
| Briefs | Le slip | lə slip |
| Sun suit | Le costume de plage | lə kɔstym də plaʒ |
| The sports wear | Les vêtements de sport | le vɛtmɑ̃ də spɔr |
| The fashion | La mode | la mɔd |
| The design | Le dessin, le modèle | lə dɛsɛ̃, lə mɔdɛl |
| The material | L'étoffe | letɔf |
| The silk | La soie | la swɑ |
| The velveteen | Le velours de coton | lə vlur də kɔtɔ̃ |

| English. | | Pronunciation. |
|---|---|---|
| The wool | La laine | la lɛn |
| The linen | La toile | la twal |
| The coat-hanger | Le porte-vêtements | lə pɔrtvɛtmɑ̃ |
| The tailor | Le tailleur | lə tajœr |
| The dressmaker | La couturière | la kutyrjɛr |
| The milliner | La modiste | la mɔdist |
| To dress | S'habiller | sabije |
| To undress | Se déshabiller | sə dezabije |
| To sew | Coudre | kudr |
| To mend | Raccommoder | rakɔmɔde |
| To darn | Repriser, ravauder | rəprize, ravode |
| Red | Rouge, rouge | ruʒ, ruʒ |
| Blue | Bleu, bleue | blø, blø |
| Green | Vert, verte | vɛr, vɛrt |
| Yellow | Jaune, jaune | ʒon, ʒon |
| Brown | Brun, brune | brœ̃, bryn |
| Grey | Gris, grise | gri, griz |
| Black | Noir, noire | nwar, nwar |
| White | Blanc, blanche | blɑ̃, blɑ̃ʃ |
| Purple | Pourpre, pourpre | purpr, purpr |
| Light and dark | Clair et foncé | klɛr e fɔ̃se |

## Phrases

| | | |
|---|---|---|
| Have you a good tailor? | Avez-vous un bon tailleur? | avevuz œ̃ bɔ̃ tajœr? |
| I want a suit made to measure | Je veux un complet fait sur mesure | ʒvøz œ̃ kɔ̃plɛ fɛ syr mzyr |
| I prefer it to a ready-made one | Je le préfère à un complet tout fait | ʒə lprefɛr a œ̃ kɔ̃plɛ tu fɛ |
| What sort of material do you stock? | Quelles étoffes tenez-vous en magasin? | kɛlz etɔf tnevuz ɑ̃ magazɛ̃? |
| I want a lounge-suit | Je veux un complet veston | ʒvøz œ̃ kɔ̃plɛ vestɔ̃ |
| Single-breasted or double-breasted? | Croisé ou droit? | krwaze u drwa? |

| English. | | Pronunciation. |
|---|---|---|
| Please line the pockets with chamois-leather | Doublez les poches avec du chamois, s.v.p. | duble le pɔʃ avɛk dy ʃamwa, sivuplɛ |
| Do you wear braces or a belt? | Portez-vous des bretelles ou une ceinture? | pɔrtevu de brətɛl u yn sɛ̃tyr? |
| The sleeves are too short | Les manches sont trop courtes | le mɑ̃ʃ sɔ̃ tro kurt |
| The trousers are too long | Le pantalon est trop long | lə pɑ̃talɔ̃ ɛ tro lɔ̃ |
| The lapels are too wide | Les revers sont trop larges | le rvɛr sɔ̃ tro larʒ |
| The jacket does not fit | Le veston n'est pas à ma taille | lə vɛstɔ̃ nepaz a ma taj |
| I should like a dark sports jacket and a pair of light flannel trousers | Je voudrais un veston sport de couleur sombre et un pantalon de flanelle claire | ʒvudrɛz ɶ̃ vɛstɔ̃ spɔr də kulɶr sɔ̃br e ɶ̃ pɑ̃talɔ̃ də flanɛl klɛr |
| The suit is well cut | Le complet est de bonne façon | lə kɔ̃plɛ ɛ də bɔn fasɔ̃ |
| Show me some coloured shirts, please | Montrez-moi des chemises de couleur, s.v.p. | mɔ̃tremwa de ʃmiz də kulɶr, sivuplɛ |
| Six starched collars | Six cols empesés | si kɔlz ɑ̃pəze |
| Have you got a blue silk tie? | Avez-vous une cravate de soie bleue? | avevuz yn kravat də swa blø? |
| Half a dozen coloured and a dozen white handkerchiefs | Une demi-douzaine de mouchoirs de couleur et une douzaine de mouchoirs blancs | yn dmi duzɛn də muʃwar də kulɶr e yn duzɛn də muʃwar blɑ̃ |
| The hat is too big for me | Le chapeau est trop grand pour moi | lə ʃapo ɛ tro grɑ̃ pur mwa |

| English. | | Pronunciation. |
|---|---|---|
| I must send my grey hat to be cleaned | Il me faut envoyer mon chapeau gris chez le dégraisseur | il mə fot ɑ̃vwaje mɔ̃ ʃapo gri ʃe lə degresœr |
| This suit must be repaired, the lining is torn | Il faut faire réparer ce complet, la doublure est déchirée | il fo fɛr repare sə kɔ̃plɛ, la dublyr ɛ deʃire |
| Please send these shoes to be soled | Envoyez ces chaussures à réparer, s.v.p. | ɑ̃vwaje se ʃosyr a repare, sivuplɛ |
| The slippers need new heels | Les pantoufles ont besoin de talons nouveaux | le pɑ̃tufl ɔ̃ bəzwɛ̃ də talɔ̃ nuvo |
| I like coloured socks | J'aime les chaussettes de couleur | ʒɛm le ʃosɛt də kulœr |
| The woollen socks have shrunk | Les chaussettes de laine se sont rétrécies | le ʃosɛt də lɛn se sɔ̃ retresi |
| The colours have run | Les couleurs ont déteint | le kulœr ɔ̃ detɛ̃ |
| Do you prefer brown or black shoes? | Préférez-vous les chaussures brunes ou les noires? | preferevu le ʃosyr bryn u le nwar? |
| The shoes are too narrow | Les souliers sont trop étroits | le sulje sɔ̃ trop etrwa |
| The toe-cap pinches | Le bout rapporté me serre | lə bu rapɔrte mə sɛr |
| A pair of brown laces, please | Une paire de lacets bruns, s.v.p. | yn pɛr də lasɛ brœ̃, sivuplɛ |
| Have you any silk underwear which is not too expensive? | Avez-vous des vêtements de dessous en soie qui ne soient pas trop chers? | avevu de vɛtmɑ̃ də dsu ɑ̃ swa ki nswapa tro ʃɛr? |

| English. | | Pronunciation. |
|---|---|---|
| Have you any knickers in light-blue? | Avez-vous des culottes bleu clair? | avevu de kylɔt blø klɛr? |
| A pink slip, please | Une combinaison rose, s.v.p. | yn kɔ̃binɛzɔ̃ roz, sivuplɛ |
| A blue striped sports-blouse | Une blouse de sports à raies bleues | yn bluz də spɔr a rɛ blø |
| The brown skirt is very smart | La jupe brune est très élégante | la ʒyp bryn ɛ trɛz elegɑ̃t |
| This is a nice two-piece suit | C'est un joli deux-pièces | sɛt œ̃ ʒɔli døpjɛs |
| It is too large for me | Il est trop grand pour moi | il ɛ tro grɑ̃ pur mwa |
| You can have it altered | Vous pouvez le faire retoucher | vupuve lə fɛr rətuʃe |
| Please show me some silk after-noon dresses | Montrez-moi, s'il vous plaît, des robes d'intérieur en soie | mɔ̃tremwa, sivuplɛ, de rɔb dɛ̃terjœr ɑ̃ swɑ |
| I need a woollen winter-dress | J'ai besoin d'une robe d'hiver en laine | ʒe bəzwɛ̃ dyn rɔb divɛr ɑ̃ lɛn |
| Have you any low-necked evening-dresses? | Avez-vous des robes de soirée décolle-tées? | avevu de rɔb də sware dekɔlte? |
| Your green dress is very becoming | Votre robe verte vous va à merve-ille | vɔt rɔb vɛrt vu va a mɛrvej |
| The coat is not warm enough | La jaquette n'est pas assez chaude | la ʒakɛt nɛpaz ase ʃod |
| I should like a red cap, a red shawl and knitted wool-len gloves | Je voudrais un béret rouge, un châle rouge et des gants de laine tricotés | ʒvudrɛz œ̃ berɛ ruʒ, œ̃ ʃal ruʒ e degɑ̃ dlɛn trikɔte |

| English. | | Pronunciation. |
|---|---|---|
| Wouldn't you prefer fur-lined gloves? | N'aimeriez-vous pas mieux des gants doublés de fourrure? | nɛmərievu pa mjø də gã duble də furyr? |
| A pair of green slippers, lined with lamb's-wool | Une paire de pantoufles vertes, doublées d'agneline | yn pɛr də pãtuflə vɛrt duble daɲəlin |

## AT THE THEATRE[1]
### Vocabulary

| The theatre | Le théâtre | lə teɑtr |
|---|---|---|
| The opera-house | L'opéra | lɔpera |
| The box-office | Le bureau de location | lə byro də lɔkasjɔ̃ |
| The tickets in advance | La location | la lɔkasjɔ̃ |
| The evening performance | La soirée | la sware |
| The matinée | La matinée | la matine |
| The cloakroom | Le vestiaire | lə vɛstjer |
| The refreshment room | Le buffet | lə byfɛ |
| The stage | La scène | la sen |
| The curtain | Le rideau | lə rido |
| The wings | La coulisse | la kulis |
| The scenery | Les décors | le dekɔr |
| The auditorium | La salle | la sal |
| The box | La loge | la lɔʒ |
| The stalls | Les fauteuils d'orchestre | le fotœj dɔrkestr |
| The dress circle | Le balcon | lə balkɔ̃ |
| The upper circle | La seconde galerie | la sgɔ̃d galri |
| The gallery | La galerie | la galri |

[1] Don't forget that as a rule no smoking is allowed in a French theatre or cinema.

| English. | | Pronunciation. |
|---|---|---|
| The pit | Le parterre | lə parter |
| The play | La pièce de théâtre | la pjɛs də teatr |
| The curtain raiser | Le lever de rideau | lə lve də rido |
| The tragedy | La tragédie | la traʒedi |
| The comedy | La comédie | la kɔmedi |
| The act | L'acte | lakt |
| The scene | La scène | la sɛn |
| The interval | L'entr'acte | lɑ̃trakt |
| The author | L'auteur | lotœr |
| The playwright | L'auteur dramatique, le dramaturge | lotœr dramatik, lə dramatyrʒ |
| The theatre attendant | L'ouvreuse [1] | luvrøz |
| The poet | Le poète | lə pɔet |
| The actor | L'acteur | laktœr |
| The actress | L'actrice | laktris |
| The producer | Le metteur en scène | lə metœr ɑ̃ sɛn |
| The part | Le rôle | lə rol |
| The prompter | Le souffleur | lə suflœr |
| The singer | Le chanteur, la cantatrice | lə ʃɑ̃tœr, la kɑ̃tatris |
| The conductor | Le chef d'orchestre | lə ʃef dɔrkestr |
| The concert | Le concert | lə kɔ̃ser |
| The piano | Le piano | lə pjano |
| The violin | Le violon | lə vjɔlɔ̃ |
| The bass | La contrebasse | la kɔ̃trəbas |
| The cello | Le violoncelle | lə vjɔlɔ̃sel |
| The flute | La flûte | la flyt |
| The drum | Le tambour, la caisse | lə tɑ̃bur, la kes |
| The harp | La harpe | la arp |
| The trumpet | La trompette | la trɔ̃pet |
| The orchestra | L'orchestre | lɔrkestr |
| The chamber music | La musique de chambre | la mysik də ʃɑ̃br |

[1] She will expect a small tip for showing you to your seat.

| English. | | Pronunciation. |
|---|---|---|
| The applause | Les applaudisse-ments | lez aplodismã |
| To applaud | Applaudir, battre des mains | aplodir, batr de mẽ |
| The variety show | Le théâtre de varié-tés | lə teatr də varjete |
| The acrobat | L'acrobate | lakrɔbat |
| The conjurer | Le prestidigitateur | lə prestidiʒitatœr |
| The dancer | Le danseur, la dan-seuse | lə dãsœr, la dãsøz |

## Phrases

| | | |
|---|---|---|
| What is on at the theatre, to-day? | Qu'est-ce qu'on joue au théâtre aujourd'hui? | kɛskɔ̃ ʒu o teatr oʒurdɥi? |
| A tragedy at the State Theatre | Une tragédie au Théâtre National | yn traʒedi o teatr nasjɔnal |
| Would you care to go to the opera? | Aimeriez-vous aller à l'opéra? | ɛmərjevuz ale a lɔpera? |
| One of Wagner's operas is being played | On joue un des opéras de Wagner | ɔ̃ ʒu œ̃ dez ɔpera də vagnɛr |
| We shan't get any tickets | Nous n'allons pas pouvoir nous pro-curer des places | nu nalɔ̃ pɑ puvwar nu prɔkyre de plas |
| The house is sold out | La salle est comble | la sal ɛ kɔ̃bl |
| Tickets must be purchased in ad-vance | Il faut acheter les billets d'avance | il fot aʃte le bijɛ davãs |
| Can I order tickets by telephone? | Est-ce que je peux retenir les billets téléphoniquement? | ɛskə ʒpø rətnir le bijɛ telefɔnikmã? |
| I should like to see a comedy | J'aimerais voir une comédie | ʒɛmrɛ vwar yn kɔmedi |

| English. | | Pronunciation. |
|---|---|---|
| Two stalls, please, if possible in the middle | Deux fauteuils d'orchestre, s.v.p., au milieu du rang, si possible | dø fotœj dɔrkɛstr, sivuplɛ, o miljø dy rɑ̃, si pɔsibl |
| Can you see well from these seats ? | Peut-on bien voir la scène de ces places ? | pøtɔ̃ bjɛ̃ vwar la sɛn də se plas ? |
| You'd better book seats in the dress circle | Vous feriez mieux de retenir des places au balcon | vufərje mjø də rətnir de plas o balkɔ̃ |
| Programmes, opera glasses ? | Programmes, jumelles ! | prɔgram, ʒymɛl ! |
| Can you get tea or coffee in the interval ? | Peut-on se procurer du thé ou du café pendant l'entr'acte ? | pøtɔ̃ sə prɔkyre dy te u dy kafe pɑ̃dɑ̃ lɑ̃trakt ? |
| Only in the refreshment room | Au buffet seulement | o byfɛ sœlmɑ̃ |
| The curtain rises (falls) | Le rideau se lève (tombe) | lə rido slɛv (tɔ̃b) |
| When does the performance start ? | Quand la représentation commence-t-elle ? | kɑ̃ la rəprezɑ̃tasjɔ̃ kɔmɑ̃stɛl ? |
| What a magnificent stage setting ! | Quelle mise en scène magnifique ! | kɛl mizɑ̃sɛn maɲifik ! |
| It was designed by an artist | Elle a été exécutée par un artiste | ɛl a ete ɛgzekyte par œ̃ artist |
| The actors act well | Les acteurs jouent bien | lez aktœr ʒu bjɛ̃ |
| The hero has not learned his part | Le héros ne sait pas son texte | lə ero nsɛ pɑ sɔ̃ tɛkst |
| The play is enthralling (boring) | La pièce est captivante (ennuyeuse) | la pjɛs ɛ kaptivɑ̃t (ɑ̃nɥijøz) |
| The production is bad | La mise en scène est mauvaise | la mizɑ̃sɛn ɛ mɔvɛz |
| The footlights are too bright | Les feux de la rampe sont trop vifs | le fø dla rɑ̃p sɔ̃ tro vif |

| English. | | Pronunciation. |
|---|---|---|
| The comedy was booed | La comédie a été sifflée | la kɔmedi a ete sifle |
| The applause was frantic (feeble) | On a applaudi frénétiquement (sans enthousiasme) | ɔna aplodi frenetikmã (sãz ãtuzjasm) |
| Yesterday was the first night | Hier on a donné la première | jɛr ɔna dɔne la prəmjɛr |
| When was it first performed ? | Quand a-t-on donné la première représentation ? | kãtatɔ̃ dɔne la prəmjɛr rəprezãtasjɔ̃ ? |
| Here are two tickets for to-night's concert | Voici deux billets pour le concert de ce soir | vwasi dø bijɛ pur lə kɔ̃sɛr də sə swar |
| Who is conducting ? | Qui est-ce qui dirige l'orchestre ? | kiɛski diriʒ lɔrkɛstr ? |
| An Italian conductor | Un chef d'orchestre italien | œ̃ ʃɛf dɔrkɛstr italjɛ̃ |
| Do you prefer classical or light music ? | Préférez-vous la musique classique ou légère ? | preferevu la myzik klasik u leʒɛr ? |
| Do you like chamber-music ? | Aimez-vous la musique de chambre ? | ɛmevu la myzik də ʃãbr ? |
| This is a famous orchestra | C'est un orchestre célèbre | sɛt œ̃ ɔrkɛstr selɛbr |
| The soloist is a great artist. She is a soprano (contralto) singer | La soliste est une grande artiste. Elle a une voix de soprano (de contralte) | la sɔlist ɛt yn grãt artist. ɛl a yn vwɑ də sɔprano (də kɔ̃tralt) |
| He is a tenor | C'est un ténor | sɛt œ̃ tenɔr |
| He beats time | Il bat la mesure | il bat la mzyr |
| Is there a good band at your hotel ? | Y a-t-il un bon orchestre dans votre hôtel ? | jatil œ̃ bɔnɔrkɛstrə dã vɔtr otɛl ? |

| English. | | Pronunciation. |
|---|---|---|
| Would you like to go to a variety show ? | Aimeriez-vous aller au théâtre de variétés ? | ɛmərjevuz ale o teɑtr də varjete ? |
| I do not like acrobatics | Je n'aime pas l'acrobatie | ʒə nɛmpɑ lakrɔbasi |
| How about the ballet ? | Et le ballet donc ? | e lbalɛ dɔ̃ ? |
| If we want to be in time we must take a taxi | Si nous voulons arriver à l'heure, il faudra prendre un taxi | si nu vulɔ̃z arive alœr, il fodra prɑ̃dr œ̃ taksi |

# CINEMA

## Vocabulary

| | | |
|---|---|---|
| The cinema | Le cinéma | lə sinema |
| The film | Le film | lə film |
| The screen | L'écran | lekrɑ̃ |
| The talkie | Le film parlant | lə film parlɑ̃ |
| The silent film | Le film muet | lə film mɥɛ |
| The cultural (nature, travelling) film | Le film documentaire | lə film dɔkymɑ̃tɛr |
| The cartoon | Le dessin animé | lə desɛ̃ anime |
| The news reel, news of the week | Le film d'actualités | lə film daktɥalite |
| The usherette | La placeuse | la plasøz |
| The close-up | La vue de premier plan | la vy də prəmje plɑ̃ |
| The film studio | L'atelier | latəlje |
| To film | Filmer | filme |

## Phrases

| English. | | Pronunciation. |
|---|---|---|
| When is the next performance? | A quand la prochaine séance? | a kɑ̃ la prɔʃɛn seɑ̃s? |
| The news reel is shown at 3.30 | On tourne le film d'actualités à trois heures trente | ɔ̃ turn lə film daktɥalite a trwɑ-zœr trɑ̃t |
| Is this a continuous performance? | Est-ce un spectacle permanent? | ɛs ɑ̃ spɛktakl pɛrmanɑ̃? |
| What is on at the big cinema? | Qu'est-ce qu'on tourne au grand cinéma? | kɛskɔ̃ turn o grɑ̃ sinema? |
| A new film is being shown | On tourne un nouveau film | ɔ̃ turn ɑ̃ nuvo film |
| Is it a serious or a comic film? | Est-ce un film sérieux ou comique? | ɛs ɑ̃ film serjø u kɔmik? |
| We had better sit at the back | Il vaudrait mieux nous asseoir au fond de la salle | il vodrɛ mjø nuz aswar o fɔ̃ dla sal |
| I should like to see a topical film | J'aimerais voir un film d'actualités | ʒɛmrɛ vwar ɑ̃ film daktɥalite |
| This is an excellent colour film | C'est un excellent film en couleurs | sɛt ɑ̃ ɛksɛlɑ̃ film ɑ̃ kulœr |
| Would you like to see a good animal film in slow motion? | Aimeriez-vous voir un bon film de bêtes, tourné au ralenti? | ɛmərjevu vwar ɑ̃ bɔ̃ film də bɛt, turne o ralɑ̃ti? |
| Is there an emergency exit? | Y a-t-il une sortie de secours? | jatil yn sɔrti də skur? |
| Can we book seats in advance? | Peut-on louer les places d'avance? | pøtɔ̃ lwe le plas davɑ̃s? |
| You have to take up the tickets half an hour before the performance starts | Il faut prendre les billets une demi-heure avant le commencement de la séance | il fo prɑ̃dr le bijɛ yn dmiœɪ avɑ̃ lə kɔmɑ̃smɑ̃ dla seɑ̃s |

## WIRELESS

### Vocabulary

| English. | | Pronunciation. |
|---|---|---|
| The broadcasting station | La station de radio-diffusion | la stasjɔ̃ də radjodifyzjɔ̃ |
| The transmission | L'émission, la transmission | lemisjɔ̃, la trɑ̃smisjɔ̃ |
| The reception | La réception | la resɛpsjɔ̃ |
| The wireless set, radio | Le poste de radio (de T.S.F.) | lə pɔst də radjo (də teesɛf) |
| The loud-speaker | Le haut-parleur | lə oparlœr |
| The battery set | Le poste à accus | lə pɔstaaky |
| The volume | Le volume | lə vɔlym |
| The adjustment | Le réglage | lə reglaʒ |
| The mains | Le secteur | lə sɛktœr |
| The aerial | L'antenne | lɑ̃tɛn |
| The frame aerial | L'antenne en cadre | lɑ̃tɛn ɑ̃ kɑdr |
| The inside aerial | L'antenne intérieure | lɑtɛn ɛ̃terjœr |
| The flex, wire | Le flexible, le fil | lə flɛksibl, lə fil |
| The case | La boîte | la bwat |
| The direct current | Le courant continu | lə kurɑ̃ kɔ̃tiny |
| The alternating current | Le courant alternatif | lə kurɑ̃ altɛrnatif |
| The disturbance | Le parasite | lə parazit |
| The short wave | L'onde courte | lɔ̃d kurt |
| The long wave | La grande onde | la grɑ̃d ɔ̃d |
| The medium wave | L'onde moyenne | lɔ̃d mwajɛn |
| The selectivity | La sélectivité | la selɛktivite |
| The disc, record | Le disque | lə disk |
| The longplaying record | Le disque micro-sillon | lə disk mikrosijɔ̃ |
| The playing table | Le tourne-disque | lə turnə disk |
| The pick-up | Le pickup | lə pikəp |
| The record player | L'électrophone | lelektrofo |
| The announcer | Le speaker, la speakerine | lə spikœr, la spikrin |

| English. | | Pronunciation. |
|---|---|---|
| The news | Les nouvelles | le nuvɛl |
| The weather report | Le bulletin météorologique | lə byltɛ̃ meteɔrɔlɔʒik |
| Television | La télévision | la televizjɔ̃ |
| The television set | { Le téléviseur | lə televizœr |
|  | Le poste de télévision | lə pɔst d televizjɔ̃ |
| The television screen | L'écran | lekrɑ̃ |
| The line | La ligne | la liɲ |
| The listener | L'auditeur | loditœr |
| To tune in | Accorder le récepteur | akɔrde lə reseptœr |
| To listen in | Se mettre à l'écoute | sə mɛtr alekut |
| To earth | Relier à la terre | rəlje ala tɛr |

### Phrases

| Can you pick up foreign stations with your set? | Pouvez-vous capter les postes étrangers avec votre poste? | puvevu kapte le pɔstz etrɑ̃ʒe avɛk vɔt pɔst? |
|---|---|---|
| I want to buy a four-valve set | Je veux acheter un poste à quatre lampes | ʒvøz aʃte œ̃ pɔst a kat lɑ̃p |
| My set is out of order | Mon poste est détraqué | mɔ̃ pɔst ɛ detrake |
| The reception is poor | La réception est mauvaise | la resɛpsjɔ̃ ɛ mɔvɛz |
| My set is subject to disturbances and fading | Mon poste est sensible aux perturbations atmosphériques et au fading | mɔ̃ pɔst ɛ sɑ̃sibl o pɛrtyrbasjɔ̃z atmɔsferik e o fadiɲ |
| Can you recommend a good wireless repairing shop? | Pouvez-vous me recommander un magasin où l'on répare les postes de radio? | puvevu mə rəkɔmɑ̃de œ̃ magazɛ̃ u lɔ̃ repar le pɔst də radjo? |

| English. | | Pronunciation. |
|---|---|---|
| Can you send someone round to have a look at it? | Pouvez-vous envoyer quelqu'un pour y jeter un coup d'œil? | puvevuz ãvwaje kɛlkœ̃ pur i ʒəte œ̃ kudœj? |
| The valves should be renewed | Les lampes devraient être renouvelées | le lãp dəvrɛt ɛtr rənuvle |
| Have I to take out a licence for my set? | Dois-je me procurer une autorisation pour mon poste? | dwaʒ mə prɔkyre yn otɔrizasjɔ̃ pur mɔ̃ pɔst? |
| The licence is taken out at the post office | On se procure l'autorisation au bureau de poste | ɔ̃ sprɔkyr lotɔrizasjɔ̃ o byro dpɔst |
| Do you often listen-in? | Vous mettez-vous souvent à l'écoute? | vu mɛtevu suvãt alekut? |
| Only when they broadcast concerts | Seulement quand on radiodiffuse des concerts | sœlmã kãtɔ̃ radjodifyz de kɔ̃sɛr |
| I like to hear features | J'aime écouter les numéros en vedette | ʒɛm ekute le nymeroz ã vədɛt |
| There is a radio play to-night at eight | On joue ce soir une pièce radiophonique | ɔ̃ ʒu sə swar yn pjɛs radjofɔnik |
| Did you hear the news? | Avez-vous écouté les nouvelles du jour? | avevuz ekute le nuvɛl dy ʒur? |
| What was the weather forecast? | Qu'est-ce que le bulletin météorologique a annoncé? | kɛskə lə byltɛ̃ meteɔrɔlɔʒik a anɔ̃se? |
| My neighbour's wireless disturbs me | Le poste de mon voisin me dérange | lə pɔst də mɔ̃ vwazɛ̃ mə derãʒ |

| English. | | Pronunciation. |
|---|---|---|
| Would you like to listen to the programme parade? | Aimeriez-vous écouter l'annonce du programme du jour? | ɛmərjevuz ekute lanɔ̃s dy program dy ʒur? |
| You have been listening to a broadcast of the Philharmonic Orchestra | Vous venez d'entendre la radio-diffusion de l'Orchestre Philharmonique | vu vne dɑ̃tɑ̃dr la radjodifyzjɔ̃ də lɔrkɛstr filarmɔnik |
| The stations have closed down for to-night | Les stations ont terminé les émissions de ce soir | le stasjɔ̃zɔ̃ tɛrmine lezemisjɔ̃ də sə swar |

## PHOTOGRAPHY

### Vocabulary

| | | |
|---|---|---|
| The camera | L'appareil photographique | laparɛj fɔtɔgrafik |
| The film | La pellicule | la pɛlikyl |
| The plate | La plaque | la plak |
| The lens | La lentille | la lɑ̃tij |
| The photograph | La photographie | la fɔtɔgrafi |
| The time exposure | La pose | la poz |
| The snapshot | L'instantané | lɛ̃stɑ̃tane |
| The dark room | La chambre noire | la ʃɑ̃br nwar |
| The negative | Le négatif, le cliché | lə negatif, lə kliʃe |
| The developer | Le révélateur | lə revelatœr |
| The print | L'épreuve, la copie | leprœv, la kɔpi |
| The printing-out paper | Le papier au citrate | lə papje o sitrat |
| Under-exposed | Sous-exposé(e) | suzɛkspoze |
| Over-exposed | Surexposé(e) | syrɛkspoze |
| To expose | Exposer | ɛkspoze |
| To adjust | Mettre au point | mɛtr o pwɛ̃ |
| To develop | Révéler, développer | revele, devlɔpe |
| To enlarge | Agrandir | agrɑ̃dir |

## Phrases

| English. | | Pronunciation. |
|---|---|---|
| May I take photographs here? | Peut-on prendre des photographies ici? | pøtɔ̃ prɑ̃dr de fotografi isi? |
| You must hand in your camera | Il vous faut déposer votre appareil | il vu fot depoze vɔtr aparɛj |
| Where can you get photographic materials? | Où peut-on se procurer les fournitures pour la photographie? | u pøtɔ̃ sprɔkyre le furnityr pur la fotografi? |
| Can I have a film? | Puis-je avoir une bobine de pellicules? | pɥiʒ avwar yn bɔbin də pɛlikyl? |
| Could you put it in for me? | Pourriez-vous la mettre dans l'appareil pour moi? | purjevu la mɛtr dɑ̃ laparɛj pur mwa? |
| Do you develop plates and films? | Est-ce que vous développez les plaques et les pellicules? | ɛskə vu devlɔpe le plak e le pɛlikyl? |
| Please let me have a proof | Donnez-moi une épreuve, s.v.p. | dɔnemwa yn eprœv, sivuplɛ |
| The photos are under-exposed | Les photographies sont sous-exposées | le fotografi sɔ̃ suz-ɛkspoze |
| Could you intensify them? | Pourriez-vous les renforcer? | purjevu le rɑ̃fɔrse? |
| Is the light too bright for a time-exposure? | Est-ce que la lumière est trop intense pour la pose? | ɛskə la lymjɛr ɛ trop ɛ̃tɑ̃s pur la poz? |
| I should like to have this photo enlarged | Je voudrais faire agrandir cette photographie | ʒvudrɛ fɛr agrɑ̃dir sɛt fotografi |

| English. | | Pronunciation. |
|---|---|---|
| How much would an enlargement cost? | Combien l'agrandissement coûterait-il? | kɔ̃bjɛ̃ lagrɑ̃dismɑ̃ kutrɛtil? |
| Have you a suitable frame? | Avez-vous un châssis qui va? | avevuz œ̃ ʃɑsi ki va? |
| Have you got a photo-album? | Avez-vous un album pour les photographies? | avevuz œ̃ albɔm pur le fɔtɔgrafi? |
| I am going to have my photo taken | Je vais me faire photographier | ʒvɛ mə fɛr fɔtɔgrafje |

## GYMNASTICS AND ATHLETICS
### Vocabulary

| | | |
|---|---|---|
| The cinder-track | La piste en cendrée | la pist ɑ̃ sɑ̃dre |
| The gymnasium | Le gymnase | lə ʒimnaz |
| The gymnastic apparatus | Les agrès de gymnastique | lezagrɛ də ʒimnastik |
| The trapeze | Le trapèze | lə trapɛz |
| The rings | Les anneaux | lezano |
| The ladder | L'échelle | leʃɛl |
| The parallel bars | Les barres parallèles | le bar paralɛl |
| The horse | Le cheval de bois, le cheval d'arçons | lə ʃval də bwɑ, lə ʃval darsɔ̃ |
| The pole | La perche | la perʃ |
| The rope | La corde | la kɔrd |
| The dumbbells | Les haltères | lezaltɛr |
| The club | La massue | la masy |
| The spring-board | Le tremplin | lə trɑ̃plɛ̃ |
| The high jump | Le saut en hauteur | lə so ɑ̃ otœr |
| The long jump | Le saut en largeur | lə so ɑ̃ larʒœr |
| The race | La course (de vitesse) | la kurs (də vitɛs) |
| The relay race | La course de (à) relais | la kurs də (a) rəlɛ |

| English. | | Pronunciation. |
|---|---|---|
| The goal | Le but | lə by(t) |
| The gym shoes | Les sandales, les chaussons | le sãdal, le ʃosɔ̃ |
| The shorts | La culotte | la kylɔt |
| To run, race | Courir, lutter de vitesse | kurir, lyte də vitɛs |
| To jump | Sauter | sote |
| To climb | Grimper | grɛ̃pe |
| To bend the knees | Fléchir les genoux | fleʃir le ʒnu |

## Phrases

| | | |
|---|---|---|
| Do you do physical jerks in the mornings? | Faites-vous des exercices physiques le matin? | fɛtvu dezɛgzɛrsis fisik lə matɛ̃? |
| Are you going to take part in the thousand metres race? | Allez-vous prendre part à la course de mille mètres? | alevu prãdr par ala kurs də mil mɛtr? |
| Who has broken the high jump record? | Qui a battu le record du saut en hauteur? | ki a baty lə rkɔr dy so ã otœr? |
| Shall we go and see them throwing the discus and the javelin? | Voulez-vous que nous allions voir le lancement du disque et du javelot? | vulevu kə nuz aljɔ̃ vwar lə lãsmã dy disk e dy ʒavlo? |
| Can you vault over the horse? | Pouvez-vous sauter le cheval-arçons? | puvevu sote lə ʃval-arsɔ̃? |
| No, but I can turn a somersault | Non, mais je peux faire la culbute | nɔ̃, mɛ ʒpø fɛr la kylbyt |
| Can you recommend someone who teaches Swedish gymnastics? | Pouvez-vous me recommander quelqu'un qui enseigne la gymnastique suédoise? | puvevu mə rəkomãde kɛlkœ̃ ki ãsɛɲ la ʒimnastik sɥedwaz? |

# FOOTBALL

## Vocabulary

| English. | | Pronunciation. |
|---|---|---|
| The game | Le jeu, la partie | le ʒø, la parti |
| The match | Le match | lə matʃ |
| The goal | Le but | lə by(t) |
| The goalkeeper | Le gardien du but | lə gardjɛ̃ dy by(t) |
| The team | L'équipe | lekip |
| The forward | L'avant | lavɑ̃ |
| The back | L'arrière | larjɛr |
| The half-back | Le demi | lə dmi |
| The goal-post | Le montant de but | lə mɔ̃tɑ̃ də by(t) |
| The referee | L'arbitre | larbitr |
| To kick | Botter | bɔte |
| To beat | Battre, vaincre | batr, vɛ̃kr |

## Phrases

| | | |
|---|---|---|
| Shall we go and watch the Paris-Bordeaux football match? | Voulez-vous que nous allions voir le match Paris-Bordeaux? | vulevu kə nuz aljɔ̃ vwar lə matʃ pari-bɔrdo? |
| Are they famous teams? | Est-ce que ce sont des équipes renommées? | ɛskə sə sɔ̃ dez ekip rənɔme? |
| What a capital shot! | Quel shoot (shot) magnifique! | kɛl ʃut (ʃɔt) maɲifik! |
| The goal is well defended | Le but est bien défendu | lə byt ɛ bjɛ̃ defɑ̃dy |
| What was the score? | Quel a été le score? (Quelle a été la marque?) | kɛl a ete lə skɔr? (kɛl a ete la mark?) |
| Paris won three one | Paris a gagné par trois à un | pari a gaɲe par trwɑ a œ̃ |

# HOCKEY

## Vocabulary

| English. | | Pronunciation. |
|---|---|---|
| The ice hockey | Le hockey sur glace | lə ɔkɛ syr glas |
| The hockey stick | La canne de hockey | la kan də ɔkɛ |
| The hockey team | L'équipe de hockey | lekip də ɔkɛ |
| The ball | La balle | la bal |

## Phrases

| | | |
|---|---|---|
| Don't kick the ball | Ne bottez pas la balle | nə bɔte pɑ la bal |
| May I pick up the ball? | Puis-je ramasser la balle? | pɥiʒ ramɑse la bal? |
| That's a foul | Ça, c'est un coup déloyal | sa, sɛtœ̃ ku delwajal |
| At half-time our side was leading | A la mi-temps notre équipe (stade) menait | ala mitɑ̃ nɔtr ekip (stad) mənɛ |
| How many goals did they score? | Combien de buts ont-ils marqués? | kɔ̃bjɛ̃ də by(t) ʒtil marke? |
| Did Lyons beat Rouen? | Est-ce que Lyon a battu Rouen? | ɛskə ljɔ̃ a baty rwɑ̃? |

# LAWN TENNIS

## Vocabulary

| | | |
|---|---|---|
| The tennis match | Le match de tennis | lə matʃ də tɛnis |
| The tennis court | Le terrain de tennis, le court, le tennis | lə tɛrɛ̃ də tɛnis, lə kur, lə tɛnis |
| The game | Le jeu, la partie | lə ʒø, la parti |
| The set | Le set | lə sɛt |
| The single(s) | Le simple | lə sɛ̃pl |

| English. | | Pronunciation. |
|---|---|---|
| The double(s) | Le double | lə dubl |
| The racket | La raquette | la rakɛt |
| The net | Le filet | lə filɛ |
| The base-line | La ligne de fond | la liɲ də fɔ̃ |
| The service line | La ligne de service | la liɲ də sɛrvis |
| The volley | La volée | la vɔle |
| The service | Le service | lə sɛrvis |
| To serve | Servir | sɛrvir |
| To take | Prendre | prɑ̃dr |
| To return | Renvoyer | rɑ̃vwaje |

## Phrases

| | | |
|---|---|---|
| Do you play tennis ? | Jouez-vous au tennis ? | ʒwevuz o tɛnis ? |
| I'm not a good player | Je ne suis pas un bon joueur | ʒənsɥipɑz œ̃ bɔ̃ ʒwœr |
| Are there any courts in the neighbourhood ? | Y a-t-il des terrains de tennis dans le voisinage ? | jatil de tɛrɛ̃ də tɛnis dɑ̃ lvwazinaʒ ? |
| You can join our tennis club if you like | Vous pouvez entrer dans notre club si vous voulez | vupuvez ɑ̃tre dɑ̃ nɔt klyb, sivuvule |
| Is the subscription very high ? | Est-ce que la cotisation est très élevée ? | ɛskə la kɔtizasjɔ̃ ɛ trez elve ? |
| Have you brought your racket with you ? | Avez-vous apporté votre raquette ? | avevuz apɔrte vɔt rakɛt ? |
| I must have my racket restrung | Il me faut faire recorder ma raquette | il mə fo fɛr rəkɔrde ma rakɛt |
| Shall we play a single (double) ? | Allons-nous jouer un simple ou un double ? | alɔ̃nu ʒwe œ̃ sɛ̃pl u œ̃ dubl ? |
| Your service ! | A vous le service ! | a vu lsɛrvis ! |

| English. | | Pronunciation. |
|---|---|---|
| The ball was out | La balle était en dehors (out) | la bal etɛt ã deɔr (ut) |
| That was a fault | C'était une faute | setɛt yn fot |
| The ball touched the net | La balle a frisé la corde | la bal a frize la kɔrd |
| You must not take the ball on the volley | Il ne faut pas renvoyer la balle de volée | ilnfopɑ rãvwaje la bal də vɔle |
| You must take it on the bound | Il faut la prendre au bond | il fo la prãdr o bɔ̃ |
| Whose set is it? | A qui le set? | a ki lə sɛt? |

## GOLF

### Vocabulary

| The links | Le links, le parcours | lə liŋks, lə parkur |
|---|---|---|
| The hole | Le trou | lə tru |
| The green | La pelouse du trou | la pluz dy tru |
| The bunker | La banquette | la bãkɛt |
| The fairway | Le parcours normal | lə parkur nɔrmal |
| The tee | Le dé, le tee | lə de, lə ti |
| The flag | Le drapeau | lə drapo |
| The club | La crosse, la canne | la krɔs, la kan |
| The golf bag | Le sac de golf | lə sak də gɔlf |
| The stroke | Le coup | lə ku |
| The handicap | Le handicap | lə ãdikap |

### Phrases

| Where is the nearest golf course | Où se trouve le parcours de golf le plus proche? | ustruv lə parkur də gɔlf lə ply prɔʃ? |
|---|---|---|
| Are you a member of the golf club? | Êtes-vous membre du club de golf? | ɛtvu mãbr dy klyb də gɔlf? |

| English. | | Pronunciation. |
|---|---|---|
| How many holes has this course ? | Combien de trous ce parcours a-t-il ? | kɔ̃bjɛ̃ də tru sə parkur atil ? |
| Shall we play a round of golf ? | Voulez - vous que nous fassions une tournée de golf ? | vulevu kə nu fasjɔ̃z yn turne də gɔlf ? |
| What is your handicap ? | Quel est votre handicap ? | kɛl ɛ vɔtr ɑ̃dikap ? |
| Hit the ball harder | Frappez la balle plus fort | frape la bal ply fɔr |

## RIDING AND RACING

### Vocabulary

| The riding horse | Le cheval de selle | lə ʃval də sɛl |
|---|---|---|
| The racer | Le cheval de course | lə ʃval də kurs |
| The thoroughbred | Le cheval pur sang | lə ʃval pyrsɑ̃ |
| The stallion | L'étalon | letalɔ̃ |
| The mare | La jument | la ʒymɑ̃ |
| The foal | Le poulain | lə pulɛ̃ |
| The bay | Le cheval bai | lə ʃval bɛ |
| The chestnut | Le cheval alezan | lə ʃval alzɑ̃ |
| The dapple grey | Le cheval gris pommelé | lə ʃval gri pɔmle |
| The white horse | Le cheval blanc | lə ʃval blɑ̃ |
| The black horse | Le cheval noir | lə ʃval nwar |
| The rider | Le cavalier, la cavalière | lə kavalje, la kavaljɛr |
| The riding breeches | La culotte de cheval | la kylɔt də ʃval |
| The riding school | L'école d'équitation | lekɔl dekitasjɔ̃ |
| The reins | Les rênes | le rɛn |
| The stirrup | L'étrier | letrije |
| The spurs | Les éperons | lez eprɔ̃ |
| The saddle | La selle | la sɛl |
| The saddle-girth | La sangle de selle | la sɑ̃gl də sɛl |
| The groom | Le palefrenier | lə palfrənje |

| English. | | Pronunciation. |
|---|---|---|
| The trotting | Le trot | lə tro |
| The galloping | Le galop | lə galo |
| The cantering | Le petit galop | lə pti galo |
| The racecourse | Le champ de courses | lə ʃã də kurs |
| The turf | Le gazon | lə gɑzɔ̃ |
| The flat race | La course plate | la kurs plat |
| The steeplechase | Le steeple-chase (le steeple) | lə stiplətʃɛs (lə stipl) |
| The hurdle-race | La course de haies | la kurs də ɛ |
| The trotting-race | La course au trot | la kurs o tro |
| The winning-post | Le poteau d'arrivée | lə pɔto darive |
| The winner | Le gagnant | lə gaɲã |
| The length | La longueur | la lɔ̃gœr |
| The bookmaker | Le bookmaker (le book) | lə bukmaker (lə buk) |
| The betting | Les paris | le pari |
| The racing stable | L'écurie de courses | lekyri də kurs |
| The stud-owner | Le propriétaire de haras | lə prɔprietɛr də arɑ |
| To back a horse | Parier (miser) sur un cheval | parije (mize) syr œ̃ ʃval |
| To ride | Monter à cheval | mɔ̃te a ʃval |
| To mount (a horse) | Enfourcher un cheval | ãfurʃe œ̃ ʃval |
| To dismount | Descendre de cheval | desãdr də ʃval |
| To kick | Ruer | rɥe |
| To buck | Faire le saut de mouton | fɛr lə so də mutɔ̃ |
| To shy | Faire un écart | fɛr œ̃n ekar |
| To bolt | S'emballer | sãbale |

## Phrases

| | | |
|---|---|---|
| Is there a riding school near here ? | Y a-t-il une école d'équitation (un manège) près d'ici ? | jatil yn ekɔl dekitasjɔ̃ (œ̃ manɛʒ) prɛ disi ? |

| English. | | Pronunciation. |
|---|---|---|
| I should like to hire a horse | Je voudrais louer un cheval | ʒvudrɛ lwe œ̃ ʃval |
| I should like to take some riding-lessons | Je voudrais prendre des leçons d'équitation | ʒvudrɛ prɑ̃dr de lsɔ̃ dekitasjɔ̃ |
| How much are the riding-lessons ? | Combien coûtent les leçons d'équitation ? | kɔ̃bjɛ̃ kut le lsɔ̃ dekitasjɔ̃ ? |
| Where can I hire a riding-outfit ? | Où peut-on louer un habit de cavalier ? | u pœtɔ̃ lwe œ̃nabi də kavalje ? |
| Have you any breeches ? | Avez-vous des culottes de cheval ? | avevu de kylɔt də ʃval ? |
| Where is my whip ? | Où est ma cravache ? | wɛ ma kravaʃ ? |
| The horse is vicious | Le cheval est vicieux (hargneux) | lə ʃval ɛ visjø (arɲø) |
| The mare is lame | La jument est boiteuse | la ʒymɑ̃t ɛ bwatøz |
| Please harness the chestnut for me | Harnachez l'alezan pour moi, s.v.p. | arnaʃe lalzɑ̃ pur mwa, sivuplɛ |
| Would you like to go to the horse-races ? | Aimeriez-vous aller au champ de courses ? | ɛmərjevuz ale o ʃɑ̃ də kurs ? |
| Where is the entrance to the racecourse ? | Où est l'entrée du champ de courses ? | wɛ lɑ̃tre dy ʃɑ̃ də kurs ? |
| Who won that last race ? | Qui a gagné la dernière course ? | ki a gaɲe la dɛrnjɛr kurs ? |
| To which stable does the winner belong ? | A quelle écurie le gagnant appartient-il ? | a kɛl ekyri lə gaɲɑ̃ apartjɛ̃til ? |
| Did you back the favourite ? | Avez-vous joué le favori ? | avevu ʒwe lə favɔri ? |
| Where is the totalisator ? | Où est le totaliseur ? | wɛ lə tɔtalisœr ? |

## HUNTING AND SHOOTING

### Vocabulary

| English. | | Pronunciation. |
|---|---|---|
| The huntsman | Le chasseur | lə ʃasœr |
| The hounds, pack | Les chiens de meute, la meute | le ʃjẽ də møt, la møt |
| The meet | Le rendez-vous de chasse | lə rãdevu də ʃas |
| The bag | Le tableau | lə tablo |
| The fox | Le renard | lə rnar |
| The rabbit | Le lapin | lə lapẽ |
| The game | Le gibier | lə ʒibje |
| The hare | Le lièvre | lə ljevr |
| The fallow deer | Le daim | lə dẽ |
| The stag | Le cerf | lə ser(f) |
| The partridge | La perdrix | la perdri |
| The pheasant | Le faisan | lə fɛzã |
| The grouse | Le tétras, le coq de bruyère | lə tetra, lə kɔk də bryjɛr |
| The setter | Le chien d'arrêt, le setter | le ʃjẽ dare, lə setɛr |
| The pointer | Le chien d'arrêt, le chien pointeur | lə ʃjẽ dare, lə ʃjẽ pwẽtœr |
| The rifle | Le fusil de chasse | lə fyzi də ʃas |
| The gun | La carabine de chasse | la karabin də ʃas |
| The butt | La crosse | la krɔs |
| The barrel | Le canon | lə kanɔ̃ |
| The trigger | La détente, la gâchette | la detãt, la gaʃet |
| The sight | Le guidon | lə gidɔ̃ |
| The cartridge | La cartouche | la kartuʃ |
| The shot | Le plomb de chasse | lə plɔ̃ də ʃas |

## Phrases

| English. | | Pronunciation. |
|---|---|---|
| Is there any chance of hunting ? | Y a-t-il des chances qu'on puisse chasser à courre ? | jatil de ʃɑ̃s kɔ̃ pɥis ʃase a kur ? |
| Would you care to go shooting hares with me ? | Aimeriez-vous aller à la chasse au lièvre avec moi ? | ɛmərjevuz ale ala ʃas o ljɛvr avɛk mwa ? |
| My father has a shoot | Mon père a une chasse gardée | mɔ̃ pɛr a yn ʃas garde |
| Is the hunting season for deer open ? | Est-ce que la saison de la chasse au cerf est ouverte ? | ɛskə la sɛzɔ̃ dla ʃas o sɛr ɛt uvɛrt ? |
| Did you bring home a good bag ? | Avez-vous fait un grand abatis de gibier ? | avevu fɛt ɶ̃ grɑ̃t abati də ʒibje ? |
| A brace of partridges and two rabbits | Une couple de perdrix et deux lapins | yn kupl də pɛrdri e dø lapɛ̃ |
| Are you a good shot ? | Êtes-vous bon tireur ? | ɛtvu bɔ̃ tirɶr ? |
| I practised target-shooting | Je me suis exercé à tirer à la cible | ʒə msɥiz ɛgsɛrse a tire a la sibl |
| Did you clean your shot-gun ? | Avez-vous nettoyé votre carabine de chasse ? | avevu netwaje vɔt karabin də ʃas ? |
| Have you ever shot big game ? | Avez-vous jamais chassé le gros gibier ? | avevu ʒamɛ ʃase lə gro ʒibje ? |
| Where can I buy a rifle ? | Où puis-je acheter un fusil de chasse ? | u pɥiʒ aʃte ɶ̃ fyzi də ʃas ? |
| Can you let me have some cartridges ? | Pouvez-vous me donner des cartouches ? | puvevu mə done de kartuʃ ? |

# FISHING

## Vocabulary

| English. | | Pronunciation. |
|---|---|---|
| The angler | Le pêcheur à la ligne | lə peʃœr ala liɲ |
| The fishing-rod | La canne à pêche, la gaule | la kan a peʃ, la gol |
| The fishing-line | La ligne de pêche | la liɲ də peʃ |
| The float | Le flotteur | lə flɔtœr |
| The fish-hook | L'hameçon | lamsɔ̃ |
| The fishing-tackle | Les articles de pêche | lezartikl də peʃ |
| The bait | L'amorce, l'appât | lamɔrs, lapɑ |
| The fly | La mouche | la muʃ |
| The net | Le filet | lə filɛ |
| The fish-pond | Le vivier | lə vivje |
| The lake | Le lac | lə lak |
| The river | Le fleuve, la rivière | lə flœv, la rivjɛr |
| The stream | Le ruisseau | lə rɥiso |
| The freshwater fish | Le poisson d'eau douce | lə pwasɔ̃ do dus |
| The salmon | Le saumon | lə somɔ̃ |
| The trout | La truite | la trɥit |
| The carp | La carpe | la karp |
| The pike | Le brochet | lə brɔʃɛ |
| The eel | L'anguille | lɑ̃gij |
| The fisherman | Le pêcheur | lə peʃœr |
| The fishing fleet | La flotille de pêche | la flɔtij də peʃ |
| The saltwater fish | Le poisson de mer | lə pwasɔ̃ də mɛr |
| The herring | Le hareng | lə arɑ̃ |
| The cod | La morue | la mɔry |
| The haddock | L'aiglefin | lɛgləfɛ̃ |
| The hake | La merluche | la mɛrlyʃ |
| The halibut | Le flétan | lə fletɑ̃ |

| English. | | Pronunciation. |
|---|---|---|
| The turbot | **Le turbot** | lə tyrbo |
| The sole | **La sole** | la sɔl |
| The whiting | **Le merlan** | lə mɛrlɑ̃ |

## Phrases

| | | |
|---|---|---|
| Do you like fishing? | **Aimez-vous pêcher à la ligne?** | ɛmevu pɛʃe ala liɲ? |
| Do I need a licence to fish? | **Ai-je besoin d'un permis de pêche?** | ɛʒ bəzwɛ̃ dœ̃ pɛrmi də pɛʃ? |
| Where can I buy fishing-tackle? | **Où peut-on acheter des articles de pêche?** | u pøtɔ̃ aʃte dez artikl də pɛʃ? |
| I have forgotten to bring my fishing-rod | **J'ai oublié d'apporter ma canne à pêche** | ʒe ublije daporte ma kan a pɛʃ |
| The bait is no good | **L'appât ne vaut rien** | lapɑ nə vo rjɛ̃ |
| Did you make a good catch? | **Avez-vous fait une bonne pêche?** | avevu fɛt yn bɔn pɛʃ? |
| The fish are biting quickly | **Les poissons mordent vite** | le pwasɔ̃ mɔrd vit |
| Can you go out with the fishing fleet? | **Peut-on sortir avec la flotille de pêche?** | pøtɔ̃ sɔrtir avɛk la flɔtij də pɛʃ? |

## SWIMMING

### Vocabulary

| | | |
|---|---|---|
| The swimming-bath | **La piscine** | la pisin |
| The swimming-pool | **La piscine en plein air** | la pisin ɑ̃ plɛnɛr |
| The bathing establishment | **L'établissement de bains** | letablismɑ̃ də bɛ̃ |
| The bathing costume | **Le costume de bain** | lə kɔstym də bɛ̃ |

| English. | French. | Pronunciation. |
|---|---|---|
| The bathing drawers | Le caleçon de bain | lə kalsɔ̃ də bɛ̃ |
| The bathing towel | La serviette de bain | la sɛrvjɛt də bɛ̃ |
| The bathing cap | Le bonnet de bain | lə bɔnɛ də bɛ̃ |
| The diving board | Le tremplin | lə trɑ̃plɛ̃ |
| To swim | Nager | naʒe |
| To dive | Plonger | plɔ̃ʒe |
| To drown | Se noyer | sə nwaje |

## Phrases

| | | |
|---|---|---|
| Shall we have a swim (bathe) ? | Voulez - vous que nous allions nager (nous baigner) ? | vulevu kə nuz aljɔ̃ naʒe (nu bɛɲe) ? |
| Can we swim in the river ? | Pouvons-nous nager dans la rivière ? | puvɔ̃nu naʒe dɑ̃ la rivjɛr ? |
| No, you must go to the swimming-pool | Non, il faut aller à la piscine | nɔ̃, il fot ale ala pisin |
| No bathing | Défense de se baigner | defɑ̃s də sə bɛɲe |
| Are you a good swimmer ? | Êtes-vous bon nageur ? | ɛtvu bɔ̃ naʒœr ? |
| Let's swim to the opposite bank | Allons à la nage jusqu'à la rive opposée | alɔ̃z ala naʒ ʒyska la riv ɔpoze |
| The current is too strong | Le courant est trop fort | lə kurɑ̃ ɛ tro fɔr |
| Can you swim on your back ? | Savez-vous nager sur le dos ? | Savevu naʒe syr lə do ? |
| He is floating | Il fait la planche | il fɛ la plɑ̃ʃ |
| Can you do the crawl ? | Savez-vous faire le crawl ? | savevu fɛr lə krol ? |
| I've got cramp in my left calf | J'ai une crampe dans le mollet gauche | ʒe yn krɑ̃p dɑ̃ lə mɔlɛ goʃ |
| Swim and help him, he has gone under | Allez à la nage le secourir, il a coulé | alez ala naʒ lə səkurir, il a kule |

| English. | | Pronunciation. |
|---|---|---|
| He was nearly drowned | Il a failli se noyer | il a faji snwaje |
| Hang on to the lifeline | Accrochez-vous au cordage de sûreté | akrɔʃevuz o kɔrdaʒ də syrte |
| Stay in the shallow water | Restez dans les basfonds | reste dã le bafɔ̃ |
| Don't swim beyond the danger-post | N'allez pas à la nage au delà du poteau avertisseur | nalepaz ala naʒ odla dy pɔto avertisœr |
| The swimming-bath is only for experienced swimmers | La piscine est réservée aux nageurs exercés | la pisin ɛ rezɛrve o naʒœr ɛgzɛrse |
| Is there a vacant bathing cabin ? | Y a-t-il une cabine de bains de libre ? | jatil yn kabin də bɛ̃ də libr ? |
| Can you recommend a pleasant seaside resort ? | Pouvez-vous me recommander une plage (une station balnéaire) agréable ? | puvevu mə rəkɔmãde yn plaʒ (yn stasjɔ̃ balneɛr) agreabl ? |
| I want to spend my holidays at the seaside | Je veux passer mes vacances au bord de la mer | ʒvø pase me vakɑ̃s o bɔr dla mɛr |

# ROWING, BOATING

## Vocabulary

| The boat | Le bateau, le canot | lə bato, lə kano |
|---|---|---|
| The rowing boat | Le bateau à rames, le canot à l'aviron | lə batoaram, lə kanoalavirɔ̃ |
| The boat-race | La course de bateaux | la kurs də bato |
| The canoe | Le canoë | lə kanɔe |
| The collapsible boat | Le canot pliant | lə kano pliã |
| The starboard | Le tribord | lə tribɔr |
| The port | Le bâbord | lə babɔr |

| English. | | Pronunciation. |
|---|---|---|
| The oar | L'aviron, la rame | lavirɔ̃, la ram |
| The rudder | La barre, le gouvernail | la bar, lə guvɛrnaj |
| The sliding seat | Le banc à glissières | lə bɑ̃ a glisjɛr |
| The crew | L'équipe | lekip |
| The oarsman | Le rameur | lə ramœr |
| The cox | Le barreur | lə barœr |
| The stroke | Le chef de nage | lə ʃef də naʒ |
| To row | Ramer | rame |
| To steer | Barrer | bare |
| To punt | Conduire à la gaffe | kɔ̃dɥir ala gaf |

## Phrases

| | | |
|---|---|---|
| Boats for hire | Canots à louer | kanoz a lwe |
| Come to the jetty | Venez au môle (à la jetée) | vənez o mol (ala ʃte) |
| There is a strong head wind | Il fait un grand vent contraire | il fɛt ɶ̃ grɑ̃ vɑ̃ kɔ̃trɛr |
| The boat has sprung a leak | Le bateau s'est fait une voie d'eau | lə bato sɛfɛt yn vwa do |
| Let's go and watch the boat-race | Allons voir la course de bateaux | alɔ̃ vwar la kurs də bato |
| Our club won by two lengths | Notre cercle a gagné de deux longueurs | nɔt sɛrkl a gaɲe də dø lɔ̃gœr |
| Are you a member of a rowing-club ? | Êtes-vous membre d'un cercle d'aviron (de canotage) ? | ɛtvu mɑ̃mbr dɶ̃ sɛrkl davirɔ̃ (də kanotaʒ) ? |
| I should like to join a club | J'aimerais entrer dans un cercle | ʒɛmrez ɑ̃tre dɑ̃z ɶ̃ sɛrkl |

## SAILING

### Vocabulary

| | | |
|---|---|---|
| The sailing | La navigation | la navigasjɔ̃ |
| The yacht | Le yacht | lə jɔt |

| English. | | Pronunciation. |
|---|---|---|
| The sailing boat | Le canot à voiles | lə kano a vwal |
| The sail | La voile | la vwal |
| The mast | Le mât | lə mɑ |
| The keel | La quille | la kij |
| The flag | Le pavillon | lə pavijɔ̃ |
| The breeze | Le vent fort, la brise | lə vɑ̃ fɔr, la briz |
| The dead calm | Le calme plat | lə kalm pla |
| The anchor | L'ancre | lɑ̃kr |
| To sail | Naviguer | navige |
| To cruise | Faire des prome-nades en mer | fɛr de prɔmnad zɑ̃ mɛr |
| To reef | Prendre les ris | prɑ̃dr le ri |

## Phrases

| | | |
|---|---|---|
| The sailing boat is anchored in the harbour | Le canot à voiles est mouillé dans le port | lə kano a vwal ɛ mwije dɑ̃ lpɔr |
| There is a fresh breeze to-day; it's good sailing weather | Il y a bonne brise aujourd'hui; il fait beau pour naviguer à la voile | ilja bɔn briz ɔʒur-dɥi; il fɛ bo pur navige ala vwal |
| Weigh the anchor | Levez l'ancre | ləve lɑ̃kr |
| Help me hoist (reef) the sails | Aidez-moi à hisser les voiles (prendre les ris) | ɛdemwa a ise le vwal (prɑ̃dr le ri) |
| Let's spend the day on the water | Allons passer la journée sur l'eau | alɔ̃ pase la ʒurne syr lo |
| Have you enough grub with you? | Avez-vous apporté assez de boulot? | avevuz apɔrte ase də bulo? |
| Do you know anything about sail-ing? | Savez-vous quelque chose de la navi-gation? | savevu kɛlkəʃoz də la navigasjɔ̃? |
| We have often cruised in the Baltic | Nous avons souvent fait des croisières dans la Baltique | nuzavɔ̃ suvɑ̃ fɛ de krwazjɛr dɑ̃ la baltik |

| English. | | Pronunciation. |
|---|---|---|
| Is this yacht sea-worthy? | Est-ce que ce yacht est navigable? | ɛskə sə jɔt ɛ navigabl? |
| We were overtaken by the storm | Nous avons été surpris par l'orage | nuzavɔz ete syrpri par lɔraʒ |
| The boat is heeling over | Le bateau donne de la bande | lə bato dɔn dla bãd |
| The boat has capsized | Le bateau a chaviré | lə bato a ʃavire |

## BOXING

### Vocabulary

| | | |
|---|---|---|
| The boxing match | Le match de boxe | lə matʃ də bɔks |
| The wrestling match | L'assaut de lutte | laso də lyt |
| The boxer | Le boxeur, le pugiliste | lə bɔksœr, lə pyʒilist |
| The wrestler | Le lutteur | lə lytœr |
| The referee | L'arbitre | larbitr |
| The champion | Le champion | lə ʃãpjɔ̃ |
| The bantam-weight | Le poids bantam, le poids coq | lə pwa bãtam, lə pwa kɔk |
| The light-weight | Le poids léger | lə pwa leʒe |
| The feather-weight | Le poids plume | lə pwa plym |
| The middle-weight | Le poids moyen | lə pwa mwajẽ |
| The heavy-weight | Le poids lourd | lə pwa lur |

### Phrases

| | | |
|---|---|---|
| Would you care to see the match for the heavy-weight championship? | Aimeriez-vous assister au match pour le championnat du poids lourd? | ɛmərjevuz asiste o matʃ pur lə ʃãpjɔna dy pwa lur? |

| English. | | Pronunciation. |
|---|---|---|
| The former world-champion was knocked out in the sixth round | L'ancien champion du monde a été mis knock-out pendant le sixiè-me round | lɑ̃sjɛ̃ ʃɑ̃pjɔ̃ dy mɔ̃d a ete mi nɔkut pɑ̃dɑ̃ lə sizjɛm raund |
| Did he hit him be-low the belt ? | Lui a-t-il donné un coup bas ? | lɥi atil dɔne œ̃ ku bɑ ? |
| He floored him with a fierce up-per-cut | Il l'a terrassé d'un terrible coup de bas en haut (d'un uppercut) | illa tɛrase dœ̃ tɛribl ku də bɑ ɑ̃ o (dœ̃n ypɛrkyt) |
| He was counted out in the third round | Il est resté sur le plancher pour le compte dans la troisième reprise | il ɛ rɛste syr lə plɑ̃ʃe pur lə kɔ̃t dɑ̃ la trwɑzjɛm rəpriz |
| Is there a match on to-night ? | Y a-t-il un match ce soir ? | jatil œ̃ matʃ sə swar ? |
| Two holders of championships are competing | Deux tenants de championnats vont concourir | dø tnɑ̃ də ʃɑ̃pjɔna vɔ̃ kɔ̃kurir |
| Did Brown defend his title ? | Est-ce que Lebrun a défendu son titre ? | ɛskə ləbrœ̃ a defɑ̃dy sɔ̃ titr ? |
| He was pushed to the ropes and threw up the sponge | Il a été bousculé sur les cordes et a jeté l'éponge | il a ete buskyle syr le kɔrd e a ʃte lepɔ̃ʒ |
| Are you an amateur boxer ? | Êtes-vous boxeur amateur ? | ɛtvuz bɔksœr ama-tœr ? |

## WINTER SPORTS

### Vocabulary

| | | |
|---|---|---|
| The skis | Les skis | le ski |
| The skiing outfit | L'équipement de ski | lekipmɑ̃ də ski |
| The skiing jump | Le saut à ski | lə so a ski |

| English. | | Pronunciation. |
|---|---|---|
| The skier | Le skieur | lə skjœr |
| The sledge | Le traîneau | lə treno |
| The runners | Les patins | le patɛ̃ |
| The bobsleigh | Le bob | lə bɔb |
| The bob-run | La piste de bob | la pist də bɔb |
| The toboggan | Le toboggan | lə tɔbɔgɑ̃ |
| The toboggan-slide | La piste de toboggan | la pist də tɔbɔgɑ̃ |
| The snow-plough | La charrue à neige | la ʃary a nɛʒ |
| The new snow | La neige nouvelle-ment tombée | la nɛʒ nuvɛlmɑ̃ tɔ̃be |
| The snow-drift | L'amoncellement de neige | lamɔ̃sɛlmɑ̃ də nɛʒ |
| The powder snow | La neige en poudre | la nɛʒ ɑ̃ pudr |
| The avalanche | L'avalanche | lavalɑ̃ʃ |
| The skates | Les patins | le patɛ̃ |
| The skating rink | La patinoire, le ska-ting | la patinwar, lə sketiŋ |

## Phrases

| | | |
|---|---|---|
| Can we hire skis here? | Peut-on louer des skis ici? | pøtɔ̃ lwe de ski isi? |
| Is there a skiing instructor in the village? | Y a-t-il un profes-seur de ski dans le village? | jatil œ̃ prɔfesœr də ski dɑ̃ lə vilaʒ? |
| Have you ever done any skiing? | Avez-vous jamais fait du ski? | avevu ʒamɛ fɛ dy ski? |
| No, I used to go in for bob-sleighing | Non, je faisais autre-fois du bob | nɔ̃, ʒə fəzɛz otrəfwa dy bɔb |
| The snow is not good for skiing | La neige n'est pas bonne pour faire du ski | la nɛʒ nepa bɔn pur fɛr dy ski |
| Where can I buy a set of skis and ski-sticks | Où peut-on acheter une paire de skis et des bâtons de ski? | u pøtɔ̃ aʃte yn pɛr də ski e de batɔ̃ də ski? |

| English. | | Pronunciation. |
|---|---|---|
| Have you ever done any stem-turns? | Avez-vous jamais fait des stemm-boggen? | avevu ʒame fe de stembɔgen? |
| Have you ever tried the Christiania? | Avez-vous jamais essayé des Christianias? | avevu ʒamez eseje de kristjanja? |
| Where is the ski-jump? | Où est la descente à ski? | we la desãt a ski? |
| Don't forget to wax your skis | N'oubliez pas de cirer vos skis | nublije pɑ də sire vo ski |
| I must adjust my bindings | Il me faut ajuster les fixations | il mə fot aʒyste le fiksasjɔ̃ |
| Shall we go up by the mountain railway and come down on the bob-sleigh? | Allons-nous monter par le chemin de fer de montagne et descendre avec le bob? | alɔ̃nu mɔ̃te par lə ʃmɛ̃tfer də mɔ̃taɲ e desãdr avek lə bob? |
| I don't like the crust on the snow | Je n'aime pas la croûte sur la neige | ʒə nem pɑ la krut syr la neʒ |
| Have you ever done any tobogganing | Avez-vous jamais fait du toboggan? | avevu ʒame fe dy tobogã? |
| The down-hill run is rather steep | La descente est assez raide | la desãt et ase red |
| Do you like skating? | Aimez-vous le patinage? | emevu lə patinaʒ? |
| Does the ice bear? | Est-ce que la glace porte? | eskə la glas port? |
| Get your skates and let's go to the skating-rink | Allez chercher vos patins et allons au skating | ale ʃerʃe vo patɛ̃ e alɔ̃z o sketiɲ |
| There is a performance of figure-skating | On donne une séance de patinage de fantaisie | ɔ̃ don yn seãs də patinaʒ də fãtezi |
| My skates are not much good for the outside-edge | Mes patins ne valent pas grand'chose pour faire des dehors | me patɛ̃ nə val pɑ grãʃoz pur fer de dəor |

| English. | | Pronunciation. |
|---|---|---|
| You have not strapped your skates on well | Vous n'avez pas bien attaché vos patins | vunave pɑ bjɛ̃n ataʃe vo patɛ̃ |

## MOUNTAINEERING

### Vocabulary

| The high mountains | Les hautes montagnes | le ot mɔ̃taɲ |
|---|---|---|
| The rock | Le rocher | lə rɔʃe |
| The glacier | Le glacier | lə glasje |
| The moraine | La moraine | la mɔrɛn |
| The chimney | La cheminée, la varappe | la ʃəmine, la varap |
| The abyss, precipice | L'abîme, le précipice | labim, lə presipis |
| The crevasse | La crevasse | la krəvas |
| The loose rocks | Les rochers branlants | le rɔʃe brɑ̃lɑ̃ |
| The blizzard | La tempête de neige | la tɑ̃pɛt də nɛʒ |
| The guide | Le guide | lə gid |
| The mountaineer | L'alpiniste | lalpinist |
| The ice-axe | Le piolet | lə pjɔlɛ |
| The rope | La corde | la kɔrd |
| The ascent | L'ascension | lasɑ̃sjɔ̃ |
| The descent | La descente | la desɑ̃t |
| To climb | Gravir une montagne, escalader | gravir yn mɔ̃taɲ, ɛskalade |

### Phrases

| Is there a guide in the village? | Y a-t-il un guide dans le village? | jatil œ̃ gid dɑ̃ lə vilaʒ? |
|---|---|---|
| I should like to ascend the glacier to-morrow morning | J'aimerais faire l'ascension du glacier demain matin | ʒɛmrɛ fɛr lasɑ̃sjɔ̃ dy glasje dmɛ̃ matɛ̃ |

| English. | | Pronunciation. |
|---|---|---|
| You must have nailed shoes | Il vous faut des brodequins cloutés | il vu fo de brɔdkɛ̃ klute |
| Do I need a rope and an ice-axe ? | Ai-je besoin d'une corde et d'un piolet ? | ɛʒ bəzwɛ̃ dyn kɔrd e dœ̃ pjɔlɛ ? |
| The ascent is very steep | L'ascension est très raide | lasɑ̃sjɔ̃ ɛ trɛ rɛd |
| You have to use irons when climbing the chimney | Il faut vous servir de crampons en escaladant la cheminée | il fo vu sɛrvir də krɑ̃pɔ̃ ɑ̃n ɛskaladɑ̃ la ʃəmine |
| Beware of the crevasses ! | Prenez garde aux crevasses ! | prəne gard o krəvas ! |
| I'm afraid we shall have to spend the night in a mountain-hut | Il nous faudra passer la nuit dans un chalet-refuge, je crains bien | il nu fodra pɑse la nɥi dɑ̃z œ̃ ʃalɛrəfyʒ, ʒə krɛ̃ bjɛ̃ |
| We might lose our way in the blizzard | Nous pourrions nous égarer dans la tempête de neige | nupurjɔ̃ nuz egare dɑ̃ la tɑ̃pɛt də nɛʒ |
| Let's see the sunrise from the peak | Allons voir le lever de soleil depuis la cime | alɔ̃ vwar lə lve də sɔlɛj dəpɥi la sim |
| Do you like mountaineering ? | Aimez-vous l'alpinisme ? | ɛmevu lalpinism ? |
| You should use your snow-goggles | Vous devriez porter des lunettes d'alpiniste | vu dəvrije pɔrte de lynɛt dalpinist |
| Can you let me have some cream for sun-burn ? | Pouvez-vous me donner de la pommade pour déhâler ? | puvevu mə dɔne dla pɔmad pur deale ? |
| Can we get some refreshments at the alpine dairy ? | Peut-on se procurer des rafraîchissements dans la laiterie alpine ? | pøtɔ̃ sprɔkyre de rafrɛʃismɑ̃ dɑ̃ la lɛtri alpin ? |

# GAMES

## Vocabulary

| English. | | Pronunciation. |
|---|---|---|
| The draughts | Le jeu de dames | lə ʒø də dam |
| The chess | Le jeu d'échecs | lə ʒø deʃɛk |
| The queen | La dame, la reine | la dam, la rɛn |
| The king | Le roi | lə rwa |
| The knight | Le cavalier | lə kavalje |
| The rook | La tour | la tur |
| The bishop | Le fou | lə fu |
| The pawn | Le pion | lə pjɔ̃ |
| The chessboard | L'échiquier | leʃikje |
| The dice | Les dés | le de |
| The billiards | Le jeu de billard, le billard | lə ʒø də bijar, lə bijar |
| The chalk | La craie | la krɛ |
| The cue | La queue | la kø |
| The game of cards | Le jeu de cartes, la partie de cartes | lə ʒø də kart, la parti də kart |
| The player | Le joueur | lə ʒwœr |
| The dummy | Le mort | lə mɔr |
| The hearts | Le cœur | lə kœr |
| The diamonds | Le carreau | lə karo |
| The spades | Le pique | lə pik |
| The clubs | Le trèfle | lə trɛfl |
| The ace | L'as | las |
| The king | Le roi | lə rwa |
| The queen | La dame | la dam |
| The jack | Le valet | lə valɛ |
| The trumps | L'atout | latu |
| To trump | Couper une carte, jouer atout | kupe yn kart, ʒwe atu |
| To shuffle | Battre les cartes | batr le kart |

| English. | | Pronunciation. |
|---|---|---|
| To deal | Donner | dɔne |
| To cut | Couper | kupe |
| To declare | Annoncer | anɔ̃se |

## Phrases

| | | |
|---|---|---|
| Shall we play billiards or cards? | Jouons-nous au billard ou aux cartes? | ʒwɔ̃nu o bijar u o kart? |
| Have you got a new pack? | Avez-vous un jeu neuf? | avevuz œ̃ ʒø nœf? |
| I have shuffled, you cut | J'ai battu les cartes, à vous de couper | ʒe baty le kart, a vu də kupe |
| Your deal | A vous la donne | a vu la dɔn |
| Who will score? | Qui va marquer les points? | ki va marke le pwɛ̃? |
| Who declares? | Qui est-ce qui annonce? | ki ɛski anɔ̃s? |
| I pass | Je passe, je renonce | ʒə pɑs, ʒə rənɔ̃s |
| Diamonds are trumps | C'est carreau atout | sɛ karo atu |
| Your play | A vous de jouer | a vu də ʒwe |
| You must follow suit | Il faut jouer dans la couleur | il fo ʒwe dɑ̃ la kulœr |
| This is my trick | Cette levée est à moi | sɛt lve ɛt a mwa |
| I must discard | Je dois écarter, je dois me défausser | ʒdwaz ekarte, ʒdwa mə defose |
| Don't look at my cards | Ne regardez pas mes cartes | nə rgarde pɑ me kart |
| Lay the cards down on the table | Mettez les cartes sur la table | mɛte le kart syr la tabl |
| I have lost 100 francs at cards | J'ai perdu cent francs aux cartes | ʒe pɛrdy sɑ̃ frɑ̃ o kart |
| He has gambled away his fortune | Il a perdu sa fortune au jeu | il a pɛrdy sa fɔrtyn o ʒø |

# TIME

## Vocabulary

| English. | | Pronunciation. |
|---|---|---|
| The wrist-watch | La montre-bracelet | la mɔ̃trəbraslɛ |
| The alarm-clock | Le réveil | lə revɛj |
| The watchmaker | L'horloger | lɔrlɔʒe |
| To repair | Réparer | repare |
| To be fast (slow) | Avancer (retarder) | avɑ̃se (rətarde) |
| To set | Régler, mettre à l'heure | regle, mɛtralœr |
| To get up | Se lever | sə ləve |
| To go to bed | Se coucher | sə kuʃe |
| Early | De bonne heure, tôt | də bɔn œr, to |
| Late | Tard, en retard | tar, ɑ̃ rtɑr |
| Punctual | Ponctuel, exact | pɔ̃ktɥɛl, ɛgzakt |
| The morning | Le matin | lə matɛ̃ |
| The noon | Le midi | lə midi |
| The forenoon | La matinée | la matine |
| The afternoon | L'après-midi | lapremidi |
| The evening | Le soir, la soirée | lə swar, la sware |
| The night | La nuit | la nɥi |
| The week | La semaine, huit jours | la smɛn, ɥi ʒur |
| The days of the week | Les jours de la semaine | le ʒur dla smɛn |
| Sunday | Dimanche | dimɑ̃ʃ |
| Monday | Lundi | lœ̃di |
| Tuesday | Mardi | mardi |
| Wednesday | Mercredi | mɛrkrədi |
| Thursday | Jeudi | ʒødi |
| Friday | Vendredi | vɑ̃drədi |
| Saturday | Samedi | samdi |
| The date | La date | la dat |
| The month | Le mois | lə mwɑ |

| English. | | Pronunciation. |
|---|---|---|
| January | janvier | ʒɑ̃vje |
| February | février | fevrie |
| March | mars | mars |
| April | avril | avril |
| May | mai | mɛ |
| June | juin | ʒɥɛ̃ |
| July | juillet | ʒɥijɛ |
| August | août | u, au |
| September | septembre | sɛptɑ̃br |
| October | octobre | ɔktɔbr |
| November | novembre | nɔvɑ̃br |
| December | décembre | desɑ̃br |
| The spring | Le printemps | lə prɛ̃tɑ̃ |
| The summer | L'été | lete |
| The autumn | L'automne | lotɔn |
| The winter | L'hiver | livɛr |
| The public holiday | Le jour de fête légal | lə ʒur də fɛt legal |
| The Christmas | la Noël | la nɔɛl, nwɛl |
| Easter | Pâques | pɑk |
| Whitsun | La Pentecôte | la pɑ̃tkot |
| The second | La seconde | la zgɔ̃nd |
| The minute | La minute | la minyt |
| The hour | L'heure | lœr |
| The moon | La lune | la lyn |
| The sun | Le soleil | lə sɔlɛj |
| The star | L'étoile | letwal |

## Phrases

| | | |
|---|---|---|
| Can you tell me the right time ? | Pouvez - vous me dire l'heure juste ? | puvevu mdir lœr ʒyst ? |
| Is your watch right ? | Est-ce que votre montre est à l'heure ? | ɛskə vɔt mɔ̃tr ɛt alœr ? |
| It is ten minutes fast | Elle avance de dix minutes | ɛl avɑ̃s də di minyt |

| English. | | Pronunciation. |
|---|---|---|
| It is a quarter of an hour slow | Elle retarde d'un quart d'heure | ɛl rətard dœ̃ kar dœr |
| It always keeps good time | Elle est toujours exacte | ɛl ɛ tuʒur ɛgzakt |
| What time is it? | Quelle heure est-il? | kɛl œr ɛtil? |
| It is eight o'clock | Il est huit heures | il ɛ ɥit œr |
| It is five minutes past eight | Il est huit heures cinq | il ɛ ɥit œr sɛ̃k |
| It is a quarter past eight | Il est huit heures et quart | il ɛ ɥit œr(z) e kar |
| Half-past eight | Huit heures et demie | ɥit œr(z) e dmi |
| A quarter to nine | Neuf heures moins le quart | nœv œr mwɛ̃ lə kar |
| Eight a.m. | Huit heures du matin | ɥit œr dy matɛ̃ |
| Eight p.m. | Huit heures du soir | ɥit œr dy swar |
| It is noon | Il est midi | il ɛ midi |
| My train leaves at 2.30 | Mon train part à deux heures trente | mɔ̃ trɛ̃ par a døz œr trɑ̃t |
| You will have to be at the station half an hour beforehand | Il vous faudra être à la gare une demi-heure d'avance | il vu fodra ɛtr ala gar yn dmi œr davɑ̃s |
| Don't be late | Ne soyez pas en retard | nə swaje pɑz ɑ̃ rtard |
| I shall be in time | Je serai à l'heure | ʒə sre a lœr |
| It is time to get up (to go to bed) | Il est temps de se lever (se coucher) | il ɛ tɑ̃ də sləve (sə kuʃe) |
| Hurry up, it is half-past seven | Dépêchez-vous, il est sept heures et demie | depeʃevu, il ɛ sɛt œr(z) e dmi |
| My watch has stopped | Ma montre s'est arrêtée | ma mɔ̃tr sɛt arɛte |
| I must take my watch to the watchmaker | Il me faut porter ma montre chez l'horloger | il me fo pɔrte ma mɔ̃tr ʃe lɔrlɔʒe |

| English. | | Pronunciation. |
|---|---|---|
| It needs cleaning | Elle a besoin d'être nettoyée | ɛl a bəzwɛ̃ dɛtr nɛtwaje |
| The glass is cracked | Le verre est fêlé | lə vɛr ɛ fɛle |
| The spring is broken | Le ressort est cassé | lə rsɔr ɛ kɑse |
| Set your watch by the station clock | Réglez votre montre sur l'horloge de la gare | regle vɔt mɔ̃tr syr lɔrlɔʒ dla gar |
| Next week there will be a concert | On donnera un concert la semaine prochaine | ɔ̃ dɔnra œ̃ kɔ̃sɛr la smɛn prɔʃɛn |
| I shall be back in a week | Je serai de retour dans huit jours | ʒə sre də rtur dɑ̃ ɥi ʒur |
| A fortnight ago I was in London | Il y a quinze jours j'étais à Londres | ilja kɛ̃z ʒur ʒetɛz a lɔ̃dr |
| It gets dark very early | Il fait nuit de très bonne heure | il fɛ nɥi də trɛ bɔn œr |
| What is the date to-day? | Le combien sommes-nous aujourd'hui? | lə kɔ̃bjɛ̃ sɔmnu oʒurdɥi? |
| To-day is the fifteenth of September | C'est aujourd'hui le quinze septembre | sɛt oʒurdɥi lə kɛ̃z sɛptɑ̃br |
| My birthday is on the tenth of October | Mon anniversaire a lieu le dix octobre | mɔ̃n anivɛrsɛr a ljø lə dis ɔktɔbr |
| Are you travelling this year? | Est-ce que vous allez en voyage cette année? | ɛskə vuz alez ɑ̃ vwajaʒ sɛt ane? |
| I came back the day before yesterday | Je suis rentré(e) avant-hier | ʒə sɥi rɑ̃tre avɑ̃tjɛr |
| I shall be leaving again to-morrow (the day after to-morrow, next week) | Je repartirai demain (après-demain, la semaine prochaine) | ʒə rəpartire dmɛ̃ (apredmɛ̃, la smɛn prɔʃɛn) |

| English. | | Pronunciation. |
|---|---|---|
| Don't arrive at the last minute | N'arrivez pas à la dernière minute | narive paz a la dernjer minyt |
| One moment, please | Un moment, s'il vous plaît | œ̃ mɔmã, sivuplɛ |
| At dawn | Au point du jour | o pwɛ̃ dy ʒur |
| At dusk | A la brune | ala bryn |
| Last year was a leap-year | L'année dernière était bissextile | lane dernjer etɛ bisɛkstil |
| Can you spare me a moment? | Pouvez-vous me donner un moment? | puvevu mə dɔne œ̃ mɔmã? |
| I have no time | Je n'ai pas le temps | ʒənepa ltã |
| He left long ago | Il est parti il y a longtemps | il ɛ parti ilja lɔ̃tã |
| How old are you? | Quel âge avez-vous? | kɛl aʒ avevu? |
| I was thirty-six in January | J'ai eu trente-six ans au mois de janvier | ʒe y trãtsiz ã o mwa dʒãvje |

## WEATHER

### Vocabulary

| English | French | Pronunciation |
|---|---|---|
| The climate | Le climat | lə klima |
| The weather | Le temps | lə tã |
| The air | L'air, l'atmosphère | lɛr, latmɔsfɛr |
| The heat | La grande chaleur | la grãd ʃalœr |
| The warmth | La chaleur | la ʃalœr |
| The cold | Le froid | lə frwa |
| The rain | La pluie | la plɥi |
| The snow | La neige | la nɛʒ |
| The sunshine | Le soleil | lə sɔlej |
| The sky | Le ciel | lə sjɛl |
| The cloud | Le nuage | lə nɥaʒ |
| The thunderstorm | L'orage | lɔraʒ |
| The thunder | Le tonnerre | lə tɔnɛr |

| English. | | Pronunciation. |
|---|---|---|
| The lightning | L'éclair | leklɛr |
| The hail | La grêle | la grɛl |
| The ice | La glace | la glas |
| The gale | Le coup de vent | lə kudvɑ̃ |
| The wind | Le vent | lə vɑ̃ |
| The breeze | Le vent fort, la brise | lə vɑ̃ fɔr, la briz |
| The fog, mist | Le brouillard, la brume | lə brujar, la brym |
| Fine | Beau (belle) | bo (bɛl) |
| Bad | Mauvais (mauvaise) | mɔvɛ (mɔvɛz) |
| Cold | Froid (froide) | frwa (frwad) |
| Warm | Chaud (chaude) | ʃo (ʃod) |
| Hot | Très chaud, brûlant | trɛ ʃo, brylɑ̃ |
| It is freezing | Il gèle | il ʒɛl |
| It is snowing | Il neige | il nɛʒ |
| It is raining | Il pleut | il plø |

## Phrases

| | | |
|---|---|---|
| What is the weather like ? | Quel temps fait-il ? | kɛl tɑ̃ fɛtil ? |
| It is fine | Il fait beau | il fɛ bo |
| It is a lovely day | C'est une belle journée | sɛt yn bɛl ʒurne |
| The weather is beautiful (dull) | Le temps est beau (couvert) | lə tɑ̃ ɛ bo (kuvɛr) |
| The weather is changeable | Le temps est variable | lə tɑ̃ ɛ varjabl |
| The weather is settled | Le temps est au beau fixe | lə tɑ̃ ɛt o bo fiks |
| It is hot (cold) | Il fait chaud (froid) | il fɛ ʃo (frwa) |
| It is rainy (foggy) | Le temps est à la pluie (au brouillard) | lə tɑ̃ ɛt a la plɥi (o brujar) |
| It is very oppressive | Il fait très lourd | il fɛ trɛ lur |

| English. | | Pronunciation. |
|---|---|---|
| Do you think the weather will remain fine? | Pensez-vous que le temps restera au beau? | pɑ̃sevu kə ltɑ̃ rɛstra o bo? |
| The wind is cold | Le vent est froid | lə vɑ̃t ɛ frwa |
| It is stormy | Le temps est à l'orage | lə tɑ̃ ɛtalɔraʒ |
| The wind has dropped | Le vent est tombé | lə vɑ̃ ɛ tɔ̃be |
| It is raining in torrents (cats and dogs) | Il pleut à torrents (des hallebardes) | il plø a tɔrɑ̃ (de albard) |
| It is pouring | Il pleut à verse | il plø avɛrs |
| I'm wet through | Je suis trempé(e) | ʒə sɥi trɑ̃pe |
| Where are my galoshes and umbrella? | Où sont mes caoutchoucs et mon parapluie? | u sɔ̃ me kautʃu e mɔ̃ paraplɥi? |
| Take a mack(intosh) | Prenez un imperméable | prənez œ̃n ɛ̃pɛrmeabl |
| Will there be a thunderstorm? | Va-t-on avoir un orage? | vatɔ̃ avwar œ̃n ɔraʒ? |
| It's thundering and lightening | Il tonne et éclaire | il tɔn e eklɛr |
| The sky is overcast | Le ciel est couvert | lə sjɛl ɛ kuvɛr |
| The sky is clear | Le ciel est clair | lə sjɛl ɛ klɛr |
| It's too sunny here, let's sit in the shade | Il fait trop de soleil ici, allons nous asseoir à l'ombre | il fɛ tro də sɔlɛj isi, alɔ̃ nuz aswar alɔ̃br |
| It is getting cold | Il commence à faire froid | il kɔmɑ̃s a fɛr frwa |
| Are you cold? | Avez-vous froid? | avevu frwa? |
| I feel hot | Je me sens chaud | ʒə msɑ̃ ʃo |
| I am perspiring, I can't stand the heat | Je transpire, je ne peux pas supporter la chaleur | ʒə trɑ̃spir, ʒə npø pɑ sypɔrte la ʃalœr |
| How many degrees is it on the thermometer? | Combien de degrés le thermomètre marque-t-il? | kɔ̃bjɛ̃ də dəgre lə tɛrmɔmɛtr markətil? |

| English. | | Pronunciation. |
|---|---|---|
| It has gone up to 22 degrees (Cent.) | Il a monté jusqu'à vingt-deux degrés | il a mõte ʒyska vɛ̃tdø dəgre |
| The glass is rising (falling) | Le baromètre monte (baisse) | lə barɔmɛtr mõt (bɛs) |
| It indicates fine weather | Il annonce du beau temps | il anõs dy bo tɑ̃ |
| It is ten degrees of frost | Nous avons dix degrés de froid | nuzavõ di dəgre də frwa |
| It's freezing hard | Il gèle dur (à pierre fendre) | il gɛl dyr (a pjɛr fɑ̃dr) |
| Is it thawing? | Dégèle-t-il? | deʒɛltil? |
| It's very slippery, be careful | Faites attention, le sol est très glissant | fɛtz atɑ̃sjõ, lə sɔl ɛ trɛ glisɑ̃ |

# PAYING A CALL, GREETINGS, REQUESTS, EXPRESSIONS OF THANKS, OF REGRET, APOLOGIES, ENQUIRIES

## Vocabulary

| | | |
|---|---|---|
| The visit, call | La visite | la vizit |
| The invitation | L'invitation | lɛ̃vitasjõ |
| The appointment | Le rendez-vous | lə rɑ̃devu |
| The party | La réunion intime | la reynjõ ɛ̃tim |
| The conversation | La conversation, l'entretien | la kõversasjõ, lɑ̃trə-tjɛ̃ |
| The talk, chat | La causerie, la causette | la kozri, la kozɛt |
| The reception | La réception | la resɛpsjõ |
| The visiting card | La carte de visite | la kart də vizit |
| To invite | Inviter | ɛ̃vite |
| To visit, call on | Rendre visite, aller voir | rɑ̃dr vizit, ale vwar |
| To ring the bell | sonner | sɔne |

| English. | | Pronunciation. |
|---|---|---|
| To arrive | arriver | arive |
| To be punctual | être à l'heure, être exact(e) | εtr alœr, εtr εgzakt |
| To be late | être en retard | εtr ᾶ rtar |
| To welcome | souhaiter la bien-venue à | swεte la bjᴇ̃vny a |
| To expect | attendre, s'attendre à | atᾶdr, satᾶdr a |
| To meet | Rencontrer, aller au-devant de | rᾶkɔ̃tre, ale odvᾶ də |
| To introduce | Présenter | prezᾶte |
| To say good-bye | Dire adieu | dir adjø |

## PAYING A CALL

| | | |
|---|---|---|
| Did you ring the bell? | Avez-vous sonné? | avevu sɔne? |
| Is Mrs. Brown at home? | Madame Lebrun est-elle visible (chez elle)? | madam ləbrᴇ̃ εtεl vizibl (ʃez εl)? |
| Come in | Entrez! | ᾶtre! |
| Mrs. Smith wishes to speak to you | Mme Lefèvre désire vous parler | madam ləfεvr dezir vu parle |
| Show the visitor in | Faites entrer le visiteur (la visiteuse) | fεtz ᾶtre lə vizitœr (la vizitøz) |
| I am (very) pleased to see you | Je suis enchanté(e) de vous voir | ʒə sɥiz ᾶʃᾶte də vu vwar |
| It is a great pleasure to me | Ça me fait beaucoup de plaisir | samfε boku də plεzir |
| The pleasure is mine | Mais c'est moi qui suis enchanté(e) | mε sε mwa ki sɥiz ᾶʃᾶte |
| Thank you for your kind invitation | Merci de votre aimable invitation | mεrsi də vɔtr εmabl ᴇ̃vitasjɔ̃ |
| It was very kind of you to invite me | C'était bien aimable à vous de m'inviter | sεtε bjᴇ̃ εmabl a vu də mᴇ̃vite |

| English. | | Pronunciation. |
|---|---|---|
| You are very kind | Vous êtes bien aimable | vuz ɛt bjɛ̃ ɛmabl |
| My parents send their kind regards | Mes parents vous font leurs amitiés | me parɑ̃ vu fɔ̃ lœrz amitje |
| Am I late (early)? | Suis-je en retard (en avance)? | sчiʒ ɑ̃ rtar (ɑ̃n avɑ̃s)? |
| May I introduce my husband? | Puis-je vous présenter mon mari? | pчiʒ vu prezɑ̃te mɔ̃ mari? |
| Here are my son and my daughter | Voici mon fils et ma fille | vwasi mɔ̃ fis e ma fij |
| Please sit down | Veuillez vous asseoir | vœje vuzaswar |
| Have some tea and cake | Voulez-vous prendre du thé et du gâteau? | vulevu prɑ̃dr dy te e dy gato? |
| Please help yourself | Servez-vous, je vous en prie | sɛrvevu, ʒvuzɑ̃pri |
| Please stay to dinner (supper) | Restez à dîner (souper), je vous en prie | rɛstez a dine (supe), ʒvuzɑ̃pri |
| Next time you must stay with us | La prochaine fois il faudra que vous passiez quelque temps chez nous | la prɔʃen fwa il fodra kə vu pasje kɛlkə tɑ̃ ʃe nu |
| Can you put me up? | Pouvez-vous m'offrir un lit? | puvevu mɔfrir œ̃ li? |
| I am sorry to say I must go | Je regrette, mais je dois partir | ʒə rəgrɛt, mɛ ʒdwa partir |
| Do stay a little longer | Restez un peu plus longtemps, je vous en prie | rɛstez œ̃ pø ply lɔ̃tɑ̃, ʒvuzɑ̃pri |
| I am sorry I can't stay any longer | Je regrette, mais je ne peux pas rester plus longtemps | ʒə rəgrɛt, mɛ ʒə npø pa rɛste ply lɔ̃tɑ̃ |
| I must not lose my train | Il ne faut pas que je manque mon train | il nfo pa kə ʒmɑ̃k mɔ̃ trɛ̃ |

| English. | | Pronunciation. |
|---|---|---|
| I hope you'll come again soon | J'espère que vous reviendrez bientôt | ʒɛspɛr kə vu rəvjɛ̃dre bjɛ̃to |
| Come whenever you like | Venez quand vous voudrez | vne kɑ̃ vuvudre |
| Many thanks for your hospitality | Merci mille fois de votre hospitalité | mɛrsi mil fwɑ də vɔtr ɔspitalite |
| Give my love to your parents | Faites mes amitiés à vos parents | fɛt mez amitje a vo parɑ̃ |
| Will you meet me for lunch to-morrow? | Voulez-vous prendre rendez-vous avec moi demain pour le déjeuner | vulevu prɑ̃d rɑ̃devu avɛk mwa dmɛ̃ pur lə deʒœne? |
| Sorry, I have a prior engagement | Je regrette, mais je ne suis pas libre | ʒə rəgrɛt, mɛ ʒə nsɥi pa libr |
| I have nothing on the day after to-morrow | Je suis complètement libre après-demain | ʒə sɥi kɔ̃plɛtmɑ̃ libr aprɛdmɛ̃ |

## GREETINGS

| | | |
|---|---|---|
| Good morning; good day | Bonjour | bɔ̃ʒur |
| Good evening; good night | Bonsoir; bonne nuit | bɔ̃swar; bɔn nɥi |
| How are you; how do you do? | Comment allez-vous; comment vous portez-vous? | kɔmɑ̃t alevu; kɔmɑ̃ vupɔrtevu? |
| Pleased to see you | Enchanté de vous voir | ɑ̃ʃɑ̃te də vu vwar |
| Haven't seen you for a long time | Il y a longtemps que je ne vous ai vu(e) | ilja lɔ̃tɑ̃ kə ʒnvuze vy |
| What a surprise to see you | Quelle surprise de vous voir | kɛl syrpriz də vu vwar |

| English. | | Pronunciation. |
|---|---|---|
| We must keep in touch | Il ne faut pas qu'on se perde de vue | il nfo pa kɔ̃ spɛrd də vy |
| Good-bye; see you again soon | Au revoir; on se reverra bientôt | o rvwar; ɔ̃ sə rvɛra bjɛ̃to |
| Pleasant journey | Bon voyage | bɔ̃ vwajaʒ |
| Good luck | Bonne chance | bɔn ʃɑ̃s |
| Keep well | Portez-vous bien | pɔrtevu bjɛ̃ |
| Don't forget us | Ne nous oubliez pas | nə nuz ublije pɑ |

## REQUESTS

| | | |
|---|---|---|
| A cup of coffee, please | Une tasse de café, s'il vous plaît | yn tɑs də kafe, sivuplɛ |
| May I trouble you for a match (a light) | Vous seriez bien aimable de me donner une allumette (du feu) | vu sərije bjɛ̃nɛmabl də mdɔne yn alymɛt (dy fø) |
| May I ask you a favour? | Puis-je vous demander une grâce? | pɥiʒ vu dmɑ̃de yn grɑs? |
| Would you be good enough to post this letter for me? | Voudriez-vous être assez aimable pour me mettre cette lettre à la poste? | vudrijevuz ɛtr asez ɛmabl pur mə mɛtr sɛt lɛtr ala pɔst? |
| Will you do me a favour | Voulez-vous me faire une faveur? | vulevu mfɛr yn favœr? |
| I have a request to make | J'ai une demande à vous faire | ʒe yn dmɑ̃d a vu fɛr |
| I don't want to be disturbed | Je ne veux pas être dérangé(e) | ʒə nvø pɑz ɛtr derɑ̃ʒe |
| She asks for help | Elle demande du secours | ɛl dmɑ̃d dy skur |
| I wish I were at home | Je voudrais être chez moi | ʒvudrɛz ɛtr ʃe mwa |

| English. | | Pronunciation. |
|---|---|---|
| Would you assist me ? | Voudriez-vous m'aider ? | vudrijevu mɛde ? |
| Your request will be granted | Votre demande sera accordée | vɔt dəmɑ̃d sra akɔrde |
| May I open the window ? | Permettez-vous que j'ouvre la fenêtre ? | pɛrmɛtevu kə ʒuvr la fnɛtr ? |
| Do you mind if I close the door ? | Ça ne vous fait rien que je ferme la porte ? | sa nvu fɛ rjɛ̃ kə ʃfɛrm la pɔrt ? |
| May I apply for the job ? | Puis - je solliciter l'emploi ? | pɥiʒ sɔlisite lɑ̃plwa ? |
| I should like to hear your opinion | Je voudrais avoir votre opinion | ʒvudrɛz avwar vɔtr ɔpinjɔ̃ |
| What do you want ? | Que désirez-vous ? | kə dezirevu ? |
| Can I help you ? | Puis-je vous aider ? | pɥiz vuz ɛde ? |
| Don't bother | Ne vous inquiétez pas | nvuz ɛ̃kjete pɑ |

## THANKS

| Thank you ; thanks | Je vous remercie ; merci | ʒvu rəmɛrsi ; mɛrsi |
|---|---|---|
| Many thanks | Merci beaucoup | mɛrsi boku |
| I'm very grateful to you | Je vous suis très reconnaissant(e) | ʒvu sɥi trɛ rəkɔnɛsɑ̃(t) |
| I'm very much obliged to you | Je vous suis bien obligé(e) | ʒvu sɥi bjɛ̃ ɔbliʒe |
| I'm deeply indebted to you | Je vous suis infiniment redevable | ʒvu sɥiz ɛ̃finimɑ̃ rədvabl |
| You are very kind (good) | Vous êtes bien aimable (bon, bonne) | vuzɛt bjɛ̃ ɛmabl (bɔ̃, bɔn) |
| You've done me a great favour | Vous m'avez fait une grande faveur | vu mave fɛt yn grɑ̃d favœr |
| I wish I could repay you | Je voudrais pouvoir vous le (la) rendre | ʒvudrɛ puvwar vu lə (la) rɑ̃dr |

| English. | | Pronunciation. |
|---|---|---|
| Pray accept my sincere thanks | Je vous prie d'accepter (d'agréer) mes remerciements sincères | ʒe vu pri daksεpte (dagree) me rə-mεrsimã sɛ̃sεr |
| I should like to thank you for the present | Je voudrais vous remercier du (pour le) cadeau | ʒvudrε vu rəmεrsje dy (purlə) kado |

## REGRETS, APOLOGIES

| | | |
|---|---|---|
| I am sorry you are ill | Je regrette que vous soyez malade | ʒə rgrεt kə vu swaje malad |
| I'm sorry for you | Je vous plains | ʒvuplɛ̃ |
| I regret the misunderstanding | Je regrette le malentendu | ʒə rgrεt lə malãtãdy |
| May I express my regrets? | Puis-je vous exprimer mes regrets? | pɥiʒ vuz εksprime me rəgrε? |
| It is very regrettable | C'est bien regrettable | sε bjɛ̃ rəgrεtabl |
| I am sorry you did not come to see me | Je regrette que vous ne soyez pas venu(e) me voir | ʒə rgrεt kə vu nə swaje pɑ vny mə vwar |
| Let me express my sympathy (condolences) | Permettez-moi de vous exprimer mes condoléances | pεrmεte mwa dvuz εksprime me kɔ̃-dɔleãs |
| Pardon. Sorry | Pardon. Je regrette | pardɔ̃. ʒə rgrεt |
| I beg your pardon | Je vous demande pardon | ʒvu dmãd pardɔ̃ |
| Please forgive me | Veuillez me pardonner | vœje mə pardɔne |
| I didn't want to hurt your feelings | Je n'ai pas voulu vous froisser | ʒne pɑ vuly vu frwase |
| It wasn't my fault | Ce n'était pas de ma faute | snetε pɑ dma fot |

| English. | | Pronunciation. |
|---|---|---|
| I didn't do it on purpose | Je ne l'ai pas fait exprès | ʒə nle pɑ fɛ ɛksprɛ |
| Don't be angry | Ne vous fâchez pas | nə vu faʃe pɑ |
| Please don't take it amiss | Ne le prenez pas de travers, je vous en prie | nəl prəne pɑ də travɛr, ʒvuz ɑ̃ pri |
| Don't think me impolite (rude) | Ne me croyez pas impoli(e) (malhonnête) | nə mkrwaje paz ɛ̃poli (malɔnɛt) |
| Please put it down to my ignorance | Mettez-le sur le compte de mon ignorance, je vous prie | mɛtelə syr lə kɔ̃t də mɔ̃n iɲɔrɑ̃s, ʒvu pri |

## ENQUIRIES

| | | |
|---|---|---|
| Where is the station? | Où est la gare? | wɛ la gar? |
| Can you direct me to the post-office? | Pouvez-vous m'indiquer le chemin du bureau de poste? | puvevu mɛ̃dike lə ʃmɛ̃ dy buro də pɔst |
| Is this the way to the theatre? | Est-ce par ici qu'on arrive au théâtre? | ɛs par isi kɔ̃n ariv o teatr? |
| Is there a bus-stop near here? | Y a-t-il un arrêt d'autobus près d' ici? | jatil ɛ̃n arɛ dotɔbys prɛ disi? |
| Where is the booking office? | Où est le guichet? | wɛ lə giʃɛ? |
| Where can I change money? | Où puis-je changer l'argent? | u pɥiʒ ʃɑ̃ʒe larʒɑ̃? |
| Where can I leave my luggage? | Où puis-je déposer mes bagages? | u pɥiʒ depoze me bagaʒ? |
| Can you get me a taxi? | Pouvez-vous me procurer un taxi? | puvevu mprɔkyre ɛ̃ taksi? |

| English. | | Pronunciation |
|---|---|---|
| Which is the best hotel? | Quel est le meilleur hôtel? | kɛl ɛ lə mɛjœr otɛl? |
| Can I have a room for the night? | Puis-je louer une chambre pour une nuit? | pɥiʒ lwe yn ʃãbr pur yn nɥi? |
| Where is the lift? | Où est l'ascenseur? | u ɛ lasãsœr? |
| Are there any letters for me? | Y a-t-il des lettres pour moi? | jatil de lɛtr pur mwa? |
| Where can I telephone? | D'où peut-on téléphoner? | du pøtõ telefɔne? |
| Where does Mr. X live? | Où M. X. demeure-t-il? | u msjø iks dmœrtil? |
| Does Mr. Y. live here? | M. Y. demeure-t-il ici? | msjø igrɛk dmœrtil isi? |
| Has anyone called? | Est-il venu quelqu'un? | ɛtil vny kɛlkœ̃? |
| Was there a telephone message for me? | A-t-on téléphoné un mot pour moi? | atõ telefɔne œ̃ mo pur mwa? |
| Can you give me any information? | Pouvez-vous me donner des renseignements? | puvevu mdɔnə de rãsɛɲəmã? |

## PUBLIC NOTICES

| | | |
|---|---|---|
| Look out! | Attention! Prenez garde! | atãsjõ! prənə gard! |
| Mind the step! | Prenez garde à la marche! | prənə gard ala marʃ! |
| Danger. High tension current | Danger! Courant à haute tension | dãʒe! kurã a ot tãsjõ |
| Private property. No admittance | Propriété privée. Défense d'entrer | prɔpriete prive. defãs dãtre |
| Keep off the grass | Défense de marcher sur les pelouses | defãs də marʃe syr le pluz |

| English. | | Pronunciation. |
|---|---|---|
| Trespassers will be prosecuted | Défense de passer sous peine d'amende | defãs də pase su pɛn damãd |
| Beware of the dog | Prenez garde au chien | prəne gard o ʃjẽ |
| Beware of pick-pockets | Attention aux pick-pockets | atãsjɔ̃ o pikpɔkɛ |
| No hawkers | Défense de colporter | defãs də kɔlpɔrte |
| You may telephone from here | On peut téléphoner | ɔ̃ pø telefone |
| Entrance | Entrée | ãtre |
| Exit ; way out | Sortie | sɔrti |
| Emergency exit | Sortie de secours | sɔrtitskur |
| Push | Poussez | puse |
| Pull | Tirez | tire |
| Road up | Attention aux travaux | atãsjɔ̃ o travo |
| Keep to the right | Tenez la droite | tne la drwat |
| Drive slowly | Allure modérée prescrite à tous les véhicules | alyr mɔdere prɛskrit a tu le veikyl |
| Diversion | Déviation | devjasjɔ̃ |
| No thoroughfare | Route barrée | rut bare |
| One-way street | Rue à sens unique | ry a sãs ynik |
| Main road ahead | Route de priorité en avant | rut də priɔrite ãnavã |
| No smoking | Défense de fumer | defãs də fyme |

## NEWSPAPERS, BOOKS

### Vocabulary

| | | |
|---|---|---|
| The newspaper | Le journal, le quotidien | lə ʒurnal, lə kɔtidjẽ |
| The bookstall | Le kiosque à journaux | lə kjɔsk a ʒurno |

| English. | | Pronunciation. |
|---|---|---|
| The newspaper vendor | Le vendeur de journaux | lə vãdœr də ʒurno |
| The periodical | Le périodique | lə perjɔdik |
| The technical (professional) journal | Le journal technique (professionnel) | lə ʒurnal tɛknik (prɔfɛsjɔnɛl) |
| The illustrated paper | Le journal illustré | lə ʒurnal ilystre |
| The monthly journal | La revue mensuelle | la rvy mãsɥɛl |
| The family journal | La revue de famille | la rvy də famij |
| The trade journal | La revue de commerce | la rvy də kɔmɛrs |
| The fashion paper | Le journal de modes | lə ʒurnal də mɔd |
| The advertisement | L'annonce | lanõs |
| The leader | L'article de fond | lartik(lə) də fõ |
| The column | La colonne | la kɔlɔn |
| The volume | Le tome, le volume | lə tom, lə vɔlym |
| The edition | L'édition | ledisjõ |
| The print | Les caractères | le karaktɛr |
| The binding | La reliure | la rəljyr |
| The publisher | L'éditeur | leditœr |
| The editor | Le rédacteur | le redaktœr |
| The poet | Le poète | lə pɔɛt |
| The author | L'auteur | lotœr |
| To print | Imprimer | ɛ̃prime |
| To read | Lire | lir |

## Phrases

| | | |
|---|---|---|
| Has the morning paper come ? | Est-ce que le journal du matin est arrivé ? | ɛskə lʒurnal dy matɛ̃ ɛt arive ? |
| Can you get me an evening paper ? | Pouvez-vous me procurer un journal du soir ? | puvevu mə prɔkyre œ̃ ʒurnal dy swar ? |

| English. | French | Pronunciation. |
|---|---|---|
| Are these the latest periodicals ? | Est-ce que ce sont les périodiques les plus récents ? | ɛskə sə sɔ̃ le perjɔdik le ply resɑ̃ ? |
| Have you read the leader ? | Avez-vous lu l'article de fond ? | avevu ly lartik(lə) də fɔ̃ ? |
| What's the news ? | Quelles sont les nouvelles ? | kɛl sɔ̃ le nuvɛl ? |
| Please let me have a weekly paper | Donnez-moi, s'il vous plaît, un journal hebdomadaire | dɔne mwa, sivuplɛ, œ̃ ʒurnal ɛbdɔmadɛr |
| Let me have a comic paper, please | Donnez-moi un journal pour rire | dɔne mwa œ̃ ʒurnal pur rir |
| Do you stock English papers ? | Tenez-vous les journaux anglais en magasin ? | tnevu le ʒurnoz ɑ̃glɛ ɑ̃ magazɛ̃ ? |
| Could you lend me your paper for a minute ? | Pourriez-vous me prêter votre journal un moment ? | purjevu mə prɛte vɔt ʒurnal œ̃ mɔmɑ̃ ? |
| Have you seen the advertisements ? | Avez-vous vu les annonces ? | avevu vy lez anɔ̃s ? |
| Could you get me a fashion paper ? | Pourriez-vous me procurer un journal de modes ? | purjevu mə prɔkyre œ̃ ʒurnal də mɔd ? |
| Have you got a map of Paris ? | Avez-vous un plan de Paris ? | avevuz œ̃ plɑ̃ də pari ? |
| Can you recom- a good guide-book ? | Pouvez-vous me recommander un bon livret-guide ? | puvevu mə rəkɔmɑ̃de œ̃ bɔ̃ livrɛgid ? |
| I want an edition of Molière in four volumes | Je cherche une édition de Molière en quatre volumes | ʒə ʃɛrʃ yn edisjɔ̃ də mɔljɛr ɑ̃ kat vɔlym |
| Have you a good French novel ? | Avez-vous un bon roman français ? | avevuz œ̃ bɔ̃ rɔmɑ̃ frɑ̃sɛ ? |

| English. | | Pronunciation. |
|---|---|---|
| Please show me some books on French art | Montrez-moi, s'il vous plaît, des livres d'art français | mɔ̃tre mwa, sivuplɛ, de livr dar frãse |
| Haven't you got a bound copy ? | N'auriez-vous pas un exemplaire relié ? | nɔrjevu paz ɛ̃n ɛgzãplɛr rəlje ? |
| This book is out of print | Ce livre est épuisé | slivr ɛt epɥize |
| Can you recommend a book by a modern author ? | Pouvez-vous me recommander un livre d'auteur moderne ? | puvevu mə rəkɔmãde ɛ̃ livr dotœr mɔdɛrn ? |
| I want a good French – English pocket dictionary | Je désire un bon dictionnaire de poche Français-Anglais | ʒə dezir ɛ̃ bɔ̃ diksjɔnɛr də pɔʃ frãse-ãgle |
| Have you a lending library ? | Avez-vous une bibliothèque de prêt ? | avevuz yn bibliɔtɛk də prɛ ? |

# THE HOUSE

## Vocabulary

| The flat | L'appartement | lapartəmã |
|---|---|---|
| The story | L'étage | letaʒ |
| The cellar | La cave | la kav |
| The attic | La mansarde | la mãsard |
| The roof | Le toit | lə twa |
| The ground floor | Le rez-de-chaussée | lə redʃose |
| The wall | Le mur | lə myr |
| The window | La fenêtre, la croisée | la fnɛtr, la krwaze |
| The door | La porte | la pɔrt |
| The key | La clé, la clef | la kle |
| The room | La pièce | la pjɛs |

| English. | | Pronunciation. |
|---|---|---|
| The floor | Le plancher | lə plɑ̃ʃe |
| The ceiling | Le plafond | lə plafɔ̃ |
| The drawing-room | Le salon | lə salɔ̃ |
| The dining-room | La salle à manger | la salamɑ̃ʒe |
| The study | Le cabinet de travail, le bureau | lə kabinɛtravaj, lə byro |
| The bedroom | La chambre à coucher | la ʃɑ̃brakuʃe |
| The dressing-room | Le cabinet de toilette | lə kabinɛtwalɛt |
| The nursery | La chambre des enfants, la nursery | la ʃɑ̃br dezɑ̃fɑ̃, la nœrzere |
| The bathroom | La salle de bain(s) | lə sal də bɛ̃ |
| The wash-basin | La cuvette (de lavabo) | la kyvɛt (də lavabo) |
| The lavatory | Le water-closet, les cabinets | lə watɛrklozɛt, le kabinɛ |
| The stairs | L'escalier | lɛskalje |
| The banisters | La rampe | la rɑ̃p |
| The furniture | L'ameublement, les meubles | lamœbləmɑ̃, le mœbl |
| The lamp | La lampe | la lɑ̃p |
| The stove | Le poêle, le calorifère, la salamandre | lə pwɑl, lə kalɔrifɛr, la salamɑ̃dr |
| The curtains | Les rideaux | le rido |
| The blind | Le store | lə stɔr |
| The carpet | Le tapis | lə tapi |
| The table | La table | la tabl |
| The chair | La chaise | la ʃɛz |
| The looking-glass | Le miroir, la glace | lə mirwar, la glas |
| The sideboard | Le buffet | lə byfɛ |
| The bell | La sonnette | la sɔnɛt |
| The bed | Le lit | lə li |
| The bedside table | La table de nuit | la tabl də nɥi |
| The pillow | L'oreiller | lɔreje |
| The blanket | La couverture | la kuvɛrtyr |
| The quilt | L'édredon | ledrədɔ̃ |

| English. | | Pronunciation. |
|---|---|---|
| The sheet | Le drap | lə dra |
| The kitchen | La cuisine | la kɥizin |
| The kitchen range | La cuisinière | la kɥizinjɛr |
| The gas cooker | Le fourneau à gaz | lə furno a gɑz |
| The electric cooker | Le fourneau électrique | lə furno elɛktrik |
| The washing machine | La machine à laver | la maʃin a lave |
| The vacuum cleaner | L'aspirateur | laspiratœr |
| The saucepan | La casserole | la kasrɔl |
| The pan | Le poêlon, la poêle | lə pwalɔ̃, la pwal |
| The tea-kettle | La bouilloire | la bujwar |
| The gas-meter | Le compteur à gaz | lə kɔ̃tœr a gɑz |
| The electric meter | Le compteur d'électricité | lə kɔ̃tœr delɛktrisite |
| The refrigerator | Le réfrigérateur | lə refriʒeratœr |
| The pantry | Le garde-manger, la dépense | lə gardmɑ̃ʒe, la depɑ̃s |
| The cook | Le cuisinier, la cuisinière | lə kɥizinjɛ, la kɥizinjɛr |
| To live | Demeurer, habiter | dmœre, abite |
| To move | Déménager | demenaʒe |
| To move in (out) | Emménager (déménager) | ɑ̃menaʒe (demenaʒe) |
| To rent | Louer | lwe |

## Phrases

| | | |
|---|---|---|
| Rooms to let | Chambres à louer | ʃɑ̃brɛz a lwe |
| Have you taken a furnished flat ? | Avez-vous loué un appartement meublé ? | avevu lwe ɛ̃n apartəmɑ̃ mœble ? |
| I want a furnished room with the use of the kitchen | Je désire une chambre meublée et l'usage de la cuisine | ʒə dezir yn ʃɑ̃br mœble e lyzaʒ dla kɥizin |

| English. | | Pronunciation. |
|---|---|---|
| Where do you live ? | Où demeurez-vous ? | u dmœrevu ? |
| I live on the second floor | Je demeure au deuxième étage | ʒə dmœr o døzjɛm etaʒ |
| I live on the top floor | Je demeure au dernier étage | ʒə dmœr o dɛrnjer etaʒ |
| Are you upstairs ? | Êtes-vous en haut ? | ɛtvuz ɑ̃ o ? |
| I want an airy and spacious room | Je désire une chambre bien aérée et spacieuse | ʒə dezir yn ʃɑ̃br bjɛ̃ aere e spasjøz |
| I am looking for a bed-sitting room | Je cherche une pièce unique avec lit | ʒə ʃɛrʃ yn pjɛs ynik avɛk li |
| I need a writing-desk and a book-case | J'ai besoin d'un bureau et d'une bibliothèque | ʒe bəzwɛ̃ dɑ̃ byro e dyn bibliɔtɛk |
| Can you give me another blanket and pillow ? | Pouvez - vous me donner encore une couverture et un oreiller ? | puvevu mə dɔne ɑ̃kɔr yn kuvɛrtyr e ɑ̃n ɔrɛje ? |
| Is there a wardrobe and a chest of drawers in the bedroom ? | Y a-t-il une garde-robe et une commode dans la chambre ? | jatil yn gardərɔb e yn kɔmɔd dɑ̃ la ʃɑ̃br ? |
| Is the bed comfortable ? | Le lit est-il conforable ? | lə li ɛtil kɔ̃fɔrtabl ? |
| I do not like the mattress | Je n'aime pas le matelas | ʒə nɛm pɑ lə matlɑ |
| It is too hard | Il est trop dur | il ɛ tro dyr |
| Save light ! | Économisez la lumière ! | ekɔnɔmize la lymjɛr ! |
| May I switch on the light ? | Puis-je allumer l'électricité (tourner le commutateur) ? | pɥiʒ alyme lelɛktrisite (turne lə kɔmytatœr ? |
| The lamp on the bedside table is broken (burnt out) | La lampe sur la table de nuit est cassée (grillée) | la lɑ̃p syr la tabl də nɥi ɛ kɑse (grije) |
| Could I have a new bulb ? | Pourrais - je avoir une lampe neuve ? | purɛʒ avwar yn lɑ̃p nœv ? |

| English. | | Pronunciation. |
|---|---|---|
| Can I have a bath ? | Puis-je prendre un bain ? | pɥiz prãdr œ̃ bɛ̃ ? |
| Where is the maid ? | Où est la bonne ? | wɛ la bɔn ? |
| She is in the kitchen | Elle est dans la cuisine | ɛl ɛ dã la kɥizin |
| When is dinner ? | A quelle heure dîne-t-on ? | akɛl œr dintɔ̃ ? |
| Could you keep lunch for me ? | Pourriez-vous me garder le déjeuner ? | purievu mə garde lə deʒœne ? |
| The table in the dining-room is laid | La table est mise dans la salle à manger | la tabl ɛ miz dã la salamãʒe |
| Bring another chair | Apportez encore une chaise | apɔrtez ãkɔr yn ʃɛz |
| Come into the drawing-room | Venez dans le salon | vne dã lsalɔ̃ |
| Take this easy chair | Prenez ce fauteuil | prəne sə fotœj |
| Where is the latch-key ? | Où est le passe-partout ? | wɛ lə paspartu ? |
| In the lock | Dans la serrure | dã la sɛryr |
| What is the month-ly rent for this flat ? | Quel est le loyer mensuel de cet appartement ? | kɛl ɛ lə lwaje mã-sɥɛl də sɛt apar-təmã ? |
| Do I pay in ad-vance ? | Dois-je payer d' avance ? | dwaʒ pɛje davãs ? |
| When can I move in ? | Quand puis-je em-ménager ? | kã pɥiʒ ãmenaʒe ? |

# COUNTRIES AND NATIONS
## Vocabulary

| | | |
|---|---|---|
| Africa | L'Afrique | lafrik |
| The African | L'Africain(e) | lafrikɛ̃ (afrikɛn) |
| African | africain(e) | afrikɛ̃ (afrikɛn) |
| Albania | L'Albanie | lalbani |

| English. | | Pronunciation. |
|---|---|---|
| The Albanian | L'Albanien(ne) | lalbanjɛ̃ (albanjɛn) |
| Albanian | albanien(ne) | albanjɛ̃ (albanjɛn) |
| Alsace-Lorraine | L'Alsace-Lorraine | lalzas-lɔrɛn |
| The Alsatian | L'Alsacien(ne) | lalzasjɛ̃ (alzasjɛn) |
| The Lorrainer | Le (la) Lorrain(e) | lə lɔrɛ̃, la lɔrɛn |
| Algeria | L'Algérie | lalʒeri |
| America | L'Amérique | lamerik |
| The American | L'Américain(e) | lamerikɛ̃ (amerikɛn) |
| American | américain(e) | amerikɛ̃ (amerikɛn) |
| Arabia | L'Arabie | larabi |
| The Arab | L'Arabe | larab |
| Arabian | arabique, arabe | arabik, arab |
| Argentine | L'Argentine | larʒɑ̃tin |
| The Argentinian | L'Argentin(e) | larʒɑ̃tɛ̃ (arʒɑ̃tin) |
| Argentinian | argentin(e) | arʒɑ̃tɛ̃ (arʒɑ̃tin) |
| Asia | L'Asie | lazi |
| The Asiatic | L'Asiatique | lazjatik |
| Asiatic, Asian | asiatique | azjatik |
| Australia | L'Australie | lostrali |
| The Australian | L'Australien(ne) | lostraljɛ̃ (ostraljɛn) |
| Australian | australien(ne) | ostraljɛ̃ (ostraljɛn) |
| Austria | L'Autriche | lotriʃ |
| The Austrian | L'Autrichien(ne) | lotriʃjɛ̃ (otriʃjɛn) |
| Austrian | autrichien(ne) | otriʃjɛ̃ (otriʃjɛn) |
| The Baltic States | Les pays baltes | le pei balt |
| Bavaria | La Bavière | la bavjɛr |
| The Bavarian | Le (la) Bavarois(e) | lə bavarwa (la ba-varwaz) |
| Bavarian | bavarois(e) | bavarwa (bavarwaz) |
| Belgium | La Belgique | la bɛlʒik |
| The Belgian | Le (la) Belge | lə (la) bɛlʒ |
| Belgian | belge | bɛlʒ |
| Brazil | Le Brésil | lə brezil |
| The Brazilian | Le (la) Brésilien(ne) | lə breziljɛ̃ (brezil-jɛn) |
| Britain | La Grande-Bretagne | la grɑ̃d brətaɲ |

| English. | | Pronunciation. |
|---|---|---|
| The Britisher, Briton | Le (la) Britannique | lə (la) britanik |
| The British | Les Britanniques | le britanik |
| British | britannique | britanik |
| Bulgaria | La Boulgarie | la bulgari |
| The Bulgarian | Le (la) Boulgare | lə (la) bulgar |
| Canada | Le Canada | lə kanada |
| The Canadian | Le (la) Canadien(ne) | lə kanadjẽ (kanadjɛn) |
| Canadian | canadien(ne) | kanadjẽ (kanadjɛn) |
| Carinthia | La Carinthie | la karẽti |
| Chile | Le Chili | lə ʃili |
| The Chilian | Le (la) Chilien(ne) | lə ʃiljẽ (la ʃiljɛn) |
| China | La Chine | la ʃin |
| The Chinese | Le (la) Chinois(e) | lə ʃinwa (la ʃinwaz) |
| Croatia | La Croatie | la krɔasi |
| Crete | La Candie | la kãdi |
| Denmark | Le Danemark | lə danmark |
| The Dane | Le (la) Danois(e) | lə danwa (la danwaz) |
| Danish | danois(e) | danwa (danwaz) |
| Egypt | L'Égypte | leʒipt |
| The Egyptian | L'Égyptien(ne) | leʒipsjẽ (eʒipsjɛn) |
| England | L'Angleterre | lãglətɛr |
| The Englishman | L'Anglais | lãglɛ |
| The Englishwoman | L'Anglaise | lãglɛz |
| The English | Les Anglais | lez ãglɛ |
| English | anglais(e) | ãglɛ (ãglɛz) |
| Esthonia | L'Esthonie, l'Estonie | lɛstɔni |
| Europe | L'Europe | lœrɔp |
| The European | L'Européen(ne) | lœrɔpeẽ (œrɔpeɛn) |
| European | européen(ne) | œrɔpeẽ (œrɔpeɛn) |
| Finland | La Finlande | la fẽlãd |
| The Finn | Le (la) Finlandais(e) | lə fẽlãdɛ (la fẽlãdɛz) |
| Flanders | La Flandre | la flãdr |

| English. | | Pronunciation. |
|---|---|---|
| The Fleming | Le (la) Flamand(e) | lə flamã (la flamãd) |
| Flemish | flamand(e) | flamã (flamãd) |
| France | La France | la frãs |
| The Frenchman | Le Français | lə frãsɛ |
| The Frenchwoman | La Française | la frãsɛz |
| The French | Les Français | le frãsɛ |
| French | français(e) | frãsɛ (frãsɛz) |
| Germany | L'Allemagne | lalmaɲ |
| The German | L'Allemand(e) | lalmã (almãd) |
| German | allemand(e) | almã (almãd) |
| Greece | La Grèce | la grɛs |
| The Greek | Le Grec, la Grecque | lə grɛk, la grɛk |
| Greek | grec, grecque | grɛk |
| Holland | La Hollande | la ɔlãd |
| The Dutchman | Le Hollandais | lə ɔlãdɛ |
| The Dutchwoman | La Hollandaise | la ɔlãdɛz |
| The Dutch | Les Hollandais | le ɔlãdɛ |
| Dutch | hollandais(e) | ɔlãdɛ (ɔlãdɛz) |
| Hungary | La Hongrie | la ɔ̃gri |
| The Hungarian | Le (la) Hongrois(e) | lə ɔ̃grwa (la ɔ̃grwaz) |
| Hungarian | hongrois(e) | ɔ̃grwa (ɔ̃grwaz) |
| Iceland | L'Islande | lislãd |
| India | L'Inde | lɛ̃d |
| The Indian | L'Hindou(e) | lɛ̃du |
| Indian | hindou(e) | ɛ̃du |
| Ireland, Eire | L'Irlande, l'Eire | lirlãd, lɛr |
| The Irishman | L'Irlandais | lirlãdɛ |
| The Irish | Les Irlandais | lez irlãdɛ |
| Irish | irlandais(e) | irlãdɛ (irlãdɛz) |
| Israel | L'Israël | lizraɛl |
| Israeli | israélite | izraelit |
| Italy | L'Italie | litali |
| The Italian | L'Italien(ne) | litaljɛ̃ (italjɛn) |
| Italian | italien(ne) | italjɛ̃ (italjɛn) |
| Japan | Le Japon | lə ʒapɔ̃ |
| The Japanese | Les Japonais | le ʒaponɛ |

| English. | | Pronunciation. |
|---|---|---|
| Jugoslavia | La Yougoslavie | la jugɔslavi |
| The Jugoslav | Le (la) Yougoslave | lə (la) jugɔslav |
| Latvia | La Lettonie, la Latvie | la lɛtɔni, la latvi |
| Lithuania | La Lithuanie | la litɥani |
| Luxembourg | Le Luxembourg | lə lyksãbur |
| Mexico | Le Mexique | lə mɛksik |
| Moravia | La Moravie | la mɔravi |
| The Netherlands | Les Pays-Bas | le peibɑ |
| New Zealand | La Nouvelle-Zélande | la nuvɛl zelãd |
| The New Zealander | Le (la) Néo-Zélandais(e) | lə neo-zelãdɛ (zelãdɛz) |
| Newfoundland | La Terre-Neuve | la tɛrnœv |
| Norway | La Norvège | la nɔrvɛʒ |
| The Norwegian | Le (la) Norvégien(ne) | lə nɔrveʒjɛ̃ (nɔrveʒjɛn) |
| Norwegian | norvégien(ne) | nɔrveʒjɛ̃ (nɔrveʒjɛn) |
| Palestine | La Palestine | la palɛstin |
| Persia | La Perse | la pɛrs |
| The Persian | Le (la) Persan(e) | lə pɛrsã (la pɛrsan) |
| Poland | La Pologne | la pɔlɔɲ |
| The Pole | Le (la) Polonais(e) | lə pɔlɔnɛ (la pɔlɔnɛz) |
| Polish | polonais(e) | pɔlɔnɛ (pɔlɔnɛz) |
| Portugal | Le Portugal | lə pɔrtygal |
| The Portuguese | Le (la) Portugais(e) | lə pɔrtygɛ (la pɔrtygɛz) |
| Prussia | La Prusse | la prys |
| The Prussian | Le (la) Prussien(ne) | lə prysjɛ̃ (la prysjɛn) |
| Prussian | prussien(ne) | prysjɛ̃ (prysjɛn) |
| Roumania | La Roumanie | la rumani |
| The Roumanian | Le (la) Roumain(e) | lə rumɛ̃ (la rumɛn) |
| Russia | La Russie | la rysi |
| The Russian | Le (la) Russe | lə (la) rys |
| Russian | russe | rys |
| Saxony | La Saxe | la saks |

| English. | | Pronunciation. |
|---|---|---|
| Scandinavia | La Scandinavie | la skɑ̃dinavi |
| Scotland | L'Écosse | lekɔs |
| The Scot, Scotsman | L'Écossais | lekɔsɛ |
| The Scotch | Les Écossais | lez ekɔsɛ |
| Scotch | écossais(e) | ekɔsɛ (ekɔsɛz) |
| Spain | L'Espagne | lɛspaɲ |
| The Spaniard | L'Espagnol(e) | lɛspaɲɔl |
| Spanish | espagnol(e) | ɛspaɲɔl |
| Sweden | La Suède | la sɥɛd |
| The Swede | Le (la) Suédois(e) | lə sɥɛdwa (la sɥɛdwaz) |
| Swedish | suédois(e) | sɥɛdwa (sɥɛdwaz) |
| Switzerland | La Suisse | la sɥis |
| The Swiss | Les Suisses | le sɥis |
| Syria | La Syrie | la siri |
| Tunis | La Tunisie | la tynizi |
| Turkey | La Turquie | la tyrki |
| The Turk | Le Turc, la Turque | lə tyrk, la tyrk |
| The United States | Les États-Unis | lez etatzyni |
| Wales | Le pays de Galles | lə pei də gal |
| The Welshman | Le Gallois | lə galwa |

## Phrases

| | | |
|---|---|---|
| What is your nationality? | Quelle est votre nationalité? | kɛl ɛ vɔt nasjɔnalite? |
| I am English (German, French, Russian) | Je suis Anglais(e) (Allemand(e), Français(e), Russe) | ʒə sɥiz ɑ̃glɛ(z) (almɑ̃(d), frɑ̃sɛ(z), rys) |
| Have you any identification papers? | Avez-vous des papiers d'identité? | avevu de papje didɑ̃tite? |
| I have an English (German, French, Russian) passport | J'ai un passeport anglais (allemand, français, russe) | ʒe œ̃ paspɔr ɑ̃glɛ (almɑ̃, frɑ̃sɛ, rys) |

| English. | | Pronunciation. |
|---|---|---|
| How long have you been here? | Depuis combien de temps êtes-vous ici? | dəpqi kɔ̃bjɛ̃ də tɑ̃ ɛtvuz isi? |
| Here is my registration card | Voici ma carte d'immatriculation | vwasi ma kart dimatrikylasjɔ̃ |
| I am French by birth | Je suis Français(e) de naissance | ʒə sqi frɑ̃sɛ(z) də nɛsɑ̃s |
| I am English by marriage | Je suis Anglaise par mon mariage | ʒə sqiz ɑ̃glɛz par mɔ̃ marjaʒ |
| From which country do you come? | De quel pays êtes-vous originaire? | də kɛl pei ɛtvuz ɔriʒinɛr? |
| I have been deprived of my nationality | J'ai été dénationalisé(e) | ʒe ete denasjɔnalize |
| You are stateless | Vous êtes sans patrie | vuz ɛt sɑ̃ patri |
| I am homeless | Je suis sans feu ni lieu | ʒə sqi sɑ̃ fø ni ljø |
| Can I claim British nationality? | Puis-je revendiquer la nationalité britannique? | pqiʒ rəvɑ̃dike la nasjɔnalite britanik? |
| Are you a naturalized Swiss? | Êtes-vous naturalisé(e) suisse? | ɛtvu natyralize sqis? |
| I want to travel to Poland | Je veux aller en Pologne | ʒvøz ale ɑ̃ pɔlɔɲ |
| My mother-tongue is French | Ma langue maternelle est le français | ma lɑ̃g matɛrnɛl ɛ lə frɑ̃sɛ |
| Are you a foreigner | Êtes-vous étranger (étrangère)? | ɛtvuz etrɑ̃ʒe (etrɑ̃ʒɛr)? |
| I have travelled through France | J'ai parcouru la France | ʒe parkury la frɑ̃s |
| He has returned from the Far East | Il est rentré d'Extrême-Orient | il ɛ rɑ̃tre dɛkstrɛm ɔrjɑ̃ |
| Are you a British subject? | Êtes-vous sujet britannique? | ɛtvu syʒe britanik? |

| English. | | Pronunciation. |
|---|---|---|
| Do you speak English (French, German)? | Parlez-vous anglais (français, allemand)? | parlevu(z) ãglɛ (frãsɛ, almã)? |
| I can only speak a little French | Je ne parle qu'un peu le français | ʒə nparl kœ pø lə frãsɛ |
| I can read it, but I cannot speak it | Je peux le lire mais pas le parler | ʒpø lə lir mɛ pa lə parle |
| I shall have to take French lessons | Il va falloir que je prenne des leçons de français | il va falwar kə ʒə prɛn de lsõ də frãsɛ |
| Can you recommend a good teacher? | Pouvez - vous me recommander un bon professeur? | puvevu mə rəkomãde œ̃ bõ profesœr? |
| Can you understand me? | Pouvez - vous me comprendre? | puvevu mə kõprãdr? |
| Please speak a little more slowly | Parlez un peu plus lentement, s.v.p. | parlez œ̃ pø ply lãtmã, sivuplɛ |
| I didn't understand you | Je ne vous ai pas compris | ʒə nvuze pa kõpri |
| Could you please translate this for me? | Pourriez-vous me traduire ceci? | purievu mə tradɥir səsi? |
| You have a good (bad) pronunciation | Vous avez une bonne (mauvaise) prononciation | vuzavez yn bɔn (movɛz) pronõsjasjõ |
| How do you spell this word? | Comment écrit-on ce mot? | kõmãt ekritõ sə mo? |
| Do you understand the Normandy dialect? | Comprenez-vous le patois normand? | kõprənevu lə patwa nɔrmã? |
| No, I need an interpreter | Non, j'ai besoin d'un interprète | nõ, ʒe bəzwɛ̃ dœ̃n ɛ̃tɛrprɛt |

## ARMY, NAVY, AIR FORCE
### Vocabulary
#### ARMY:

| English. | | Pronunciation. |
|---|---|---|
| The soldier | Le soldat | lə sɔlda |
| The automatic rifle | Le fusil-mitrailleur | lə fyzimitrajœr |
| The bayonet | La baïonnette | la bajɔnɛt |
| The tommy gun | La mitraillette | la mitrajɛt |
| The ammunition | Les munitions | le mynisjɔ̃ |
| The gun | Le canon | lə kanɔ̃ |
| The heavy howitzer | L'obusier lourd | lɔbyzje lur |
| The flame-thrower | Le lance-flammes | lə lɑ̃sflɑm |
| The smoke mortar | Le lance-fumée | lə lɑ̃sfyme |
| The atomic bomb | La bombe atomique | la bɔ̃b atɔmik |
| The H bomb | La bombe H | la bɔ̃b aʃ |
| The rocket | La fusée | la fyze |
| The tank | Le char d'assaut | lə ʃərdaso |
| The camouflage | Le camouflage | lə kamuflaʒ |
| The barracks | La caserne | la kazɛrn |
| The garrison | La garnison | la garnizɔ̃ |
| The army of occupation | L'armée d'occupation | larme dɔkypasjɔ̃ |
| The town major | Le commandant d'armes | lə kɔmɑ̃dɑ̃ darm |
| | | |
| RANKS : | Les Rangs : | le rɑ̃ : |
| The private | Le simple soldat | lə sɛ̃plə sɔlda |
| The trooper | Le cavalier | lə kavalje |
| The gunner | L'artilleur | lartijœr |
| The sapper | Le sapeur, le soldat du Génie | lə sapœr, lə sɔlda dy ʒeni |
| The signaller | Le signaleur | lə siɲalœr |
| The orderly | Le planton | lə plɑ̃tɔ̃ |
| The lance-corporal | Le soldat de première classe | lə sɔlda də prəmjɛr klɑs |
| The corporal | Le caporal | lə kapɔral |

| English. | | Pronunciation. |
|---|---|---|
| The sergeant | Le sergent | lə sɛrʒɑ̃ |
| The second lieu-tenant | Le sous-lieutenant | lə suljøtnɑ̃ |
| The lieutenant | Le lieutenant | lə ljøtnɑ̃ |
| The captain | Le capitaine | lə kapitɛn |
| The major | Le commandant | lə kɔmɑ̃dɑ̃ |
| The lieutenant-colonel | Le lieutenant-colonel | lə ljøtnɑ̃ kɔlɔnɛl |
| The colonel | Le colonel | lə kɔlɔnɛl |
| The major-general | Le général de bri-gade | lə ʒeneral də brigad |
| The lieutenant-gen-eral | Le général de divi-sion | lə ʒeneral də divizjɔ̃ |
| The general | Le général | lə ʒeneral |
| The field marshal | Le maréchal | lə mareʃal |

### NAVY:

| | | |
|---|---|---|
| The fleet | La flotte | la flɔt |
| The man-of-war | Le bâtiment de guerre | lə bɑtimɑ̃ də gɛr |
| The battleship | Le cuirassé de ligne | lə kɥirase də liɲ |
| The cruiser | Le croiseur | lə krwazœr |
| The destroyer | Le contre-torpilleur | lə kɔ̃trətɔrpijœr |
| The motor torpedo-boat | Le torpilleur à mo-teur | lə tɔrpijœr a motœr |
| The submarine | Le sous-marin | lə sumarɛ̃ |
| The mine-sweeper | Le dragueur de mines | lə dragœr də min |
| The depth charge | La grenade sous-marine | la grənad sumarin |
| The range | La distance, la di-rection, la portée | la distɑ̃s, la dirɛk-sjɔ̃, la pɔrte |
| The port, harbour | Le port | lə pɔr |
| The convoy | Le convoi | le kɔ̃vwa |
| To sink | Couler | kule |
| To scuttle | Saborder | sabɔrde |

| English. | Les Rangs : | Pronunciation.<br>le rɑ̃ : |
|---|---|---|
| RANKS : | | |
| The ordinary sea-man | Le matelot | lə matlo |
| The telegraphist | Le télégraphiste | lə telegrafist |
| The stoker | Le chauffeur | lə ʃofœr |
| The petty officer | L'officier marinier | lɔfisje marinje |
| The chief petty officer | Le premier maître | lə prəmje mɛtr |
| The sub-lieutenant | L'enseigne de vais-seau | lɑ̃sɛɲ də vɛso |
| The lieutenant | Le lieutenant de vaisseau | lə ljøtnɑ̃ də vɛso |
| The lieutenant-commander | Le capitaine de cor-vette | lə kapitɛn də kɔrvɛt |
| The commander | Le capitaine de frégate | lə kapitɛn də fregat |
| The captain | Le capitaine de vaisseau | lə kapitɛn də vɛso |
| The submarine commander | Le capitaine de sous-marin | lə kapitɛn də su-marɛ̃ |
| The admiral | L'amiral | lamiral |

|  | AIR FORCE : |  |
|---|---|---|
| The pilot | Le pilote aviateur | lə pilɔtavjatœr |
| The wireless opera-tor | L'opérateur de T.S.F. | lɔperatœr də teɛsɛf |
| The crew | L'équipage | lekipaʒ |
| The fighter | L'avion de chasse | lavjɔ̃ də ʃas |
| The bomber | Le bombardier | lə bɔ̃bardje |
| The jet plane | L'avion à réaction | lavjɔ̃ a reaksjɔ̃ |
| The high-explosive bomb | La bombe à explosif brisant | la bɔ̃b a ɛksplozif brizɑ̃ |
| The incendiary bomb | La bombe incen-diaire | la bɔ̃b ɛ̃sɑ̃djɛr |
| The air raid | L'attaque aérienne | latak aerjɛn |

| English. | | Pronunciation. |
|---|---|---|
| The attack | L'attaque | latak |
| The A.R.P. | La Défense Passive, D.P. | la defãs pasiv, depe |
| The ground personnel | Le personnel non-navigant | lə pɛrsɔnɛl nõnavigã |
| The tarmac | La piste d'envol | la pistdãvɔl |
| The aerodrome | L'aérodrome | laerɔdrom |
| The barrage balloon | Le ballon de barrage | lə balõ də baraʒ |
| To take off | Décoller | dekɔle |
| To land | Atterrir (amerrir = to alight on water) | atɛrir (amɛrir) |
| To crash | S'écraser sur le sol | sekrɑze syr lə sɔl |
| RANKS : | Les Rangs : | le rã |
| The aircraftman | Le soldat aviateur | lə sɔlda avjatœr |
| The leading aircraftman | Le soldat aviateur de première classe | lə sɔlda avjatœr də prəmjɛr klɑs |
| The sergeant | Le sergent | lə sɛrʒã |
| The warrant officer | Le sous-officier breveté | lə suzɔfisje brəvte |
| The pilot officer | Le sous-lieutenant aviateur | lə suljɔtnã avjatœr |
| The flying officer | Le lieutenant aviateur | lə ljɔtnã avjatœr |
| The flight lieutenant | Le capitaine aviateur | lə kapitɛn avjatœr |
| The squadron leader | Le commandant | lə kɔmãdã |
| The wing commander | Le lieutenant-colonel | lə ljɔtnã kɔlɔnɛl |
| The group captain | Le colonel, le commandant de groupe | lə kɔlɔnɛl, lə kɔmãdã də grup |
| The air commodore | Le général de brigade | lə ʒeneral də brigad |

| English. | | Pronunciation. |
|---|---|---|
| The air vice-marshal | Le général de division | lə ʒeneral də divizjɔ̃ |
| The air marshal | Le maréchal | lə mareʃal |
| The war | La guerre | la gɛr |
| The battle | La bataille | la batɑj |
| The victory | La victoire | la viktwar |
| The defeat | La défaite | la defɛt |
| The armistice | L'armistice | larmistis |
| The peace treaty | Le traité de paix | lə trɛte də pɛ |
| The prisoner of war | Le prisonnier de guerre | lə prizɔnje də gɛr |
| The camp | Le camp | lə kɑ̃ |
| To call up | Mobiliser, appeler sous les drapeaux | mɔbilize, aple su le drapo |
| To demobilise | Démobiliser | demɔbilize |
| To serve | Servir dans l'armée, faire son service militaire | sɛrvir dɑ̃ larme, fɛr sɔ̃ sɛrvis militɛr |
| To fight | Se battre | sə batr |
| To shoot | Tirer | tire |
| To conquer | Vaincre, conquérir | vɛ̃kr, kɔ̃kerir |

## Phrases

| | | |
|---|---|---|
| Were you in the army? | Avez-vous fait votre service militaire? | avevu fɛ vɔt sɛrvis militɛr? |
| In which service were you? | Dans quelle arme avez-vous servi? | dɑ̃ kɛl arm avevu sɛrvi? |
| I served with the engineers | J'ai servi dans le Génie | ʒe sɛrvi dɑ̃ lə ʒeni |
| I was a private in an armoured formation | J'ai été soldat dans un groupe de combat blindé | ʒe ete sɔlda dɑ̃z œ̃ grup də kɔ̃ba blɛ̃de |
| What is your military rank? | Quel est votre rang militaire? | kɛl ɛ vɔt rɑ̃ militɛr? |
| I am an officer | Je suis officier | ʒə sɥiz ɔfisje |

| English. | | Pronunciation. |
|---|---|---|
| How long were you in the army? | Combien de temps avez-vous servi dans l'armée? | kɔ̃bjɛ̃ də tã avevu sɛrvi dã larme? |
| I served in the navy | J'ai servi dans la marine de guerre | ʒe sɛrvi dã la marin də gɛr |
| I joined up three years ago | Je me suis engagé il y a trois ans | ʒə msɥiz ãgaʒe ilja trwaz ã |
| Were you called up? | Avez-vous été appelé sous les drapeaux? | avevuz ete aple su le drapo? |
| I volunteered | Je me suis engagé comme volontaire | ʒə msɥiz ãgaʒe kɔm vɔlɔnter |
| I am an airman | Je suis aviateur | ʒə sɥiz avjatœr |
| Did you take part in an air raid? | Avez-vous pris part à une attaque aérienne? | avevu pri par a yn atak aerjɛn? |
| I belonged to the ground personnel | J'appartenais au personnel non-navigant | ʒapartnɛz o pɛrsɔnel nɔ̃navigã |
| Were you a submarine captain? | Étiez-vous capitaine de sous-marin? | etjevu kapitɛn də sumarɛ̃? |
| No, I was a lieutenant on a cruiser | Non, j'étais lieutenant à bord d'un croiseur | nɔ̃, ʒetɛ ljøtnã a bɔr dœ̃ krwazœr |
| The ship was sunk, the crew was saved | Le vaisseau a été coulé mais l'équipage a été sauvé | lə vɛso a ete kule mɛ lekipaʒ a ete sove |
| How many men-of-war are lying in the harbour? | Combien de bâtiments de guerre y a-t-il dans le port? | kɔ̃bjɛ̃ də batimã də gɛr jatil dã lə pɔr? |
| The fleet has put out to sea | La flotte a pris la mer | la flɔt a pri la mɛr |
| I was a parachutist | J'étais parachutiste | ʒetɛ paraʃytist |

| English. | | Pronunciation. |
|---|---|---|
| How long did your training last? | Combien de temps votre formation militaire a-t-elle duré? | kɔ̃bjẽ də tã vɔt fɔrmasjɔ̃ militɛr atɛl dyre? |
| We took the fortress by storm | Nous avons pris la forteresse d'assaut | nuzavɔ̃ pri la fɔrtrɛs daso |
| They established a bridgehead | Ils ont établi une tête de pont | ilz ɔ̃t etabli yn tɛt də pɔ̃ |
| The enemy is in full retreat | L'ennemi est en pleine retraite | lɛnmi ɛt ã plɛn rətrɛt |
| The army was beaten (annihilated) | L'armée a été battue (anéantie) | larme a ete baty (aneãti) |
| Were you decorated in the war? | Avez-vous été décoré pendant la guerre? | avevuz ete dekɔre pãdã la gɛr? |
| Were you wounded? | Avez-vous été blessé? | avevuz ete blɛse? |
| He is disabled | Il est estropié | il ɛt ɛstrɔpje |
| In which hospital were you? | Où avez-vous été hospitalisé? | u avevuz ete ɔspitalize? |
| I am going on leave | Je vais en permission | ʒə vɛz ã pɛrmisjɔ̃ |
| He is demobilised | Il est démobilisé | il ɛ demɔbilize |
| I am invalided out | Je suis réformé | ʒə sɥi refɔrme |
| He is fit (unfit) for service | Il est apte (inapte) au service | il ɛt apt (inapt) o sɛrvis |
| I was a prisoner of war | J'ai été prisonnier de guerre | ʒe ete prizɔnje də gɛr |
| When were you taken prisoner? | Quand vous a-t-on fait prisonnier? | kã vuz atɔ̃ fɛ prizɔnje? |
| Shortly before the armistice | Peu de temps avant l'armistice | pø də tã avã larmistis |

| English. | | Pronunciation. |
|---|---|---|
| How long did you serve in the W.R.N.S. ? | Combien de temps avez-vous servi dans le service auxiliaire féminin de la marine ? | kɔ̃bjɛ̃ də tɑ̃ avevu sɛrvi dɑ̃ lsɛrvis oksiljer femnɛ̃ dla marin ? |
| I joined the A.T.S. at the beginning of the war | Je me suis engagée au commencement de la guerre dans le service auxiliaire féminin de l'armée | ʒəmsɥiz ɑ̃gaʒe o kɔmɑ̃smɑ̃ dla ger dɑ̃ lsɛrvis oksiljer femnɛ̃ də larme |
| She is an officer in the W.A.A.F. | Elle est officier dans le service auxiliaire féminin de la R.A.F. | ɛl ɛt ɔfisje dɑ̃ lsɛrvis oksiljer femnɛ̃ dla raf |
| My sister is a Red Cross nurse | Ma sœur est infirmière de la Croix Rouge | ma sœr ɛt ɛ̃firmjer dla krwɑ ruʒ |

B

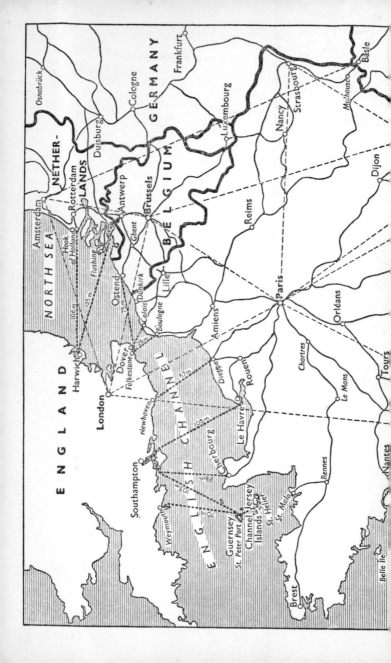